OECD Tax Policy Studies



# Taxation of SMEs in OECD and G20 Countries

No. 23

OECD

BETTER POLICIES FOR BETTER LIVES

This work is published under the responsibility of the Secretary-General of the OECD. The opinions expressed and arguments employed herein do not necessarily reflect the official views of OECD member countries.

This document and any map included herein are without prejudice to the status of or sovereignty over any territory, to the delimitation of international frontiers and boundaries and to the name of any territory, city or area.

**Please cite this publication as:**
OECD (2015), *Taxation of SMEs in OECD and G20 Countries*, OECD Tax Policy Studies, No. 23, OECD Publishing, Paris.
*http://dx.doi.org/10.1787/9789264243507-en*

ISBN 978-92-64-24346-0 (print)
ISBN 978-92-64-24350-7 (PDF)

Series: OECD Tax Policy Studies
ISSN 1990-0546 (print)
ISSN 1990-0538 (online)

The statistical data for Israel are supplied by and under the responsibility of the relevant Israeli authorities. The use of such data by the OECD is without prejudice to the status of the Golan Heights, East Jerusalem and Israeli settlements in the West Bank under the terms of international law.

**Photo credits:** Cover © selensergen/Thinkstock

Corrigenda to OECD publications may be found on line at: *www.oecd.org/about/publishing/corrigenda.htm*.

# *Foreword*

Fostering the development of small and medium-sized enterprises (SMEs) is rightly a cross-cutting priority of the Turkish G20 Presidency. SMEs are the economic backbone of many of our economies and they serve as key engines for job creation. This study, *Taxation of SMEs in OECD and G20 Countries,* examines the influence of tax systems on a range of challenges faced by SMEs, including decisions relating to their creation, form and growth. SMEs make up the vast majority of business entities and contribute strongly to employment and economic growth, spanning the full breadth of industries and sectors, and differing in their propensity to innovate and grow. At the same time, SMEs face particular challenges in relation to their access to finance. The tax system plays a dual role: at times, as a tool to assist in overcoming these challenges, and at others, as an obstacle.

Understanding the role of the tax system in the decisions of SME owners and managers is therefore critical in providing policy solutions to support their success. This study provides insights into the influence of tax systems on SMEs in 39 OECD and G20 countries, including Argentina, Australia, Austria, Brazil, Belgium, Canada, Chile, China (People's Republic of), the Czech Republic, Denmark, Estonia, Finland, France, Germany, Greece, Hungary, Iceland, India, Ireland, Israel, Italy, Japan, Korea, Luxembourg, Mexico, the Netherlands, New Zealand, Norway, Poland, Portugal, the Slovak Republic, Slovenia, South Africa, Spain, Sweden, Switzerland, Turkey, the United Kingdom, and the United States.

*Taxation of SMEs in OECD and G20 Countries* finds that rather than being neutral in their impact on SMEs and their decisions, tax systems often provide incentives for SMEs to incorporate, and to distribute income in the form of capital, particularly in the form of capital gains, which is often lower-taxed. In addition, some tax systems can disproportionately affect SMEs relative to large enterprises, to the extent that they treat profits and losses asymmetrically, have a bias towards debt over corporate equity, and impose relatively higher compliance costs.

Governments take many measures to reduce these impacts, providing tax preferences and simplification measures targeted at SMEs. Tax preferences are also intended to assist with other challenges faced by SMEs, and to support their creation and growth. This study discusses these measures and encourages careful targeting of any special tax rules for SMEs, to ensure they meet their policy objectives in a cost-effective way. It cautions against introducing preferences or simplification measures that create further distortions or complexities.

The taxation of SMEs, and the provision of SME-specific tax rules can, if carefully designed, play a useful role in addressing the challenges and the disproportionately high tax compliance burdens faced by SMEs. *Taxation of SMEs in OECD and G20 Countries* provides cross-country comparison and analysis that can assist policymakers in designing tax policy to support the creation, innovation and growth of SMEs in G20 countries and beyond!

Angel Gurría

# *Acknowledgements*

This study was prepared under the guidance of Working Party No. 2 of the OECD Committee on Fiscal Affairs and the Working Party on SMEs and Entrepreneurship, and was approved for publication by the OECD Committee on Fiscal Affairs and the OECD Committee on Industry, Innovation and Entrepreneurship. Comments and information provided by Delegates from these committees and by other national officials are gratefully acknowledged. Input provided by the Delegates to Working Party No 2. of the Committee on Fiscal Affairs in response to the questionnaire is particularly appreciated.

The study was prepared and co-ordinated by Michelle Harding of the OECD's Centre for Tax Policy and Administration (CTPA), under the guidance of Thomas Neubig and David Bradbury. Richard Clarke, Korstiaan Kool, Dimitra Koulouri and Anna Milanez, all from CTPA, also made significant authoring contributions. The study was developed in consultation with Kris Boschmans, Lucia Cusmano and Miriam Koreen from the OECD's Centre for Entrepreneurship, SMEs and Local Development, who also contributed to the drafting of the study.

Contributions and assistance from other OECD officials to the development of the study are also gratefully acknowledged: Piet Battiau, Bert Brys, Tibor Hanappi, Martin Jares, Marta Jimenez-Blanco, Elena Miola, Maurice Nettley, Dominique Paturot and Kurt Van Dender from CTPA, and Mariarosa Lunati and Gueram Sargsyan, from the OECD's Statistics Directorate. Martine Monza, Michael Sharratt and Violet Sochay provided invaluable administrative assistance.

# *Table of contents*

## Figures



## Tables

## Boxes

# Abbreviations and acronyms

| | |
|---|---|
| ACE | Allowance for corporate equity |
| AGE | Annual gross earnings |
| AMW | Annual minimum wage |
| AP | Adjusted profits |
| AW | Average wage |
| BEN | Annual benefits |
| CEO | Chief Executive Officer |
| CIT | Corporare income tax |
| CPP | Canada Pension Plan |
| CRA | Canadian Revenue Agency |
| CTPA | Centre for Tax Policy and Administration |
| DMI | Declared monthly income |
| GDP | Gross domestic product |
| EC | European Commission |
| EI | Employment insurance |
| EIS | Enterprise Investment Scheme |
| EMPR | Employer social security contribution |
| EU | European Union |
| FBT | Fringe-benefits tax |
| GST | Goods and Services Tax |
| HMRC | Her Majesty's Revenue and Customs |
| HST | Harmonised Sales Tax |
| IBFD | International Bureau of Fiscal Documentation |
| IMF | International Monetory Fund |
| ITC | Input Tax Credits |
| KOSGEB | Small and Medium Enterprises Development Organisation |
| MGE | Monthly gross earnings |
| MGEc | Monthly gross earnings – Conventional |

| | |
|---|---|
| MWFD | Federal District of Mexico City |
| NTCP | Non-tax compulsary payment |
| OECD | Organisation for Economic Co-operation and Development |
| PIT | Personal income tax |
| REPECO | Régimen de Pequeños Contribuyente |
| RFC | Federal Taxpayer Registry |
| RIF | Régimen de Incorporación Fiscal |
| SCP | Silent partnerships |
| SEIS | Seed Enterprise Investment Scheme |
| SII | Revenue body of Chile |
| SKAT | Danish Tax Administration |
| SME | Small and medium enterprise |
| SSC | Social Security Contribution |
| TDS | Witholding tax |
| TUBITAK | Scientific and Technological Research Council of Turkey |
| T | (Annual) central government income tax payable |
| Ts | (Annual) sub-central income tax |
| TY | Taxable income measured for central government tax purposes |
| TYs | Taxable income modified for sub-central government purposes |
| UN | United Nations |
| VAT | Value added tax |
| VCLP | Venture Capital Limited Partnership |
| VCT | Venture Capital Trust |
| WBSO | Wet Bevordering Speur- en Ontwikkelingswerk |
| WGE | Weekly gross earnings |
| WTO | World Trade Organisation |

# Executive summary

In most countries, small and medium-sized enterprises (SMEs) represent more than 95% of all firms. SMEs account for a large proportion of total employment and contribute significantly to national and global economic growth. They are also strongly heterogeneous: across and within industries and sectors; in their innovation behaviours; and in their profitability and growth potential. Importantly, SMEs also generate a significant share of all taxable business income in most economies.

SMEs are important for their contribution to employment, economic growth, innovation and the diversity and competition that they can bring to markets. As a large and important part of all national economies, SMEs often face challenges to their viability and growth, some of which are created by market failures, capital market imperfections and compliance costs.

This study examines the tax policy and tax administration arrangements affecting SMEs in OECD and G20 countries, drawing on the results of a questionnaire completed by 38 countries and on existing OECD databases. Based on the experiences of these countries, the study considers the influence that general tax rules and special tax measures can have on a number of economic margins, including the decision to enter self-employment, decisions over business form and whether to incorporate, the form of distribution of SME income, the size and growth of the business, decisions relating to investment, employment and finance, and compliance with tax rules.

Ideally, a country's tax system should be neutral with regard to its impact on business decisions, including the creation, form and growth of SMEs. However, the study finds that many of the tax systems examined provide incentives to incorporate and to distribute income in the form of capital, particularly as capital gains. In addition, certain features of the tax system may inadvertently disadvantage SMEs relative to larger enterprises. These features included the asymmetric treatment of profits and losses, a bias towards debt over equity and higher fixed costs associated with tax and regulatory compliance regimes.

The study notes that one of the most important issues affecting SMEs is the disproportionately high impact that regulatory requirements and the costs of tax compliance have on them. Even though many tax requirements may appear to be relatively "neutral" for businesses of all sizes, the significant fixed costs associated with compliance represent a higher cost for SMEs as a percentage of sales and income, and consequently have a greater adverse impact upon SMEs than larger businesses.

Another key issue affecting SMEs, which has been exacerbated since the financial crisis, relates to their limited access to finance for growth and expansion. With limited access to equity financing, SMEs also face considerable constraints in relation to debt financing. Availability of debt finance and the terms upon which it is granted to SMEs means that they are more finance-constrained and generally face greater costs in accessing finance than their larger competitors.

Against this backdrop, many governments provide support to SMEs through non-tax programmes, such as credit programmes, as well as through special tax rules, including both tax preferences and simplification measures for SMEs. This study presents details of the range and scope of special SME tax rules currently provided by governments. These measures include special small business corporate tax rates in fifteen jurisdictions; more generous tax deductions, tax credits or tax exemptions; preferences that apply directly to the owner or investor of the SME, providing relief for initial investment, ongoing income, or on disposal of the SME's assets; and special simplification rules, including special presumptive tax regimes for small enterprises reported in seventeen countries and special SME replacement taxes (presumptive or cash flow) reported in six countries.

While many of these special SME tax rules are designed to support the growth and profitability of SMEs, their design and introduction can have distortive impacts by giving businesses an incentive to remain small or to split up into different businesses to continue benefiting from the preferential tax treatment. These preferences need to be carefully targeted and designed to overcome the specific economic or tax difficulties identified or to provide support to companies providing positive spillovers to the economy.

After assessing some of the benefits and disadvantages of various approaches, the study highlights and identifies some principles to guide governments when developing and implementing measures to encourage the creation, growth and innovation of SMEs.

Some of the key findings include:

- SMEs often face higher tax compliance costs, in relative terms, due to their smaller size. When designing and implementing tax policies, governments should consider whether certain measures have a disproportionate impact on SMEs. Many countries provide special provisions and simplification measures that are designed to reduce the tax compliance costs of SMEs.
- The heterogeneity of the SME population means careful targeting is required to ensure that any government interventions, including tax preferences, achieve their stated policy objectives. With the exception of the disproportionately high compliance costs on SMEs, the size of a business alone may not be sufficient justification for government intervention in the form of special rules. Careful targeting of special tax rules can reduce their costs and potential distortions while ensuring that the intended goals are met.
- There may be a particular case for targeting preferences and simplification measures toward younger SMEs, who are most affected by finance and cash flow difficulties, face barriers to entry and growth from incumbent firms, are more likely to grow than older SMEs, face the highest compliance cost burdens and are likely to have higher spillover effects from innovation. Nonetheless, even within this group, measures should be carefully targeted to address the specific problem (e.g. access to finance, compliance costs) or particular objective (e.g. innovation). Young, small firms are also the riskiest and most likely to go out of business.
- Caution is needed to ensure that tax preferences or simplification measures do not introduce further distortions. These distortions can result in incentives to alter economic activity in unintended ways to benefit from special tax rules, horizontal inequities in the treatment of different firms or individuals depending on their characteristics, or the creation of additional barriers to SME growth owing to the creation of sized-based thresholds which provide incentives to remain under that threshold, whether artificially or by restraining growth.

- When introducing special tax rules for SMEs, care should be taken to ensure that these measures do not increase complexity. The costs associated with tracking eligibility, keeping specific records and interacting with the tax system for multiple different preferences or simplification measures can increase the complexity of the system. In this regard a simpler general tax system may be more advantageous to SMEs than a series of simplification measures.
- Process simplifications, particularly through targeted use of technology, offer many advantages in lowering compliance costs by streamlining and reducing the steps required to comply. They can, therefore, be a powerful tool to enhance compliance and reduce its costs.

The taxation of SMEs is an important issue given their importance to the economies of countries. Careful design of government programmes for SMEs, including special tax rules, can address market failures and the disproportionately high compliance burdens faced by SMEs. Consideration of the heterogeneity of the SME sector and the different challenges faced by SMEs and their owners need to be considered in the design of the taxation rules as governments endeavour to promote the creation, innovation and growth of SMEs.

*Chapter 1*

# The role of SMEs in domestic economies

*This chapter provides an overview of SME characteristics in OECD and G20 countries. It firstly considers their role in domestic economies, examining their contribution to employment, value-added and exports. It then considers characteristics of SMEs for tax purposes, considering their share of total taxable business income, their average taxable income at the entity level, and whether their income is subject to single or double-level taxation.*

## 1.1. Introduction

This chapter describes some overarching characteristics of small and medium-sized enterprises (SMEs) in OECD and G20 countries. In particular, it considers their role in the economy and their characteristics relevant for tax purposes, including their taxable business income and tax status as single or double-taxed entities. It draws on existing OECD databases as well as data on taxable income and business form that were reported by the 38 countries that replied to a questionnaire on the taxation of SMEs distributed in March 2015. This information is intended to provide context for the discussion of tax policy and administration issues in the remainder of the study.

The chapter uses definitions of SMEs which are based on either the number of employees or the annual turnover, using categories that are consistent with the European Commission's definition of micro, small and medium-sized enterprises (see Box 1.1 for a fuller description of how SMEs can be defined). Recognising that countries use a number of definitions of SMEs, the later chapters of the study consider SMEs as defined in national jurisdictions for the purpose of the measure being addressed.

This chapter is structured as follows. Section 1.2 considers the role of SMEs in the economy through their contribution to employment, value-added, exports and innovation. It also considers their survival rates. Section 1.3 considers tax characteristics of SMEs, including the amount of taxable business income from entities of different sizes and tax statuses. Section 1.4 concludes.

### Box 1.1. Defining SMEs

There is no single agreed definition of a SME, nor is there a sole criterion that determines SME status. A variety of definitions are applied in OECD and G20 countries, though almost all make references to SMEs as non-subsidiary, independent economic entities that are not controlled by a large or medium-sized enterprise. Common categories used in the definition, however, include the number of employees, annual turnover and the size of the balance sheet (net assets).

A commonly-used categorisation for SMEs is provided by the European Commission (Recommendation 2003/361/EC of 6 May 2003). The commission classifies micro, small and medium-sized enterprises based on their number of employees and either turnover or balance sheet total, stating that SMEs are "enterprises which employ fewer than 250 persons and which have an annual turnover not exceeding EUR 50 million, and/or an annual balance sheet total not exceeding EUR 43 million". Within this definition, a small enterprise is defined as having less than 50 employees and turnover or balance sheet of less than EUR 10 million; and a microenterprise as a firm with less than 10 employees and a balance sheet or turnover below EUR 2 million.

Many non-EU OECD and G20 countries use alternative definitions. Canada defines SMEs as firms with fewer than 500 employees, while a number of countries cap the limit for a SME at a lower number of employees, such as 100 in Israel and 19 in New Zealand. Chile uses an annual turnover cap of UF 100 000 (CLP 2.49 billion, EUR 3.59m) to define SMEs, the Russian Federation has a RUB 1 000 million (EUR 16.76 million) turnover limit, India places upper bounds of INR 100 million (EUR 1.38 million) and INR 50 million (EUR 0.69 million) on investment in plant and machinery, and equipment, respectively, and Indonesia requires net assets worth less than IDR 200 million (EUR 13 250) and ownership by an Indonesian national as two of five necessary criteria for SMEs. Further, within China, Japan, Korea and Mexico, the definition of a SME varies depending on the sector being examined.

Box 1.1. **Defining SMEs** *(continued)*

Definitions within countries may be set to reflect different country-specific considerations. These often relate to economic, financial, political and social settings or concerns, and thus greater harmonisation of definitions both within and across countries has proved challenging. Furthermore, within-country differences may exist for data collection purposes. For example, some banks and financial institutions do not use national statistical definitions for a SME but a different definition to collect data on SME financing

The definition of a SME may also vary for tax purposes. For example, eligibility for the reduced SME tax rate in Luxembourg is based on the level of taxable income, whereas in Canada and Japan it is based on the capital of the business. France and Spain use a gross turnover test to determine eligibility for their concessionary SME rates. Businesses in Belgium, on the other hand, are only eligible for the reduced SME rates if they meet requirements relating not just to taxable income, but also to the activities of the company, the shareholding, the dividend yield and the remuneration of the managers of the business.

## 1.2. SMEs' contribution to domestic economies

Based on the definition of SMEs used by the European Commission (less than 250 employees and less than EUR 50 million of turnover), responses to the questionnaire indicate that SMEs account for almost all firms, representing over 99% of all firms in each country. In all countries, micro-firms (defined as firms with less than 10 persons employed) are the most common form of enterprise: they account for between 78% of firms in Japan and 96% of all firms in Denmark, India, the Netherlands, Spain and Sweden).[1]

SMEs are a diverse group of entities, differing largely in terms of size, from micro-enterprises to medium-sized companies. They operate in a wide range of sectors, as shown in Figure 1.1 within the service provision sector.

Figure 1.1. **Composition of SMEs in the service sector, 2012**

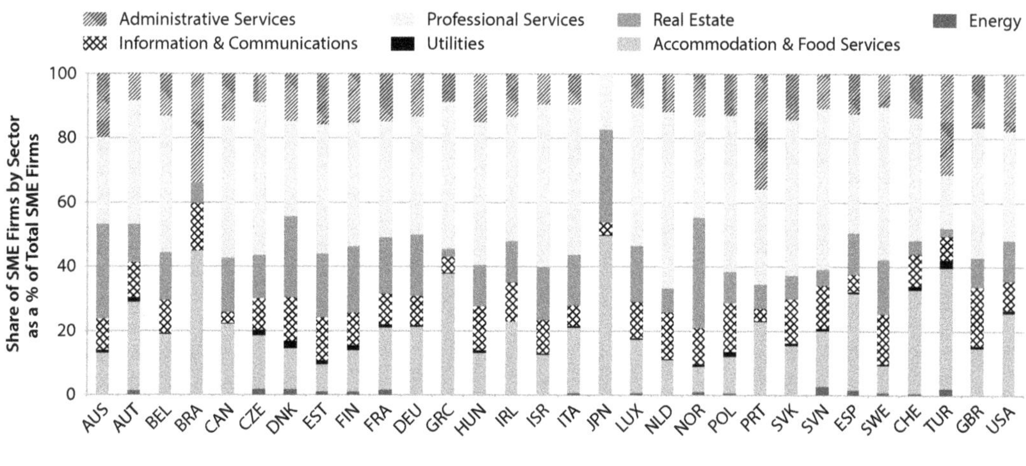


*Source:* OECD Structural and Demographic Business Statistics, http://dx.doi.org/10.1787/sdbs-data-en.

SMEs also vary markedly in terms of their competition, propensity to innovate and growth potential. Some SMEs are new firms that tend to grow quickly while many remain small firms. Across all firms, OECD (2014) estimates that high-growth firms (defined as firms with average employee growth of more than 20% per year over three years and with more than ten employees at the outset) account for between two and six per cent of the firm population, with 1% of the population of firms being "gazelle" firms – high-growth firms in their first five years of employing staff.

This section considers the importance of SMEs in economies with respect to a number of characteristics, including their contribution to employment, value-added, exports and innovation. It concludes by looking at their survival rates. Information in this section has been drawn from the Structural and Demographic Business Statistics database, *Entrepreneurship at a Glance* (OECD, 2015) and questionnaire responses.

## *Employment*

SMEs contribute significantly to total employment. In all countries for which data was provided, with the exception of India, SMEs account for over half of total employees,[2] whether defined by the number of employees or by the amount of turnover.

Figure 1.2 shows the number of persons employed by firms with less than 250 employees (left-hand panel) and with a turnover smaller than EUR 50 million (right-hand panel), as a percentage of total employment. The remaining percentage of total employment is provided by large firms (i.e. those classified above these thresholds). The figure shows that although countries vary in the proportion of employment provided by SMEs, as a whole, SMEs employ at least 60% of persons employed in all but four countries for which data was reported (Australia, France, India and Luxembourg). They account for over 75% of persons employed in Chile, Estonia, Japan and New Zealand, with firms with less than 250 employees employing 66% of the labour force on average, and 77% for businesses with an annual turnover of less than EUR 50 million. The low proportion of those hired by SMEs in India may reflect the presence of unregistered firms that account for a significant proportion of employment.

Figure 1.2. **Relative contribution of SMEs to total number of persons employed, 2014**

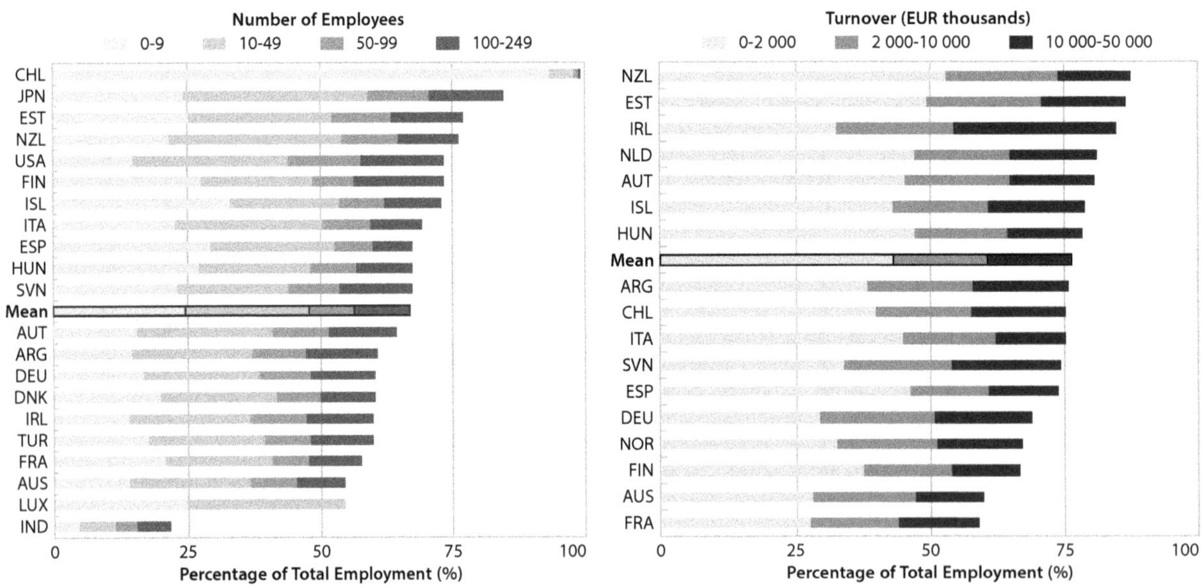


*Source:* Responses to an OECD questionnaire, *Survey on the Taxation of Small and Medium-Sized Enterprises,* 2015. See Annex B for country details and caveats. The mean is the unweighted average of the countries shown in each graph.

Micro-enterprises (i.e. less than 10 persons employed, or less than EUR 2 million in turnover) in particular account for a significant share of employment. Together with small enterprises (less than 50 employees or turnover smaller than EUR 2 million) they provide the greatest share of employment, accounting for at least 30% of total employment across all countries, except India, and over 50% in Estonia, Japan and New Zealand. However, in some countries, such as the United States, businesses without employees may be "independent contractors" and are similar to workers.[3]

The contribution of SMEs to employment differs by sector. In the service sector, a greater proportion of employment is found in SMEs than in the manufacturing sector, partly reflecting the capital intensive nature of manufacturing, although SMEs account for over 50% of employment in both sectors in all countries except Germany, Russia and the United States. SMEs operating in the service sector employ a greater percentage of employees than those in the manufacturing sector in all countries except the Netherlands, Portugal and the United Kingdom. Figure 1.3 shows the proportion of total employment in each sector in SMEs across countries.

Figure 1.3. **Employment, SME share, manufacturing and services (2012 or latest available year)**

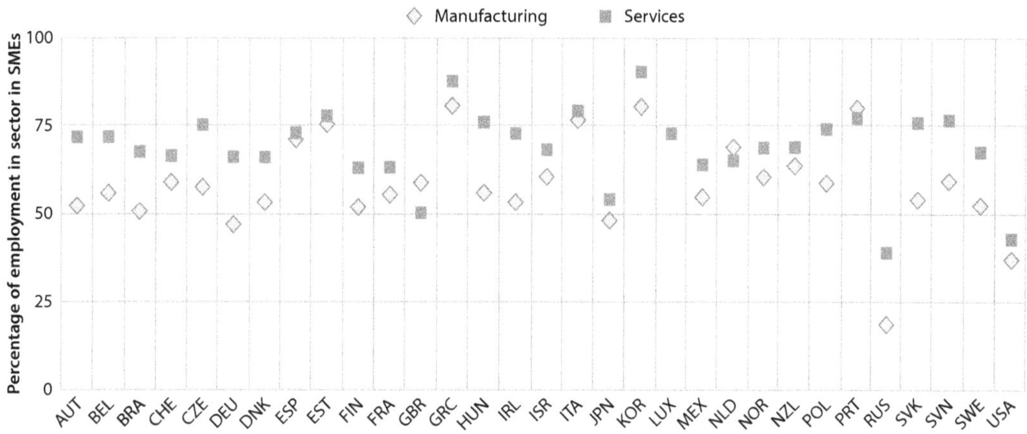


*Source:* Calculations based on OECD (2015), *Entrepreneurship at a Glance 2015*, OECD Publishing, Paris. Figures for Ireland and Israel are for 2011. Figures for Mexico are for 2009. Data for Japan are provided by the Small and Medium Enterprise Agency in Japan, using the 2012 Economic Census for Business Activity (MIC, METI) in Japan, and show the share of enterprises with less than 300 employees.

SMEs employ around 60% of employees in the manufacturing sector despite making up over 99% of the firm population. Micro-enterprises also play a more significant role in the services sector than in the manufacturing sector, accounting on average for around 34% of total employment in the service sector and 14% in manufacturing (OECD, 2015).

## *SME contribution to value-added and exports*

In most economies, SMEs account for a considerable proportion of value-added (defined as the difference between production and intermediate consumption), although the proportion is lower than for the number of persons employed due to the typically lower labour productivity of SMEs compared to larger firms. SMEs' share of value-added, however, varies by sector and also by country, with SMEs in certain sectors (such as transportation, storage, gas, steam and air conditioning) contributing more to value-added in some countries than larger firms, although the relevant sectors differ between countries. The proportion of value-added derived from SMEs at an economy-wide level is shown in Figure 1.4 for 31 countries.

Figure 1.4 shows that the proportion of value-added from SMEs ranges from just over 30% in Mexico to 84% in Luxembourg, with SMEs in most countries accounting for between 55 to 75% of value-added. A significant proportion of this comes from the smallest SMEs, due to their greater numbers. Large enterprises account for comparably more value-added on a firm by firm basis; on average, they account for 42% of value-added despite accounting for less than 1% of firms (OECD, 2015).

Figure 1.4. **Value added, by enterprise size (2012 or latest available year)**

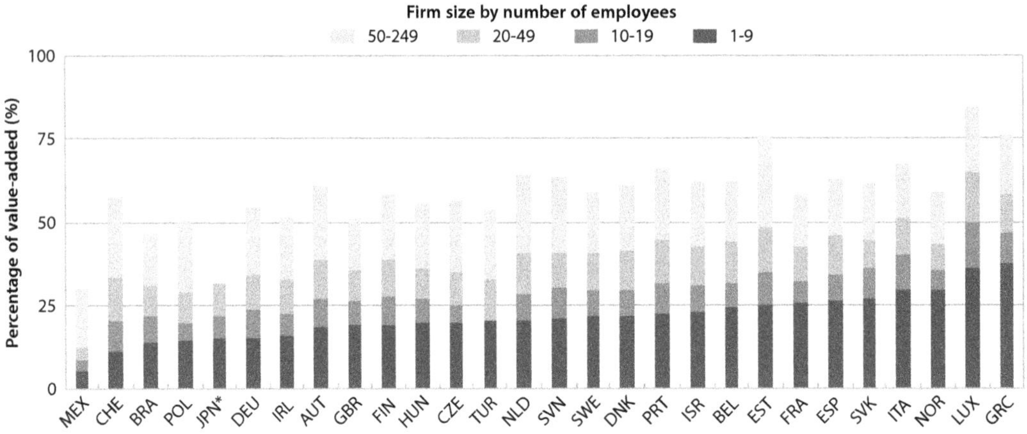


*Source:* OECD (2015), *Entrepreneurship at a Glance 2015*, OECD Publishing, Paris.

* Data for Japan for the 50 to 249 size class is not shown as the data collected for Japan does not separately identify these enterprises.

The share of direct exports from SMEs varies significantly across countries, ranging from just over 6% in Mexico to over 54% in Ireland. SMEs account for less than half of total exports in all but two countries, as shown in Figure 1.5. Notably, within the SME sector, it is medium-sized enterprises (enterprises with between 50 and 250 employees), rather than micro or small enterprises, which contribute most to exports in each country, with the exception of Ireland.

Figure 1.5. **Export by enterprise size class (2012 or latest available year)**

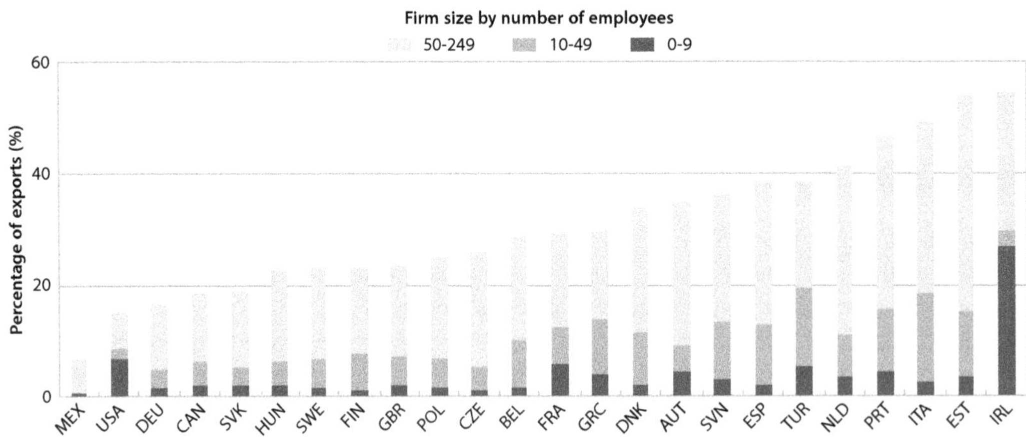


*Source:* OECD (2015), *Entrepreneurship at a Glance 2015*, OECD Publishing, Paris.

Figure 1.5 notes only the direct contribution to exports made by SMEs. SMEs may also make indirect contributions to exports as suppliers of larger exporting businesses. Preliminary estimates of the scale of this impact suggest that it can significantly exceed the direct effect (OECD, 2015).

SMEs are also increasingly involved in global value chains as partners, suppliers and distributors of large and multinational companies. This presents a range of opportunities, including benefits from involvement in new, global and niche markets for the provision of specialised products and services, the ability to outsource non-core activities, and co-operation with partners both upstream and downstream (OECD, 2008). Firms that are able to respond quickly and to innovate are better-positioned to play a part in these global value chains (OECD, 2014). Tax settings that are conducive to growth and that support SME finance and innovation are part of the broad backdrop necessary to promote SME involvement in global value chains.

In all countries for which data were reported, higher shares of large firms are involved in innovation activity than SMEs. On average, in these countries, 27% of SMEs engaged in some form of innovation against 55% of larger enterprises. This may reflect the greater impact of barriers to innovation (such as lack of funding, or the high costs of innovation) on smaller than larger enterprises (OECD, 2014).

### *Survival*

Younger businesses tend to have a high failure rate than older firms, with over half of enterprises failing by the fifth year of their operation. Data for a selection of countries in Table 1.1 indicates the successive survival rates of new enterprises (regardless of their size) in the first five years of their operation. While this will be affected by prevailing macroeconomic conditions which can differ between years, it indicates the high rate of volatility among younger firms.

Table 1.1. **Survival rates of new businesses in first five years of operation, 2012**

| Country | Year 1 | Year 2 | Year 3 | Year 4 | Year 5 |
|---|---|---|---|---|---|
| Austria | 87% | 77% | 66% | 60% | 55% |
| Czech Republic | 84% | 63% | 54% | 48% | 43% |
| Hungary | 70% | 53% | 41% | 32% | 27% |
| Italy | 83% | 69% | 53% | 45% | 38% |
| Luxembourg | 91% | 75% | 66% | 58% | 50% |
| Portugal | 85% | 68% | 56% | 46% | 39% |
| Slovenia | 84% | 70% | 52% | 48% | 43% |
| Spain | 74% | 60% | 45% | 36% | 29% |

*Source:* OECD calculations based on OECD Structural and Demographic Business Statistics, http://dx.doi.org/10.1787/sdbs-data-en.

## 1.3. Taxable income and tax status of SMEs

This section discusses characteristics of SMEs from a tax perspective, drawing on data reported by G20 and OECD countries in questionnaire responses. It considers first the total taxable business income of SMEs (at the entity level), looking at the share of total taxable income of different sized SMEs and the average taxable income for firms of different sizes. It then considers the proportion of entities at different size levels that are double-taxed (i.e. where SME income is taxed at both the entity and the personal level) and the respective contributions to taxable business income from single-taxed and double-taxed entities.

### *Taxable income*

Taxable business income at the entity level includes taxable income from single-taxed entities (reported as personal income) as well as business-level income from double-taxed entities. It does not include personal income from double-taxed entities in the form of dividends or capital gains, to include this would be double-counting. However, taxable income at the entity level will not necessarily include all SME income, particularly for owner-operated business as it will not include SME income paid as labour income to the owner. The labour income of the owner of a SME, whether single or double-taxed, will typically be deductible against business income and treated as taxable personal income of the owner.[4]

The share of SMEs in total business income differs markedly across the countries which provided data in response to the questionnaire. These results are summarised in Figure 1.6, which indicates the relative contribution to total taxable business income at the entity level reported within countries by different sized firms. The left hand side of the figure shows the break-down by the number of people the SME employs, while the right hand side is broken-down by the annual turnover of firms. The remaining contribution is derived from large firms, defined as firms with more than 250 employees and turnover greater than EUR 50 million, respectively.

Figure 1.6. **SMEs relative contribution to total taxable business profits at entity level, 2014**

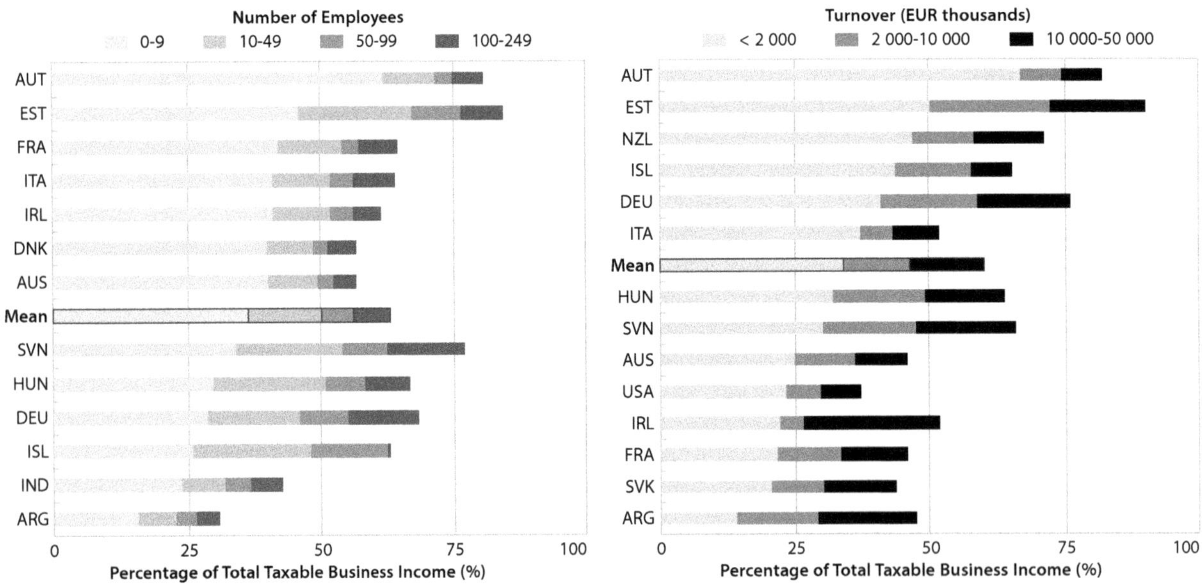


*Source:* Responses to an OECD questionnaire, *Survey on the Taxation of Small and Medium-Sized Enterprises*, 2015. See Annex B for country details and caveats. The mean is the unweighted average of the countries shown in each graph.

Figure 1.6 shows that the amount of taxable business income of firms with less than 250 employees ranges between 31% of total business income in Argentina to 85% in Estonia, averaging 63% for the countries for which data is available. A similar pattern is observed for firms with turnover of less than EUR 50 million, whose share of total taxable business income ranges from 38% of total business income in the United States to 90% in Estonia, averaging 63% among the countries that provided data.

The smallest category of firms by employment (i.e. those with nine employees or fewer) accounts for a larger share of taxable income than firms with 10-250 employees, averaging 35%, seven percentage points more than the three other SME categories combined. A similar picture can also be seen for firms with the lowest level of annual turnover (less than EUR 2 million), averaging 34%; in all but two countries these firms contribute over 20% of taxable income, while in the majority of countries this rises to over 30% of taxable income.

The greater contribution of the smallest SMEs to total taxable business income is largely due to their high share in the firm population in each country. Although the share of total business income is larger for the smallest SMEs than for larger entities, average taxable income per firm increases relatively steadily with firm size, both on an unweighted average basis across the countries that provided this data and also within each of the individual countries.

Figure 1.7 illustrates the average total taxable business income at entity level reported by single and double-taxed firms across the countries that provided data. For the figure on the left-hand panel, firm size is categorised by the number of employees, and on the right-hand side, by annual turnover. The underlying data for each country is presented in Annex B.

The average total taxable business income for both single and double-taxed firms increases quasi-exponentially as the size of the business increases. The average total taxable business income at entity level of double-taxed micro-enterprises is EUR 47 000 compared to EUR 12.1 million for the largest firms (by employees) and EUR 22 000 compared to EUR 22.1 million (by turnover). At all business sizes – defined by number of employees – double-taxed firms have higher average taxable income than single-taxed firms. The difference between the two is relatively small when the size of the business is small, but the gap between the two firm structures widens as the size of the firm increases.

Figure 1.7. **Unweighted country averages of total taxable business profits at entity level for single-taxed and double-taxed firms, 2014**

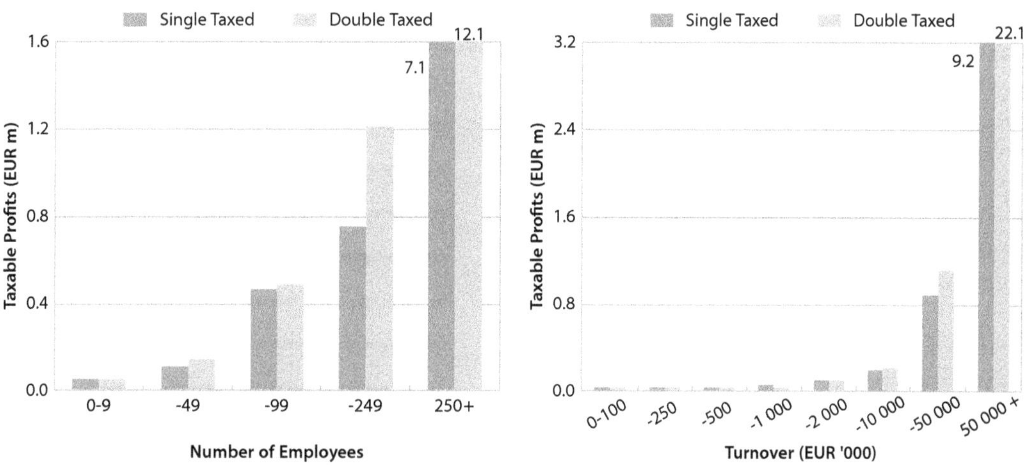


*Source:* Responses to an OECD questionnaire, *Survey on the Taxation of Small and Medium-Sized Enterprises*, 2015. Countries included are AUS, AUT, DNK, EST, FRA, DEU, HUN, IND, IRL, ITA, NZL, SVN (left-hand panel) and AUS, AUT, CAN, EST, FRA, DEU, HUN, ISL, IRL, ITA, KOR, NZL, POR, SVN, USA (right-hand panel). Individual country calculations and caveats are provided in Annex B.

Both the increasing levels of taxable income with entity size and the higher levels of taxable income in double-taxed entities are representative of the patterns observed at individual country level, which are shown individually in Annex B.

### *Tax status of enterprises as single- or double-taxed*

The income of SMEs may be taxed at the personal level only, or at both the entity level and again at the personal level when the income is distributed to the owners or investors. In many but not all cases, the tax status of a SME follows its legal form, with unincorporated entities generally being single-taxed and incorporated entities generally being double-taxed – although this assumption is not true for all countries, as described in Chapter 2. Incorporation may offer a number of advantages to business, including in many cases limited liability of the shareholders, improved access to capital markets and increased ease of business continuity.[5] However, the formation of an incorporated business is generally more costly in terms of legal fees in establishing and registering articles of incorporation, compared with setting up an unincorporated business, and typically has higher ongoing costs.

Double-level taxation of businesses is increasingly common as business size increases, whether measured by employment or by turnover. Across all countries for which data was provided in response to the questionnaire, larger entities are more likely to be doubled-taxed than smaller entities. This likelihood increases as firm size increases, whether measured

Figure 1.8. **Proportion of double-taxed entities by firm size, 2014**

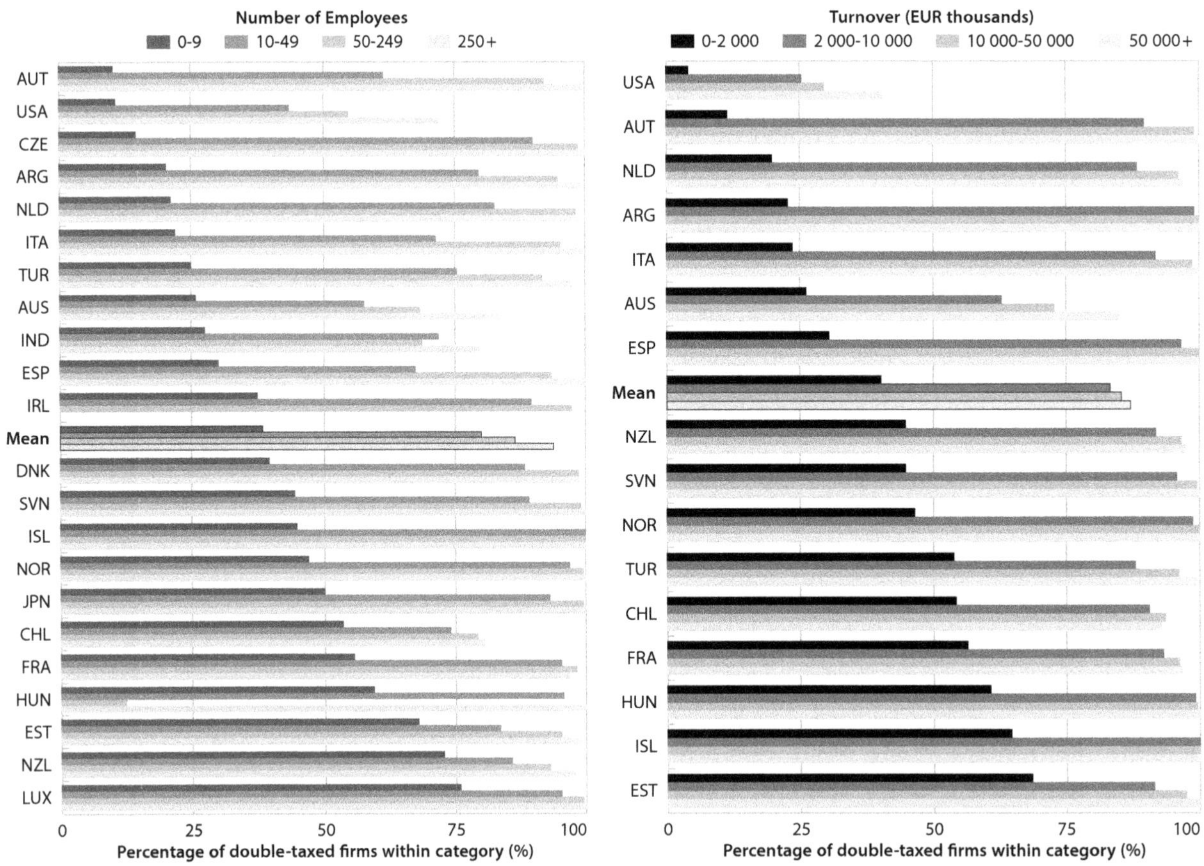


*Source:* Responses to an OECD questionnaire, *Survey on the Taxation of Small and Medium-Sized Enterprises*, 2015. See Annex B for country details and caveats. The mean is the unweighted average of the countries shown in each graph.

in terms of number of employees or turnover, where all countries except the United States (which allows flow-through taxation of many incorporated entities so that they are taxed only at the personal level) report that over 60% of large firms are taxed at both the entity and the personal level. The most marked difference in tax status is observed between micro and small enterprises: that is, in firms on either side of the boundary marked by ten employees or turnover of more than EUR 2 million. As double-tax status often, but not necessarily, follows incorporation, this implies that firms are more likely to incorporate as they grow in size. An unweighted average of the respondents to the questionnaire illustrates that 38% of firms with nine or fewer employees have double-tax status. The number of firms with double-tax status rises to 79% and 86% for businesses with 10-49 employees and 50-249 employees, while the rate for enterprises with 250 employees or more is 94 percent. The equivalent rates for firms classified by turnover size follow a similar pattern; 40 percent, 83 percent, 85% and 87% for businesses with turnover smaller than EUR 2 million, between EUR 2 and 10 million, between EUR 10 and 50 million and over EUR 50 million, respectively.

Figure 1.8 illustrates the proportion of entities of each size that are taxed at both the entity and the personal level. It shows entities by the number of employees working in firms (left-hand side) and by the amount of firm turnover (right-hand side). Countries are ranked by the share of microenterprises.

### *Business income by tax status*

The amount of total taxable business income reported by single and double-taxed entities also varies considerably between countries. Figure 1.9 shows the relative share of total taxable business income of single and double-taxed firms of all sizes in each country which provided this information.

Figure 1.9. **Contribution to total taxable business profits at entity level by firm structure, 2014**

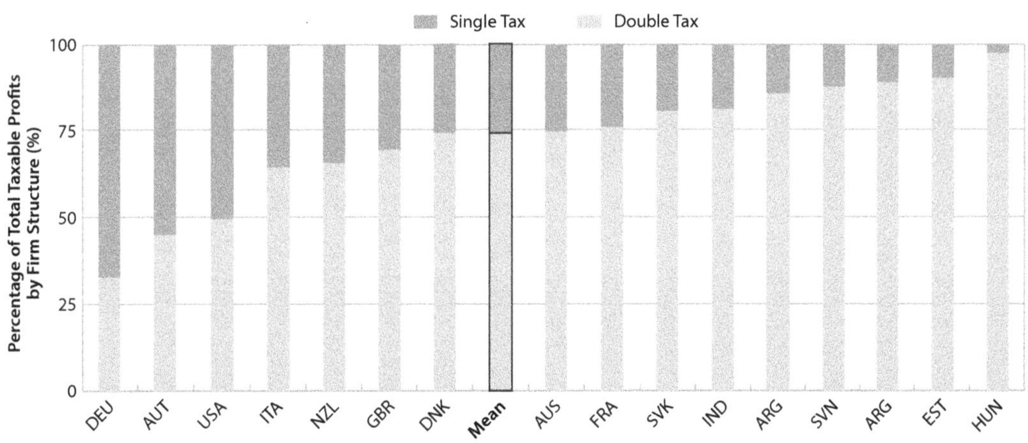


*Source:* Responses to an OECD questionnaire, *Survey on the Taxation of Small and Medium-Sized Enterprises*, 2015. See Annex B for country details and caveats. The mean is the unweighted average of the countries shown in the graph.

In all countries other than Austria, Germany and the United States, double-taxed enterprises report a greater share of taxable business income than single-level taxed entities. This is partially linked to the fact that double-taxed entities typically report higher levels of taxable income than single-taxed entities. On average, double-taxed firms reported 74% of total taxable income. A significant factor in the difference between the contributions to taxable firms across countries is the overall level of double-level taxation of entities within those countries. For example, in Austria and the United States around 13% of businesses are subject to double-level taxation, compared to 33% and 58% in Slovenia and Estonia, respectively.

## 1.4. Conclusions

SMEs are a strongly diverse group, spanning all sectors of the economy. They differ in terms of employment, from micro-enterprises with less than ten employees and less than EUR 2 million in turnover to medium-sized enterprises with up to 250 employees and EUR 50 million in turnover. They also differ in whether they export or innovate; and growth rates differ strongly among SMEs, from high-growth young enterprises to businesses that fail in the early years of their operation.

In all of the countries measured, SMEs make up over 99% of all firms. The large numbers of SMEs mean that they contribute significantly to total employment, particularly in the service sector. The number of micro-enterprises means that they account for a substantial share of employment in most of the jurisdictions considered. Micro-enterprises also account for a significant share of value-added, although the higher labour productivity of larger firms means that the share of value-added from SMEs is lower, relative to their share in employment. Medium-sized enterprises and larger firms contribute more to exports, although SMEs indirect contribution to exports as suppliers and partners of larger firms should not be underestimated.

From a tax perspective, SMEs report the largest proportion of total taxable business income, with much of this being reported by micro-enterprises due to their share in firm population. Taxable income rises steadily with firm size, as does the proportion of firms subject to double-level taxation. On average, double-level taxed firms are more profitable than single-level taxed firms of the same size, and consequently they report a greater share of total taxable income.

The following chapters examine the different dimensions of tax policy and administration that affect SMEs of different sizes, forms and activities. Those tax dimensions can affect a number of important economic margins at which SME owners, investors and managers make decisions.

## Notes

1. Full information for each country is provided in Annex B, showing the number of firms (as a proportion of total firms) at different levels of turnover in each country, by single- and double-taxed status.
2. Data provided in the questionnaire was on the number of persons employed, not the full-time equivalent employment.
3. The distinction between an independent contractor and an employee depends on the specific facts. In the United States, the general rule is that an individual is an independent contractor if the payer has the right to control only the result of the work and not what will be done and how it will be done. The earnings of a person who is working as an independent contractor are subject to Self-Employment Tax (United States Internal Revenue Service, 2015).

4. Labour income of owners is not deductible in the United States if the SME is organised as a sole proprietorship or partnership.

5. The United States is an exception in that limited liability of shareholders is not limited to corporate entities and may explain why most SMEs in the United States are organised in single-taxed entities discussed below.

## References

European Commission (2005), *The new SME definition: User guide and model declaration*, EC Publishing, Brussels, http://ec.europa.eu/enterprise/policies/sme/files/sme_definition/sme_user_guide_en.pdf.

Fowkes, R., J. Sousa and N. Duncan (2015), "Evaluation of Research and Development Tax Credit", HMRC Working Paper 17, https://www.gov.uk/government/uploads/system/uploads/attachment_data/file/413629/HMRC_WorkingPaper_17_R_D_Evaluation_Final.pdf.

Government of India (2006), *Definitions of Micro, Small & Medium Enterprises,* www.dcmsme.gov.in/ssiindia/defination_msme.htm.

Government of Indonesia (1995), *Small Enterprise Act No. 9 of 1995 (UNDANG UNDANG REPUBLIK INDONESIA NOMOR 9 TAHUN 1995 TENTANG USAHA KECILL)*, www.dcmsme.gov.in/Policies/highlights_of_internatinal_policies/Indonesia%20Policy.pdf.

New Zealand Ministry of Economic Development (2011), *SMEs in New Zealand: Structure and Dynamics 2011*, www.med.govt.nz/business/business-growth-internationalisation/pdf-docs-library/small-and-medium-sized-enterprises/structure-and-dynamics-2011.pdf.

OECD (2015), *Entrepreneurship at a Glance 2015*, OECD Publishing, Paris, http://dx.doi.org/10.1787/entrepreneur_aag-2015-en.

OECD (2014), *Entrepreneurship at a Glance 2014*, OECD Publishing, Paris, http://dx.doi.org/10.1787/entrepreneur_aag-2014-en.

OECD (2008), *Enhancing the Role of SMEs in Global Value Chains*, OECD Publishing, Paris, http://dx.doi.org/10.1787/9789264051034-en.

OECD, WTO and World Bank Group (2014), *Global Value Chains: Challenges, Opportunities, and Implications for Policy*, Report prepared for submission to the G20 Trade Ministers Meeting Sydney, Australia, 19 July 2014, www.oecd.org/tad/gvc_report_g20_july_2014.pdf.

# Chapter 2

# Income taxation of SMEs

*This chapter describes the different tax regimes that apply to SME income under both corporate and personal tax regimes. Firstly, the chapter provides a framework for considering the influence of tax policy issues on the decisions of SME owners, before considering the link between legal and tax status. Secondly, the chapter considers the taxation of SMEs taxed only at the personal level, estimating the marginal tax rates at different levels of SME income. Thirdly, the chapter discusses the taxation of SMEs which are double-taxed, considering taxation at the corporate level and subsequent taxation at the personal level when the income is distributed to the owner. Finally, the chapter concludes by discussing the impact of income taxation on the decisions of SME owners.*

## 2.1. Introduction

This chapter describes the different tax regimes that apply to income from SMEs under personal and corporate income tax regimes. It describes the general rules rather than preferences that apply in some cases, which are described in Chapter 3 of this study. The study considers tax rules as they apply to SMEs operating in a domestic context and does not consider cross-border or international tax issues that may arise for SMEs engaged in transnational activity.[1]

Section 2.2 of this chapter provides an overview of the framework and assumptions used in this chapter. Section 2.3 discusses the taxation of SMEs when they are taxed only at the personal level. Section 2.4 discusses the taxation of SMEs that are subject to taxation at both the business and personal levels. Section 2.5 concludes by discussing the impact of income taxes at different economic margins.

## 2.2. Framework and assumptions

The way in which SME income is taxed, and the different forms of taxation depending on the form of the business or distribution of income, can influence a number of decisions made by the owner. These decisions include whether to move into self-employment from employment (or unemployment), whether to operate a SME formally or informally, whether to incorporate the business or not, and decisions about whether income should be distributed as dividends, capital gains, or as compensation for labour (i.e. wages). The decisions do not occur linearly and may be revisited throughout the life and growth of the SME. They are summarised in Figure 2.1.

Many of these decisions will be affected by a myriad of factors not examined in this study, such as the ability of SMEs to attract finance or the availability of limited liability. However, examining marginal statutory tax rates that apply to different forms of income and to unincorporated and incorporated SMEs can provide some indication of the influence of the tax system on each of these economic margins.

This chapter reviews the income taxation of SMEs considering personal and corporate income taxes. In most countries, the taxation of a SME under personal and corporate taxes will depend on its business form: typically, unincorporated SMEs are taxed only at the personal level whereas incorporated SMEs are taxed first at the corporate level and then again when profits are distributed at the personal level, subject to any integration measures between these levels of taxation. When corporate taxes apply, differential rates may be applied for business under a certain size threshold. In some countries, the nature of the tax treatment may differ from the legal status of the firms, where in some circumstances unincorporated businesses are taxed at both the corporate and personal levels, or incorporated businesses may be taxed only at the personal level. Table 2.1 summarises the extent to which taxation follows the legal form of the entity in 37 countries.

In addition to personal and corporate income taxes, social security contributions (SSCs) may also apply to SME income. Thirty-two OECD countries levy SSCs, with Australia and New Zealand being the only exceptions. Contributions are levied on both employees and employers and separately on the self-employed. Germany and Japan do not have compulsory self-employed SSCs and Poland has compulsory self-employed SSCs paid as a lump sum. Employee and employer SSCs are typically levied on labour income alone, whereas self-employed SSC are generally levied on total taxable business income, including both labour and capital income. The design of these systems varies, as described more fully in Annex C.

Figure 2.1. **Influence of taxation on SME economic margins**

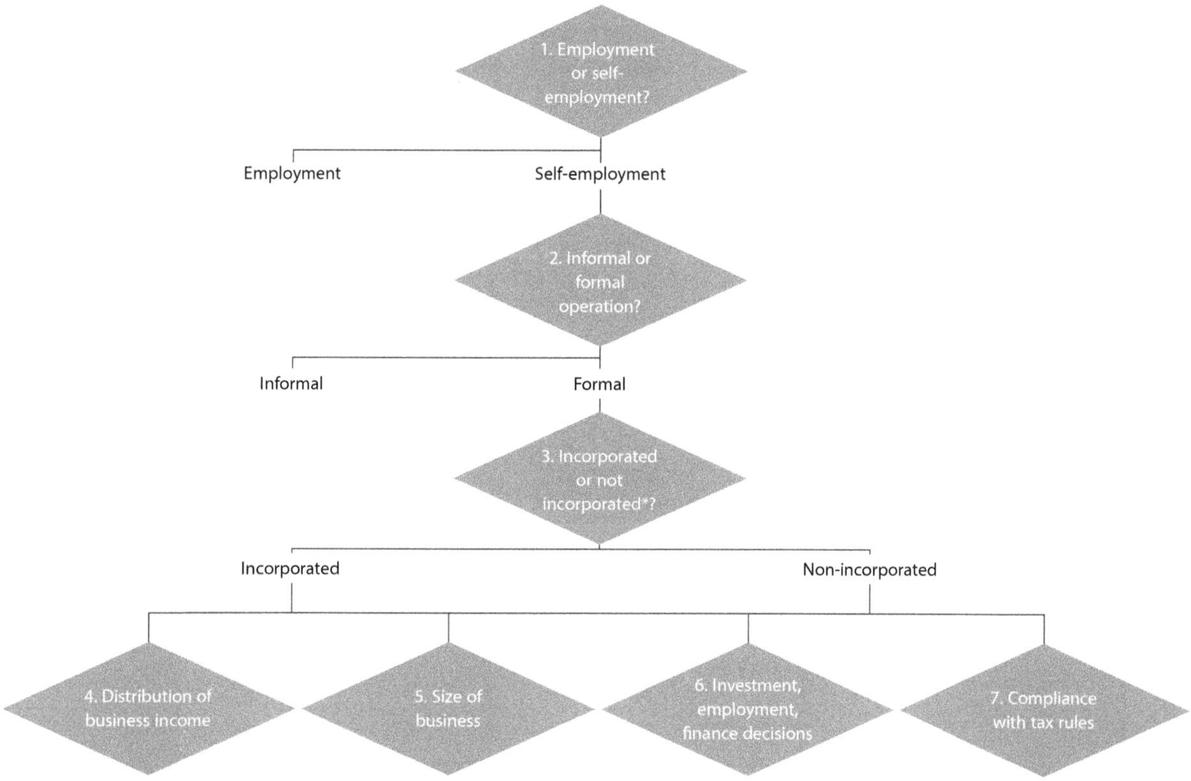


* This assumes that the tax consequences of incorporation are to add a layer of taxation at the entity level. This may not be the case for all entities as in some countries, some incorporated entities are taxed only at the personal level, or some unincorporated entities may be subject to taxation at both the entity and personal level. Table 2.1 provides a brief description of these exceptions.

In some countries, SMEs may be taxed under special taxation regimes that differ from standard personal or corporate income tax rules. Examples of these regimes include presumptive taxes that base the calculation of tax on a proxy for income (e.g. turnover or number of employees) or the specific SME tax regimes existing in Hungary and Mexico. Eligibility for these schemes may be based on an entity's size, capitalisation, income, or age. These systems are described in Chapter 4.

Tax preferences may also affect the overall tax liability for a SME. Many countries apply preferential taxation of capital gains made on SME investments, or provide enhanced credits or deductions in respect of SME tax calculations. These are described in Chapter 3 but are not taken into account in this analysis of the general tax rules.

The tax rates reported in this chapter are statutory rates rather than effective rates as they do not include tax base considerations that determine the extent to which taxable business income differs from economic income, or the impact of tax credits in reducing tax liabilities. The way in which the tax base is calculated, particularly with regard to allowable deductions, may differ by entity type. Similarly, some tax credits are only available to one form of entity. For these reasons, cross-country comparisons of these rates require caution and care in the analysis. To the extent that tax base and tax credit provisions do not differ based on the form of entity, within country comparisons of single and double-taxed entities are useful as the tax rates provide an indication of the difference in effective tax rates between these forms. Where deductions and tax credits apply specifically to SMEs but not to other business forms, these are described in chapter 3, but are not taken into account in this analysis.

The marginal statutory tax rates shown in this chapter generally assume that the taxpayer is subject to the top marginal rate. However, not all SME owners face top personal rates so there is some discussion of rates faced at lower levels of income. Further assumptions specific to each form of taxation are described in the relevant subsections of this paper.

Table 2.1. **Single and double level taxation and relationship with incorporation**

| | Tax follows legal form | Unincorporated entities taxed under corporate income taxes | Incorporated entities taxed only under personal income taxes |
|---|---|---|---|
| Argentina | Y | | |
| Australia | Y | | |
| Austria | Y | | |
| Belgium | Y | | |
| Brazil | | Y SCP (silent partnerships) | |
| Canada | | Y Corporate-equivalent tax regime applies to publicly-traded partnerships and trusts (other than real estate investment trusts) | Y Co-operative corporations can distribute earnings as tax-deductible patronage dividends which are taxable only at the member level. |
| Chile | | Y *Sociedad de hecho*; a *Fondo de inversion privado* if it does not comply with the requisites for being taxed as such; co-ownerships; and an *Empresario individual* (individual business person) will be taxed under the Business Profits Tax. | Y *Sociedades professionales* and (as of 1 Jan 2017) any *Sociedad* with only individuals as owners or participants, may opt to pay the personal tax. |
| China | Y | | |
| Czech Republic | Y | | |
| Denmark | | | Y Partnership companies and limited partnerships |
| Estonia | | | Y Firms only subject to PIT |
| Finland | | | Y Partnerships and limited partnerships, although losses are quarantined at the entity level |
| France | | Y A fiscally-transparent tax regime applies to unincorporated entities (*sociétés créees de fait*), who can opt to be taxed under corporate tax. | Y Fiscally-transparent companies (including *sociétés civiles, sociétés en nom collectif, entreprises unipersonnelles en participation*) can opt to be taxed under corporate tax.<br><br>Companies with limited liability status taxed under CIT (*sociétés anonymes, sociétés par actions simplifiées, sociétés à responsabilité limitée*) can opt, under conditions, to be taxed only at the personal level for five years of creation of an unlisted company the capital of which is owned at least for 50% by individuals and at least for 34% by the company's president and or CEO and their family members. |
| Germany | Y | | |
| Greece | Y | | |
| Hungary | | Y Trust funds | |
| Iceland | | | Y Limited partnership companies, associate limited companies or general partnership companies that do not apply for independent tax status |
| India | | Y Partnership firms or limited liability partnerships | |
| Ireland | Y | | |
| Italy | Y | | |
| Japan | Y | Y Trusts (other than group investment trusts etc. and only where certain requirements are met) | |

Table 2.1. **Single and double level taxation and relationship with incorporation** *(continued)*

| | Tax follows legal form | Unincorporated entities taxed under corporate income taxes | Incorporated entities taxed only under personal income taxes |
|---|---|---|---|
| Korea | Y | | |
| Luxembourg | Y | | |
| Mexico | | Y Trusts and non-profit entities | |
| Netherlands | | Y Some partnerships | |
| New Zealand | | Y Unit trusts and Maori authorities | Y Look-through companies |
| Poland | | | Y Limited partnerships |
| Portugal | | | Y |
| Slovak Republic | | | Y Limited partnerships |
| Slovenia | Y | | |
| South Africa | Y | | |
| Spain | Y | | |
| Sweden | Y | | |
| Switzerland | | Y Associations and trusts; investment funds | |
| Turkey | | Y Partnerships, if double-tax status is requested | Y Unlimited companies |
| United Kingdom | Y | | |
| United States | | Y Check the box partnerships can elect taxation as corporations. Certain publicly traded partnerships taxed as corporations | Y S corporations (no more than 100 shareholders, under certain conditions). Certain kinds of funds (RICs and REITs) generally face single level of tax. |

*Source:* Responses to an OECD questionnaire, *Survey on the Taxation of Small and Medium-Sized Enterprises*, 2015.

## 2.3. Single-level taxation of SME income

This section discusses the taxation of SMEs that are subject to tax only at the personal level of the owner or owners. SMEs taxed only at the personal level are typically unincorporated businesses. They include both sole proprietors with or without employees and businesses with two or more owners, for example, general or limited partnership structures. In both cases, net business income typically flows through to the owner and is taxed at the personal level according to the relevant personal income tax structure. In certain cases, income from incorporated businesses may also flow-through to the owners and be treated as their personal income for tax purposes. These include look-through companies in New Zealand and S-corporations in the United States. Given the similar tax treatment of sole proprietorships and partnerships, the discussion in the paper around personal taxation of unincorporated business income concentrates on the sole proprietorship case.

In most countries, net unincorporated business income is taxed together with other personal taxable income, including employment income, according to the graduated personal income tax rate schedule applicable in that country. In countries with a dual income tax system, income from unincorporated businesses is divided into a business component (often based on a measure of a return to capital), which is taxed at business income tax rates (or, in the case of Norway, subject to a shielding deduction at the personal level), and a return to labour, which is included with other income from labour and taxed accordingly.

Box 2.1 provides further information on dual tax systems in Finland, Denmark and Sweden.

### Box 2.1. Taxation of business income under dual income tax systems

Under the dual income tax system operating in **Finland**, income from capital and earned income are treated separately. In particular, income from capital is subject to national income tax rate at a rate of 30% below EUR 30 000 and at 33% above this, while earned income is subject to national income tax at progressive rates and to municipal income tax and church tax at flat rates (depending on the municipality and church) and to social security contributions. Net business income generated by sole proprietorships and partnerships is distributed to their owners and taxed only in the personal income taxation of the owners. Net business income is divided into a capital income component and an earned income component in the personal taxation of owners using a formal division rule. The general division rule states that net business income is treated as capital income to a maximum amount of 20% of net capital used in the business (at the end of the previous tax year), with earned income determined as the residual amount of net business income. However, unlike the owners of partnerships, owners of sole proprietorships can also choose a) to have their net business income treated as capital income to a maximum amount of 10% of the net capital used in a business (at the end of the previous tax year), or b) have their whole net business income treated as earned income. Income from labour is subject to combined personal taxes and social security contributions (at the threshold for the highest income tax rate) of 62%. Dividends earned by natural persons on shares in non-listed companies are taxed in a different manner. Dividend income up to a maximum post-corporate tax return of 8% on the investor's shareholding is treated as capital income, with the remainder treated as earned income. Twenty-five per cent of the capital income dividend component (up to a maximum of EUR 150 000, and 85% beyond this limit) is taxable as capital income. Seventy-five per cent of the earned income dividend component is taxable as earned income.

Under the dual income tax system operating in **Denmark**, capital income, personal income (including employment income and business income), dividend and capital gains income from shares and controlled foreign company income are treated separately. Taxable income, consisting of the aggregate of personal income and capital income less general deductions, is subject to national income tax at progressive rates and to municipal income tax and church tax at a flat rate (depending on the municipality), with employment income subject to social security contributions. Income from shares up to DKK 49 200 is subject to national income tax at a flat rate of 27%, with a 42% rate applying above this limit. A special regime for business income of individuals allows income retained in a reserve to be taxed at a 24.5% rate (corresponding to the rate of corporate income tax). When income is withdrawn from the reserve, it is taxed as personal income at progressive rates with a credit for the 24.5% (reserve) tax. Income from labour is subject to combined personal taxes and social security contributions (at the threshold for the highest income tax rate) of 56%.

Under the dual income tax system operating in **Sweden**, capital income, business income and employment income are calculated separately, with net business income and net employment income aggregated to determine earned income. Capital income is subject to national income tax at a flat rate of 30% (20% for dividend income from a closely held company), while employment income is subject to national income tax at progressive rates, to municipal income tax at a flat rate (depending on the municipality) and to social security contributions. A special regime for business income of individuals allows income retained in an "expansion fund" to be subject to tax at a 22% rate (equal to the corporate income tax rate). When income is withdrawn from the expansion fund it is either taxed as employment income, or, if optional "positive interest allocation" rules are utilised, is split into a capital income component and an employment income component [with a credit for the 28% (reserve) tax]. Income from labour is subject to combined personal taxes and social security contributions (at the threshold for the highest income tax rate) of 69%.

There is a wide range of diversity in income levels within single-level taxed SMEs, as discussed further in Box 2.2. Consequently, the applicable marginal tax rates and social security contributions (SSCs) payable vary considerably between SMEs. To consider the difference that the level of income of the SME and its owner makes, this study considers tax rates on single-taxed enterprises at two levels of income: firstly, at the marginal tax rate where the top personal income tax threshold applies, and secondly, at the level of the average wage.

### Box 2.2. Single-taxed entities and levels of taxable income

As detailed in Chapter 1, the SME population is vastly different in terms of number of employees, turnover, the sectors that SMEs are involved in, exports and growth potential. There are consequently significant differences in the taxable income of SMEs. While taxable income tends to increase with size, as shown in Chapter 1, there remains significant variation in levels of taxable income reported by entities within each size group.

Single-taxed SMEs encompass a wide range of actors and entity types, not all of which correspond to the image of a small business. One example includes SMEs which provide a platform through which a sole proprietor offers professional services to larger companies, for example, a consultant. These types of SMEs typically have no (or a very limited number of) employees and in many ways, do not strongly differ economically from employees. As they are primarily a vehicle for supplying the labour of the owner, they may also have minimal deductions for tax purposes. Another example relates to providers of professional services, such as doctors or lawyers, who may operate alone or in partnerships. To the extent that these SMEs have higher incomes than the average SME income, the marginal rate at the top personal tax threshold may be a useful indicator. A third group of SMEs are those engaged in substantive business activity, providing goods and services to the public, often with a number of employees in addition to the owners. Each of these types of single-taxed SMEs has very different characteristics for tax purposes, including the level of taxable business income.

To better define the small business sector, Knittel (et al., 2011) developed two tests to determine whether reported business income was derived from "'substantial operations'… carried out in a 'businesslike' manner". The first of these tests was to determine whether the activity generated or had the potential to generate non-negligible income. For this test, a minimum of USD 10 000 of income or deductions was applied. The second test determined whether the business was making businesslike deductions (for example, rent employment, or payment to other firms for goods and services), so excluded entities that reported less than 5 000 of deductions. To identify small businesses in the remaining population, a threshold of USD 10 million of income and deductions was set.

Using this approach, the amount of small business income for different owners was identified, as set out in the following table:

**Average income from small businesses and from other sources for small business owners in the United States, 2010, USD**

| | Taxpayers with flow-through income | | With small business income/loss | | | | | |
|---|---|---|---|---|---|---|---|---|
| | | | With employees | | No employees | | All | |
| | Flow-through income | Adjusted gross income | Small business income | Adjusted gross income | Small business income | Adjusted gross income | Small business income | Adjusted gross income |
| Median | 2 500 | 44 800 | 14 200 | 90 700 | 3 400 | 47 700 | 4 700 | 54 400 |
| Mean | 18 500 | 92 100 | 47 100 | 202 200 | 10 700 | 92 300 | 18 600 | 113 400 |

*Source:* Information provided by the United States Treasury Department.

Box 2.2. **Single-taxed entities and levels of taxable income** *(continued)*

When considering the applicable rate for small businesses, these results demonstrate that the top marginal rate in the United States applies only to a small proportion of the small business population. The top marginal rate applies to income above USD 310 000, whereas the average income of SME owners, even with all other sources of income included is well below this level. Estimating tax rates at the average wage level (USD 53 000 in 2010), as shown in the table in this box may, therefore, be more representative of the small business population.

This result is also consistent with information provided in the questionnaire responses, where many countries report average levels of taxable profits of singled-taxed entities that are well below the top marginal tax rate threshold. These results are presented in full in the Annex.

Table 2.2 shows the marginal statutory tax rates applying to the net income of SMEs taxed only at the personal level. The second column shows the marginal rate applying to net personal income at the top statutory threshold under personal income taxes from SMEs (or to the labour income component, in the case of dual income systems) in each country, exclusive of self-employed SSCs. This shows the marginal rate at the earnings level where the top statutory personal income tax rate first applies and may therefore differ from the top statutory rate. The third column shows the amount by which the tax rate increases after self-employed SSCs have been taken into account. The level of SSCs has been determined as at the top personal income tax (PIT) threshold, rather than as at the top SSC threshold. This is consistent with the approach taken in *Taxing Wages* (OECD, 2015a) to the calculation of top marginal PIT rates. Where applicable, deductibility of SSCs under personal income taxes has been taken into account. The fourth column shows employee SSCs at the threshold for the top marginal PIT rate. The fifth column shows the threshold above which the top marginal personal income tax rate applies and at which self-employed SSCs have been calculated. Further detail on the rates and thresholds of self-employed SSCs can be found in Annex C.

Table 2.2. **Top marginal personal income tax rates, thresholds and social security contributions[a], 2014**

| | Top marginal rate, excl SSCs (%)[b] | Self-employed SSC differential (percentage points) | Employee SSC differential (percentage points) | Threshold at which top rate applies (EUR, thousands) |
|---|---|---|---|---|
| Australia | 47 | | | 122 |
| Austria | 50 | | | 647 |
| Belgium | 45 | 22 | 14 | 47 |
| Canada | 50 | | | 150 |
| Chile | 40 | | | 118 |
| Czech Republic[c] | 15 | 15 | 11 | 4 |
| Denmark | 56 | | | 66 |
| Estonia | 21 | 34 | 2 | 2 |
| Finland | 49 | 13 | 8 | 108 |
| France | 54 | | 1 | 561 |
| Germany | 47 | | | 260 |
| Greece | 46 | | | 112 |

Table 2.2. **Top marginal personal income tax rates, thresholds and social security contributions[a], 2014** *(continued)*

| | Top marginal rate, excl SSCs (%)[b] | Self-employed SSC differential (percentage points) | Employee SSC differential (percentage points) | Threshold at which top rate applies (EUR, thousands) |
|---|---|---|---|---|
| Hungary[d] | 16 | 46 | 19 | - |
| Iceland | 44 | | | 63 |
| Ireland | 51 | 4 | 4 | 100 |
| Israel | 50 | | | 171 |
| Italy | 48 | | | 300 |
| Japan | 51 | | 0 | 159 |
| Korea | 39 | | 4 | 127 |
| Luxembourg | 44 | 1 | 1 | 164 |
| Mexico | 35 | 0.2 | 0.3 | 170 |
| Netherlands[e] | 50 | | 3 | 59 |
| New Zealand | 33 | | | 44 |
| Norway | 39 | 11 | 8 | 103 |
| Poland | 21 | 23 | 18 | 24 |
| Portugal | 50 | | 11 | 281 |
| Slovak Republic | 22 | | 13 | 40 |
| Slovenia | 39 | | 22 | 95 |
| Spain | 52 | | | 305 |
| Sweden | 57 | 12 | | 68 |
| Switzerland | 36 | 6 | 6 | 247 |
| Turkey | 36 | | | 38 |
| United Kingdom | 45 | 2 | 2 | 186 |
| United States | 46 | 3 | 2 | 310 |
| Unweighted mean | 42 | 14 | 8 | 154 |
| Median | 46 | 12 | 5 | 118 |

*Notes:* a. Social security contributions have been calculated as at the top PIT threshold. This means that in many countries the top SSC threshold has been exceeded.

b. This is the marginal rate at the earnings level where the top statutory personal income tax rate first applies and is taken from Table I.7 of the OECD Tax Database (OECD, 2015b). The rate takes account of the effects of tax credits, the deductibility of sub-central taxes against central government taxes, etc.

c. In the Czech Republic, personal income tax is levied on employee income calculated as gross wages plus employer social security contributions. This leads to a top marginal rate, excluding SSCs, of 20.1% on employee income. The rate of SSC contributions for the self-employed is 29.2%; however, this applies only to 50% of the tax base.

d. The 46% rate for self-employed SSCs in Hungary assumes that wages are above the minimum tax base for each of the components of the SSC (150% of minimum wage for health insurance and the labour market contribution, 112.5% of minimum wage for the social contribution tax and 100% of minimum wage for the pension contribution).

e. Figures for the Netherlands exclude the impact of the SME profit exemption (which exempts 14% of the profits of single-taxed entities from taxation) and the deduction for entrepreneurs (a fixed deduction of EUR 7 280). Both are discussed further in Chapter 3. These reduce the marginal tax rates on SME profits and increase the effective threshold for the top marginal rate. The impact of these reductions is shown in Table 2.7.

*Source:* OECD calculations based on OECD (2015b), *OECD Tax Database*, www.oecd.org/tax/tax-policy/tax-database.htm. The calculations for France assume that the maximum level of self-employed contribution has been reached.

In moving from employment to self-employment (in the form of a sole proprietor), there are two main changes to taxes payable, based on the calculations in Table 2.2 at the top marginal rate. For countries which separate the taxation of labour and capital from small business income, the taxpayer will face a lower average tax rate on their income due to the lower rates applied on the business income component. The second change is due to the difference in SSCs payable, moving from employee and employer SSCs to self-employed contributions, and in some cases, to changes to the base for SSC calculations.[2] Table 2.2 also shows the additional tax payable under self-employed and employed contributions. Although within individual countries this can vary markedly, self-employed contributions are greater at the level of the top personal threshold in most countries and on an unweighted average basis, in many cases as the self-employed do not have an employer making social security contributions on their behalf.

However, as seen in Box 2.2, the top marginal rate will not apply to the full SME population. Depending on the level of the threshold applied, it may only apply to a small proportion of owners of SMEs in some countries. For this reason, Table 2.3 shows the marginal tax rates applying to net income at the level of the average wage in each country. The second column shows the marginal rate applying to net personal income from SMEs at 100% of the average wage (or to the labour income component, in the case of dual income systems) in each country, exclusive of self-employed SSCs. This information has been taken from *Taxing Wages* (OECD, 2015a). The third column shows the amount by which the tax rate increases after self-employed SSCs have been taken into account at 100% of the average wage, including any effect of deductibility if relevant. The fourth column shows the level of employee SSCs that apply at this income level. The fifth column shows the level of the average wage in 2014. Further detail on the rates and thresholds of self-employed SSCs can be found in Annex C.

Table 2.3. **Marginal personal income tax rates less cash contributions and social security contributions[a] at 100% AW, 2014**

| | Marginal rate at AW, excl. SSCs (%) | Self-employed SSC differential (percentage points) | Employee SSC differential (percentage points) | The average wage (EUR, thousands) |
|---|---|---|---|---|
| Australia | 34 | | | 54 |
| Austria | 31 | 18 | 18 | 43 |
| Belgium | 42 | 22 | 13 | 46 |
| Canada | 30 | 10 | 5 | 34 |
| Chile | - | | 7 | 9 |
| Czech Republic[b] | 15 | 15 | 11 | 11 |
| Denmark | 34 | | 8 | 53 |
| Estonia | 21 | 34 | 2 | 12 |
| Finland | 37 | 16 | 8 | 43 |
| France | 30 | 29 | 14 | 37 |
| Germany | 41 | | 11 | 46 |
| Greece | 35 | | | 20 |
| Hungary | 16 | 46 | 19 | 10 |
| Iceland | 38 | | | 44 |
| Ireland | 48 | 4 | 4 | 34 |
| Israel | 33 | | | 28 |

Table 2.3. **Marginal personal income tax rates less cash contributions and social security contributions[a] at 100% AW, 2014** *(continued)*

| | Marginal rate at AW, excl. SSCs (%) | Self-employed SSC differential (percentage points) | Employee SSC differential (percentage points) | The average wage (EUR, thousands) |
|---|---|---|---|---|
| Italy | 31 | 22 | 9 | 30 |
| Japan | 27 | | 1 | 35 |
| Korea | 17 | | 4 | 28 |
| Luxembourg | 37 | 15 | 12 | 55 |
| Mexico | 18 | 7 | 1 | 6 |
| Netherlands[c] | 46 | 5 | | 49 |
| New Zealand | 30 | | | 34 |
| Norway | 36 | 11 | 8 | 65 |
| Poland | 10 | 26 | 17 | 10 |
| Portugal | 32 | | 11 | 17 |
| Slovak Republic | 30 | | | 10 |
| Slovenia | 21 | | 22 | 18 |
| Spain | 28 | 21 | 6 | 26 |
| Sweden | 25 | 22 | 7 | 45 |
| Switzerland | 22 | 8 | 5 | 74 |
| Turkey | 18 | | 15 | 10 |
| United Kingdom | 30 | 9 | 2 | 44 |
| United States | 32 | 13 | 8 | 38 |
| Unweighted mean | 30 | 10 | 7 | 33 |
| Median | 30 | 8 | 6 | 34 |

*Notes:* a. Social security contributions have been calculated as those applying at 100% of the average wage. When the top SSC threshold has been exceeded, this is shown as zero.

b. In the Czech Republic, personal income tax is levied on employee income calculated as gross wages plus employer social security contributions. This leads to a top marginal rate, excluding SSCs, of 20.1% on employee income. The rate of SSC contributions for the self-employed is 29.2%; however, this applies only to 50% of the tax base.

c. Figures for the Netherlands exclude the impact of the SME profit exemption (which exempts 14% of the profits of single-taxed entities from taxation) and the deduction for entrepreneurs (a fixed deduction of EUR 7 280). Both are discussed further in Chapter 3. These reduce the marginal tax rates on SME profits and increase the effective threshold for the top marginal rate. The impact of these reductions is shown in Table 2.7.

*Source:* OECD calculations based on OECD (2015b), *OECD Tax Database*, www.oecd.org/tax/tax-policy/tax-database.htm. The calculations for France assume that the maximum level of self-employed contribution has been reached. For Hungary, which has a flat rate of personal tax, the SSC rate at the lowest minimum SSC threshold is shown.

At the level of the average wage, the marginal tax rate applicable to labour earnings is lower in almost all countries, as in almost all countries the threshold for the top marginal rate is above the level of the average wage (with exceptions being the Czech Republic, Estonia, Hungary and Ireland). Social security contributions are however often higher than at the threshold for the top marginal rate, as more countries apply both self-employed and social security contributions at the average wage.[3] For social security contributions, this is the case in Finland, Hungary, Luxembourg, Poland, Sweden, Switzerland, the United Kingdom and the United States. Self-employed contributions add more to the total marginal rate than employee social security contributions, on a simple average basis. However inter-country differences are strong, with self-employed contributions being greater in most countries at the level of the average wage, as before, often due to the fact that self-employed persons do not have employers making contributions on their behalf.

If the owner of the SME has other income that is in excess of the top marginal rate thresholds, the average marginal statutory rates shown for SME income in Table 2.2 will also be the average statutory tax rate on that income (except under a dual income tax system). For individuals without other sources of income, or with lower levels of other income, SME income will be taxed at lower rates under the marginal income tax system, meaning the average of the statutory tax rates on SME income will vary depending on the level of taxable income.

Table 2.4 shows the average tax rates on SME income at different levels of personal income on labour income, assuming the tax payer has no other income, that are calculated using the *Taxing Wages* model (OECD, 2015a). The table excludes self-employed SSCs. Average rates are compared at different levels of the average wage. The average wage is used as a basis of comparison across countries given that the total income generated by a SME may be influenced by many other variables in these countries that would render comparisons at a given level of business income less useful, for example, GDP per capita, wage earnings per capita, or labour productivity.

Table 2.4 shows that there is a wide variation in the average tax rates applied to labour income, with the increases in tax rates on different levels of small business income, measured in multiples of the average wage. This variation is a function of the tax rate systems and structures in each country, including the relationship between the average wage and the top marginal tax rate applied to personal income. Both the unweighted mean and median demonstrate the pattern shown in most countries, where most of the increase in the average tax rate takes place between the first and third multiple of the average wage, with the increase in average rates tapering off after this as the average wage level in most countries increases past the threshold for the top marginal rate.

Table 2.4. **Average personal tax rates (excl. SSCs) at different levels of average wage income, 2014**

| | Average tax rate at multiples of the average wage (AW) (%) | | | | |
|---|---|---|---|---|---|
| | 100% of AW | 200% of AW | 300% of AW | 400% of AW | 500% of AW |
| Australia | 23 | 31 | 35 | 38 | 40 |
| Austria | 17 | 26 | 32 | 35 | 37 |
| Belgium | 28 | 37 | 40 | 42 | 43 |
| Brazil | 0 | 4 | 9 | 13 | 16 |
| Canada | 16 | 25 | 32 | 36 | 38 |
| Chile | 0 | 1 | 2 | 3 | 4 |
| China | 0 | 4 | 8 | 12 | 15 |
| Czech Republic | 12 | 16 | 17 | 18 | 18 |
| Denmark | 36 | 44 | 48 | 50 | 51 |
| Estonia | 18 | 19 | 20 | 20 | 20 |
| Finland | 23 | 32 | 38 | 40 | 42 |
| France | 15 | 22 | 26 | 30 | 33 |
| Germany | 19 | 30 | 35 | 37 | 39 |
| Greece | 9 | 22 | 27 | 30 | 33 |
| Hungary | 16 | 16 | 16 | 16 | 16 |
| Iceland | 28 | 35 | 38 | 40 | 41 |

Table 2.4. **Average personal tax rates (excl. SSCs) at different levels of average wage income, 2014** *(continued)*

| | Average tax rate at multiples of the average wage (AW) (%) | | | | |
|---|---|---|---|---|---|
| | 100% of AW | 200% of AW | 300% of AW | 400% of AW | 500% of AW |
| India | 0 | 3 | 10 | 17 | 21 |
| India[a] | 0 | 3 | 9 | 16 | 20 |
| Indonesia | 0 | 2 | 3 | 5 | 7 |
| Ireland | 16 | 32 | 37 | 40 | 42 |
| Israel | 9 | 19 | 24 | 27 | 31 |
| Italy | 22 | 31 | 34 | 37 | 39 |
| Japan | 8 | 14 | 20 | 26 | 30 |
| Korea | 5 | 12 | 17 | 22 | 25 |
| Luxembourg | 18 | 27 | 32 | 36 | 37 |
| Mexico | 9 | 15 | 17 | 19 | 21 |
| Netherlands[b] | 16 | 32 | 38 | 41 | 43 |
| New Zealand | 17 | 25 | 27 | 29 | 30 |
| Norway | 21 | 29 | 32 | 34 | 35 |
| Poland | 7 | 8 | 11 | 14 | 16 |
| Portugal | 16 | 27 | 31 | 34 | 36 |
| Slovak Republic | 9 | 13 | 15 | 17 | 18 |
| Slovenia | 11 | 18 | 23 | 25 | 26 |
| South Africa | 12 | 20 | 25 | 29 | 31 |
| Spain | 17 | 25 | 32 | 36 | 38 |
| Sweden | 17 | 35 | 42 | 46 | 48 |
| Switzerland | 11 | 18 | 23 | 26 | 28 |
| Turkey | 12 | 18 | 20 | 22 | 25 |
| United Kingdom | 14 | 25 | 32 | 36 | 37 |
| United States | 17 | 24 | 28 | 30 | 32 |
| Unweighted mean | 14 | 21 | 25 | 28 | 30 |
| Median | 15 | 22 | 26 | 29 | 31 |

*Note:* a. Results for the minority case where the employee is in a firm with over 20 employees.

b. Figures for the Netherlands exclude the impact of the SME profit exemption (which exempts 14% of the profits of single-taxed entities from taxation) and the deduction for entrepreneurs (a fixed deduction of EUR 7 280). Both are discussed further in Chapter 3. These reduce the average tax rates on SME profits and increase the effective threshold for the top marginal rate. The impact of these reductions is shown in Table 2.7.

*Source:* Calculations based on OECD (2015a), *Taxing Wages 2013-2014*, OECD Publishing, Paris, for a single taxpayer with no children.

## 2.4. Double-level taxation of SME income

This subsection discusses the tax treatment of SMEs that are subject to taxation at both the entity level and again at the personal level when profits are distributed, either as dividends or capital gains (on realisation). Any integration between the corporate and personal levels of taxation will be relevant to determining the total level of taxation on SME income.

Double taxation most commonly applies to incorporated SMEs, where the separate legal status of the entity confers a separate status for tax purposes. However, in some countries, unincorporated entities may also be taxed at both the corporate and personal level. Examples of these include certain trust funds (for example in Hungary, New Zealand, Mexico and Switzerland), or limited partnerships that are able to be taxed as corporations in India. Table 2.1 provides more information on unincorporated entities that are taxed at both the corporate and personal levels.

This subsection begins with a discussion of taxation at the corporate level and is followed by a consideration of the taxation of income from SMEs at the personal level on dividends, capital gains, or labour income, including any applicable integration measures between the two levels of taxation.

### *Taxation at the entity level*

Net income of SMEs subject to double level taxation is taxed first under the corporate tax system. Most countries apply a single statutory corporate income tax (CIT) rate (including relevant federal and state taxes) to the full amount of taxable profits of incorporated businesses, regardless of the size of the company or the amount of taxable income. However, fourteen countries tax SME income using graduated small business corporate tax rates. These rates apply to SME income under a particular level, often in conjunction with other eligibility criteria based on the turnover or capitalisation of the business.

Table 2.5 shows the basic statutory corporate tax rates in 37 countries. It also shows statutory small business tax rates and income thresholds where these are applicable, together with any other eligibility criteria. Where a series of graduated small business rates apply at different levels of income, Table 2.5 shows each of the rates and thresholds that apply.

Table 2.5. **Basic and small business corporate tax rates, thresholds and eligibility criteria, 2014**

| | Basic CIT rate (%) | Small business CIT rate(s) (%) | Threshold(s) (income, EUR thousands) | Notes and other eligibility criteria for small business rates |
|---|---|---|---|---|
| Argentina | 35 | | | |
| Australia [a] | 30 | | | |
| Austria | 25 | | | |
| Belgium [b] | 33.99 | 24.978<br>31.93<br>35.535 | 25<br>90<br>323 | Applicable when total taxable income is less than EUR 322 500. In order to qualify for the reduced rates, the company must fulfil additional conditions, relating to the activity of the company, the shareholding, the yield on the capital and the directors' remuneration. |
| Canada | 26.3 | 15.2 [c] | 341 | Applies to qualifying active business income of Canadian-controlled private corporations when taxable capital is less than CAD 10 000 000. Relief is phased out between CAD 10 000 000 and CAD 15 000 000 |
| Chile | 20 | | | |
| Czech Republic | 19 | | | |
| Denmark | 24.5 | | | |
| Estonia | 21 | | | |
| Finland | 20 | | | |
| France | 31.33 [d] | 15 | 38 | Applicable where turnover does not exceed EUR 7.63 million and at least 75% of ownership is held by natural persons (or by companies owned at least 75% by natural persons) |
| Germany | 29.8 | | | |
| Greece | 26 | | | |
| Hungary | 19 | 10 | 1 620 | |

Table 2.5. **Basic and small business corporate tax rates, thresholds and eligibility criteria, 2014** *(continued)*

| | Basic CIT rate (%) | Small business CIT rate(s) (%) | Threshold(s) (income, EUR thousands) | Notes and other eligibility criteria for small business rates |
|---|---|---|---|---|
| Iceland | 20 | | | |
| India | 30.9<br>32.445 | 33.99 | 124<br>1 235 | |
| Ireland | 12.5 | | | Full relief is available for the first three years of operation for companies incorporated after 1 October 2008 and that have started a new trade for CIT up to EUR 40 000 and partial relief for CIT up to 60 000. |
| Israel | 26.5 | | | |
| Italy | 27.5 | | | |
| Japan | 34.62 | See notes | See notes | Basic corporate tax rate is 32.11% from April 2015 and 31.33% from April 2016. For corporations whose capital is JPY 100 million or less, there are special measures that mean a reduced tax rate (15%) is applied to part of their income (up to JPY 8 million per year) |
| Korea | 24.2 | 11 | 143 | |
| Luxembourg | 29.2 | 28.2 | 15 | Applies only to income under EUR 15 000 |
| Mexico | 30 | | | Reductions apply to primary sector companies:<br>Taxpayers with an income up to 20 annual minimum wages (AMW) per associate (with a total limit of 200 AMW) are exempted from the corporate income tax, while those with an income over this threshold benefit from a 30% reduction until their income reaches 423 AMW. Additionally, companies or associations of producers with an income up to 4 230 AMW receive a 30% income tax reduction. |
| Netherlands | 25 | 20 | 200 | |
| New Zealand | 28 | | | |
| Norway | 27 | | | |
| Poland | 19 | | | |
| Portugal[e] | 31.5 | 18.5<br>24.5<br>27.5<br>29.5 | 15<br>1 500<br>7 500<br>35 000 | Except for the 18.5% rate, these tax rates apply to all companies with income below the respective thresholds |
| Slovak Republic | 22 | | | |
| Slovenia | 17 | | | |
| South Africa | 28 | 0<br>7<br>21 | 5<br>25<br>38 | Enterprises with a turnover below EUR 1 300 000 |
| Spain | 30 | 25 | 300 | SMEs with a turnover below EUR 5 000 000 and an average payroll of less than 25 employees are eligible for a 20% rate. |
| Sweden | 22 | | | |
| Switzerland | 21.1 | | | |
| Turkey | 20 | | | |
| United Kingdom | 21 | 20<br>21.25 | 372<br>1 860 | Rates as of 1 April 2014. From 1 April 2015 the basic rate was reduced to 20% and the small business rate abolished. |
| United States | 39.1 | 20.02<br>29.89<br>38.76<br>43.64<br>38.51<br>39.39<br>42.26 | 38<br>57<br>75<br>252<br>7 537<br>11 306<br>13 818 | |

Table 2.5. **Basic and small business corporate tax rates, thresholds and eligibility criteria, 2014** *(continued)*

| | Basic CIT rate (%) | Small business CIT rate(s) (%) | Threshold(s) (income, EUR thousands) | Notes and other eligibility criteria for small business rates |
|---|---|---|---|---|
| Unweighted mean (all) | 25.45 | 21.41 | - | |
| Median (all) | 25.50 | 21.07 | - | |
| Unweighted mean (countries with small business rates) | 29.09 | 18.69 | - | |
| Median (countries with small business rates) | 29.22 | 20.00 | - | |

*Notes:* a. Since 1 July 2015, companies with an annual turnover of less than AUD 2 million have had their tax rate reduced by 1.5 percentage points to 28.5 per cent. Unincorporated small businesses with annual turnover less than AUD 2 million will receive a 5 per cent discount on tax payable (capped at AUD 1 000).

b. As in the Tax Database, the Allowance for Corporate Equity has not been taken into account. All rates listed (standard CIT and small business rates) include a 3% austerity surcharge.

c. This includes corporate tax at the central government level at 11% and an additional 4.2% (average) at the provincial/territorial level. In April 2015, the Canadian government announced that the 11% federal government corporate tax rate for small businesses would be gradually reduced to 9% by 2019.

d. Companies not eligible for the small business rate also pay a solidarity surcharge which brings the CIT rate for these companies to 34.4%.

e. Assumes a subnational tax rate of 1.5% at all levels of federal taxation.

*Sources:* OECD (2015b), *OECD Tax Database*, www.oecd.org/tax/tax-policy/tax-database.htm, IBFD (2015), *IBFD Tax Research Platform*, accessed at http://online.ibfd.org/kbase, and responses to an OECD questionnaire, *Survey on the Taxation of Small and Medium-Sized Enterprises*, 2015.

Table 2.5 shows that fourteen countries have lower corporate income tax rates for small businesses below a prescribed threshold. The largest differences between the basic and small business rates are found in Canada, France, South Africa and the United States. Across the whole group of countries considered, small business rates reduce the corporate tax rate by four percentage points on average. Across countries with a small business rate, the difference between the unweighted mean of the lowest small business rate and the basic rate is ten percentage points (nine percentage points if the median rates are measured). The level of income threshold differs between countries, with countries with higher thresholds typically offering a lesser reduction than those that apply small business rates only to the very smallest levels of income.

A number of approaches are used in applying small business corporate tax rates:

- Lower tax rate on first tranche(s) of profits, regardless of total income level: for example, Korea and the Netherlands tax the first amount of corporate profits at a lower small business rate, up to a small business profit threshold, regardless of the size of the company;

- Withdrawal of tax relief at higher profit levels: for example, the United States applies a tiered CIT rate structure that taxes small business profits at lower rates, but withdraws this tax relief when taxing firms with significant profits through the use of rates above the basic corporate tax rate for higher brackets of corporate income, before returning to the basic corporate rate;

- Reduced CIT rates for corporations with income below a certain level: Other countries including Luxembourg and Belgium apply reduced CIT rates only to firms with taxable profits less than a small business profit threshold; once a business exceeds this income threshold, full basic corporate tax rates apply to the entirety of the firm's income;
- Eligibility for small-business rates determined by non-income criteria instead of or in addition to income criteria: Japan uses a test based on the capital amount of the enterprise to determine eligibility for a small business rate, while France and Spain rely on a gross turnover test. Canada limits application of its small business tax rate to qualifying active business income of Canadian-controlled private corporations (CCPCs), while using a capital test to withdraw small business tax rate relief. Firms that meet these eligibility criteria are eligible for a reduced rate of corporate tax on the first tranche of their profits. Belgium requires that the company also meet non-income criteria relating to their activities, shareholdings, capital yield and directors' remuneration.

For entities that are taxed under basic CIT rates, the average statutory rate at different levels of income will be the same as the marginal statutory rate. For those entities subject to different rates based on their level of income, the average statutory rate will increase as income passes the relevant thresholds, converging, in first and last case described above, on the basic corporate tax rate as income increases.

Figure 2.2. **Average statutory CIT rates at different levels of business income (measured by multiples of the average wage), 2014**

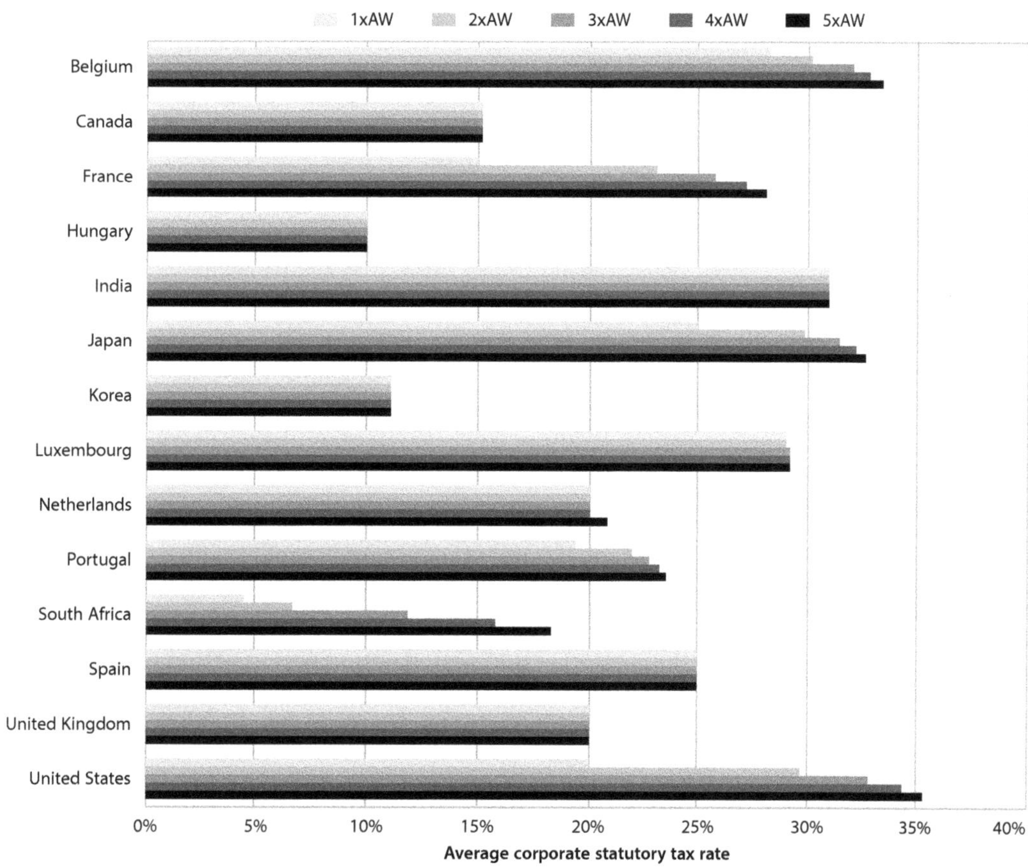


*Source:* OECD calculations based on OECD (2015b), *OECD Tax Database*, www.oecd.org/tax/tax-policy/tax-database.htm, responses to an OECD questionnaire, *Survey on the Taxation of Small and Medium-Sized Enterprises*, 2015, and IBFD (2015), *IBFD Tax Research Platform*, accessed at http://online.ibfd.org/kbase.

To compare the average corporate tax rates at different income levels in countries with more than one corporate income tax rate, Figure 2.2 presents the average statutory CIT rates at different levels of wage income. As before, average wage income is used as a means of comparison across countries. Figure 11 assumes that the firms shown meet all of the eligibility criteria for the small business rates.

Figure 2.3 shows average statutory corporate income taxes, including small business rates and thresholds, for the same fourteen countries, at a range of different taxable income levels.

Figure 2.3. **Average statutory CIT rates under small-business rates at different levels of business income, 2014**

(G20 countries, left-hand panel; non-G20 OECD countries, right-hand panel)

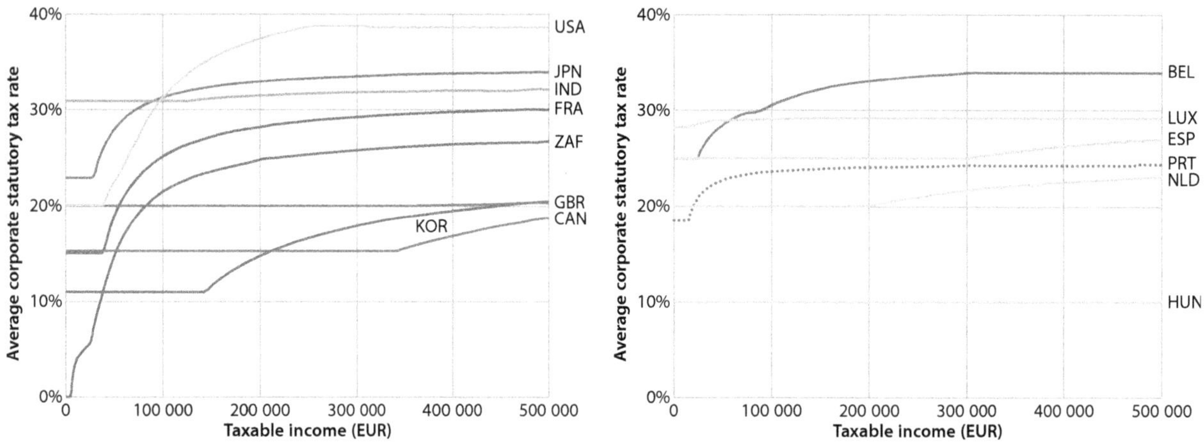


*Source:* OECD calculations based on OECD (2015b), *OECD Tax Database*, www.oecd.org/tax/tax-policy/tax-database.htm, IBFD (2015), *IBFD Tax Research Platform*, accessed at http://online.ibfd.org/kbase, and questionnaire responses.

Figures 2.2 and 2.3 show the variation in the impact of small business corporate tax rates at different levels of small business income. In many countries, small business rates markedly reduce the amount of tax payable at lower levels of SME income (particularly among the G20 countries); whereas in others the difference in average tax rates is much smaller. Figure 2.3 shows the level of the first relevant threshold in each country (except Hungary, where the threshold of HUF 500 million (EUR 1.6 million) is beyond the right-hand side of the scale) at the point which the average tax rate starts increasing. If the change in rates is relatively significant, the impact of the small business rates and thresholds is to impose a sharply increasing average tax rate on SME income, as seen, for example in France, Japan, South Africa and the United States, in the left-hand panel of Figure 2.3. Canada, which also has a larger differential between the small business tax rates and the basic rate does not show this pattern because the threshold at which the small business rate ceases to apply is comparatively high, meaning that the average tax rate beyond this point increases more slowly. This pattern is also seen on Figure 2.2, where the increase in tax rates at different levels of the average wage (which is again used as a proxy for levels of business income) is sharper in these countries. In countries where the thresholds are relatively higher (for example, in Hungary or Spain) or where the small business tax rate differential is relatively small (e.g. India, Luxembourg and the United Kingdom) the increase in the average statutory tax rate at different levels of business income is much less marked.

### *Taxation at the personal level*

After taxation at the corporate level, the income from incorporated SMEs may be subject to a second level of taxation at the individual shareholder level when they are distributed to the owner. Taxation at the personal level will depend on the form in which the income is received and on any available integration mechanisms between corporate and personal level taxation.

There are three possible forms in which the income can be received. Distributed after-tax corporate profits are normally subject to shareholder-level dividend taxation, while capital gains on shares that result from the retention of after-tax profits may be subject to capital gains taxation upon the disposition of shares. Finally, the wage income of an owner for hours worked in the business, deductible for corporate income tax purposes, is subject to personal income tax. This subsection considers each in turn.

The owner or owners of a small business can receive post-corporate tax income from the business in the form of dividend income. How dividend income is taxed at the personal level will differ depending on the degree of corporate and personal integration in the country concerned. Under a classical income system, dividend income is included together with other income and is taxed at personal rates, with no integration relief for corporate tax paid. Under this system, there is double-taxation. To reduce this, modified classical systems apply in several OECD countries, which apply a lower rate of taxation to dividend income than to other forms of personal income. Another method of reducing double taxation is to tax only a portion of the dividends received at the personal level. Several OECD countries use a final withholding tax rate to apply a lower rate of taxation to capital income than to other forms of personal income. Finally, a group of countries apply imputation credits, taxing individual taxpayers on the grossed up value of the dividends but allowing tax credits to offset corporate tax paid, thus reducing or eliminating the amount of double taxation.

These forms of integration also affect the benefit of reduced corporate tax rates on small business income. To the extent these methods double tax business income, any benefit from the reduced rates on small business income will be partially reduced by taxes at the personal level, so that the amount of the reduction in small business rates is reduced by the net of shareholder tax rate. For example, if a business earns EUR 100 and faces a corporate tax rate of 25%, EUR 75 will be taxable at the personal level (assuming the profits are distributed as dividends) under a classical system. If a small business corporate tax rate of 15% applies, EUR 85 will be taxable at the personal level. Where double taxation exists, the value of the small business rate to the shareholder (assuming income is not retained and later distributed as untaxed capital gains) will depend on the rate of tax they pay at the personal level. This impact will be reduced in systems where double taxation is lessened or avoided.

The form of integration between the corporate and personal levels will affect the resulting tax rate on dividend income and therefore the difference between tax rates on single and double-taxed entities. Where a full classical system applies, corporate tax will add a second level of taxation to the owner, increasing the marginal statutory tax rate on business income. Different forms of integration may, however, have the opposite effect, where lower taxes on corporate income combined with lower withholding or capital rates, and the removal of SSCs, reduce the marginal statutory rate on business income.

If post-corporate tax profits of a SME are reinvested, the resulting capital gains may be taxed again at the personal level, subject to any preferences applicable to the sale of shares from SMEs (see Chapter 3 for an overview of these). Capital gains are typically taxed on realisation at their nominal level, although Chile, Israel, Mexico and Portugal adjust the amount of the nominal gain for inflation. In many countries, shares that have been held for longer than a set period may benefit from a reduction or exemption from capital gains taxation. Either part or all of the gains from the sale of shares may be included in taxable income and may be subjected to tax at personal rates, special capital gains rates, or withholding rates (see Harding, 2013, for further information).

Finally, profits from the business can, in the case of owner-operators, be distributed in the form of labour income. Where labour income is a deductible expense for the business, no corporate income tax will be paid at the entity level. At the personal level, labour income will be taxed at the applicable marginal tax rate on labour income and will also be subject to employee and employer SSCs.

Table 2.6 shows the marginal statutory tax rates applying to each scenario. The first two columns show the top statutory rates on labour income inclusive and exclusive of employee SSCs (effectively assuming that employer contributions do not affect wages). The third and fourth columns show the combined rate of tax on dividend income in each country, including integration between entity and personal levels, where used. The third column shows the combined rate under the basic CIT rate, whereas the fourth column shows the combined rate at the first step of the small business rate.[4] The fifth and sixth columns show the combined tax rates on capital gains, including integration, under basic and small business tax rates, respectively. Capital gains rates assume that the shares had been held beyond any holding period test prior to sale and are based on Harding (2013) and consultations with national officials.

Table 2.6. **Labour tax rate, employee SSCs[a] and combined statutory rates on dividends under basic and small business taxation, 2014**

| | Top marginal rate on labour[b] | | Combined corporate and personal rates on dividends | | Combined corporate and personal rates on capital gains[c] | |
|---|---|---|---|---|---|---|
| | excl SSCs (%) | Employee SSC differential (percentage points) | Combined rates under basic CIT rates (%) | Reduction in combined rates due to small business CIT rates (percentage points) | Combined rates under basic CIT rates (%) | Reduction in combined rates due to small business CIT rates (percentage points) |
| Australia | 47 | | 47 | | 42 | |
| Austria | 50 | | 44 | | 39 | |
| Belgium | 45 | 14 | 51 | -7 | 34 | -9 |
| Canada | 50 | | 51 | -2 | 40 | -9 |
| Chile | 40 | | 40 | | 21 | |
| Czech Republic | 15 | 11 | 31 | | 19 | |
| Denmark | 56 | | 56 | | 48 | |
| Estonia | 21 | 2 | 21 | | 33 | |
| Finland[d] | 49 | 8 | 42 | | 39 | |
| France | 54 | 1 | 64 | -10 | 54 | -14 |
| Germany | 47 | | 49 | | 44 | |
| Greece | 46 | | 33 | | 26 | |
| Hungary | 16 | 46 | 32 | -8 | 19 | -9 |
| Iceland | 44 | | 36 | | 32 | |
| Ireland | 51 | 4 | 55 | | 44 | |

Table 2.6. **Labour tax rate, employee SSCs[a] and combined statutory rates on dividends under basic and small business taxation, 2014** *(continued)*

| | Top marginal rate on labour[b] | | Combined corporate and personal rates on dividends | | Combined corporate and personal rates on capital gains[c] | |
|---|---|---|---|---|---|---|
| | excl SSCs (%) | Employee SSC differential (percentage points) | Combined rates under basic CIT rates (%) | Reduction in combined rates due to small business CIT rates (percentage points) | Combined rates under basic CIT rates (%) | Reduction in combined rates due to small business CIT rates (percentage points) |
| Israel | 50 | | 49 | | 38 | |
| Italy[e] | 48 | | 46 | | 42 | |
| Japan | 51 | 0 | 50 | -11 | 42 | -13 |
| Korea | 39 | 4 | 51 | -9 | 24 | -13 |
| Luxembourg | 44 | 1 | 43 | -1 | 29 | -1 |
| Mexico | 35 | 0.3 | 42 | | 30 | |
| Netherlands | 50 | 3 | 44 | -4 | 39 | -4 |
| New Zealand | 33 | | 33 | | 28 | |
| Norway | 39 | 8 | 47 | | 37 | |
| Poland | 21 | 18 | 34 | | 31 | |
| Portugal | 50 | 11 | 51 | | 44 | |
| Slovak Republic[f] | 22 | 13 | 33 | | 33 | |
| Slovenia | 39 | 22 | 38 | | 20 | |
| Spain[g] | 52 | | 49 | -4 | 44 | -4 |
| Sweden | 57 | | 45 | | 40 | |
| Switzerland | 36 | 6 | 37 | | 21 | |
| Turkey | 36 | | 34 | | 20 | |
| United Kingdom | 45 | 2 | 45 | -1 | 38 | -1 |
| United States | 46 | 2 | 60 | 0 | 49 | -1 |
| Unweighted mean | 42 | 8 | 44 | -2 | 35 | -2 |
| Median | 46 | 5 | 44 | -2 | 37 | -4 |

*Notes:* a. Social security contributions have been calculated as at the top PIT threshold. This means that in many countries the top SSC threshold has been exceeded.

b. This is the marginal rate at the earnings level where the top statutory personal income tax rate first applies and is taken from Table I.7 of the OECD Tax Database (OECD, 2015b).

c. Personal tax rates on capital gains have been reduced by 25% to approximate the impact of deferral of taxation until realisation.

d. Combined rates for Finland show the tax rate for listed dividends, which is also the maximum combined rate for non-listed dividends (if they are taxed wholly as capital income). However, non-listed dividends are taxed at lower rates (between 26-30%, depending on the amount of the income and the capital of the distributing company).

e. In Italy, the taxation of non-qualified dividends and capital gains at the personal level was increased from 20% to 26% from 1 July 2014. The combined rates shown here include the new rate of 26%.

f. The combined statutory rate on dividends in the Slovak Republic includes health contributions of 14% which are levied at the personal level, but the maximum effective assessment base is not taken into account.

g. Spain applies a progressive tax regime to capital gains, with rates as follows: EUR 0-6 000 in capital gains, 21%; EUR 6-24 000, 25%; over 24 000, 27%.

*Source:* OECD calculations based on OECD (2015b), *OECD Tax Database*, www.oecd.org/tax/tax-policy/tax-database.htm. Capital gains rates were taken from Harding, M. (2013), *Taxation of Dividend, Interest and Capital Gain Income*, OECD Taxation Working Paper, and from discussions with national officials, are for sales of long-held shares and do not consider any different treatments that may apply to liquidated SMEs.

Taxes on capital gains can be deferred, often for many years, since most tax systems only tax capital gains when realised, not as they accrue over time. Deferral can significantly reduce the net present value of taxes on income earned through the accumulation of unrealised capital gains. This can occur when a small business owner chooses to receive lower wage compensation in return for growing "sweat equity" in the business in the form of unrealised capital gains. In Table 2.6, the combined tax rates on capital gains include the impact of corporate taxation, the relevant integration method between company and personal taxes, personal tax rates, and the benefit of tax deferral. To approximate the impact of deferral in reducing the effective tax rate on capital, the effective tax rates shown in the table have been calculated using the personal tax rate applying to capital gains in each country, reduced by 25%.[5] The amount by which deferral reduces the effective tax rate on capital gains on SME business income depends on the appreciation rate, the discount rate and the time for which the asset is held. A 25% reduction in the effective tax rate can occur under a number of combinations of these factors and is consistent, for example, with a holding period of 10 years, an appreciation rate of 6% and an annual discount rate of 7%.

Table 2.6 shows that whether tax rates are higher on labour, dividends or capital gains income will depend not only on the respective rates applied to each form of income but also on the method of integration between corporate and personal taxation, the existence of small business rates for entity income, the level of SSCs and any capital gains tax exemptions that apply. For most countries, income received in the form of capital gains income faces the lowest combined statutory tax rates (even where small business tax rates are not taken into account). Capital gains tax rates are often lower than tax rates on other income and a significant number of countries allow exemptions for capital gains on shares held for longer than a set period to be exempt from taxation. Moreover, the impact of deferred taxation of capital gains (i.e. when gains are taxed on a realisation rather than an accrual basis) also reduces the effective tax rate on capital gains income (assuming the interest rate is higher than zero). For all but ten countries, income received in the form of labour is the highest taxed. For the remaining ten, dividends face the highest tax rate (seven when the impact of small business rates is considered).

The unweighted mean and median also follow these patterns. When the impact of SSCs is included, the highest average rates are found on labour income, although not significantly higher than dividends. Capital gains tax rates are the lowest, on an unweighted average basis. This implies that for many countries, the tax system provides incentives for incorporated SMEs to distribute their income as lower-taxed capital gains. This impact is particularly pronounced when other preferences on the sale or disposal of SME assets are considered; for example, further reductions or exemptions from capital gains tax, or gift and inheritance tax preferences. These are described in Chapter 3.

## 2.5. Comparisons and conclusions

Table 2.7 summarises tax rates that apply to different forms of SMEs. The second and third columns show the case of a SME owner subject to taxation at only the personal level, at 100% of the average wage and at the threshold for the top marginal rate, respectively. For such a SME owner, profits are taxable as the personal income of the owner under personal income taxes (with part of the income taxed as capital income in dual income tax systems). Self-employed SSCs apply to the total level of taxable income. In most countries, the top threshold is above the average wage, leading to lower income taxes on labour income earned at 100% of the average wage. However, in many cases, the level of self-employed contributions is also higher at this level of income than at the threshold for the top marginal rate, in some cases cancelling out the reduction in labour tax rates.

The last three columns show the situation of SMEs subject to taxation at both the entity and personal levels, subject to top marginal rates. At the entity level, income will be taxed at either basic or small business rates that apply to income from SMEs. The second column shows the combined statutory rates applied to dividend income from a small business, including corporate taxation at small business rates (where applicable) and the top dividend marginal tax rate for the taxpayer, together with any integration mechanisms that apply. The third column shows the same information for income distributed in the form of capital gains income. It assumes that the shares were held longer than any applicable holding period test prior to sale, halving the relevant capital gains tax rate applied at the personal level to approximate the advantage of deferring taxation. The final column shows the case of an owner-operator of a SME who pays themselves in labour income at the top marginal statutory tax rate, which is deductible at the corporate level and subject to employee and employer SSCs.

In summarising the combined statutory tax rates for top rate taxpayers under the four different kinds of business income, Table 2.7 indicates that income distributed through a double-taxed entity in the form of capital gains is likely to be the lowest taxed for a SME owner at the top marginal rate. This is the case for all countries except for Estonia and the Slovak Republic and is also reflected in the unweighted mean and median tax rates applicable to each of the four forms of entity. Dividend income is typically the second-lowest taxed (when small business tax rates apply at the entity level); with the impact of lower corporate tax rates and personal/corporate integration outweighing the impact of the additional level of taxation in all but nine countries. This is also reflected in the average rates shown in Table 2.7. Labour income, whether received as an employee of the SME or as sole-proprietor income, is typically the highest taxed form of income for a top-rate taxpayer who owns a SME.

Table 2.7. **Marginal tax rates on different forms of business income, 2014**

| | Single-level taxation | | Double-level taxation (typically, for incorporated SMEs) | | |
|---|---|---|---|---|---|
| Nature of income | Labour or business | | Dividends | Capital gains | Labour |
| Corporate tax | None | | Basic or small business rates | | Deductible against corporate income |
| Personal tax | Labour (at 100% AW) | Labour (at top marginal rate threshold)[a] | Dividend, incl. integration (at top marginal rate) | Capital gains,[b] incl. integration (at top marginal rate) | Labour (at top marginal rate) |
| SSCs | Self-employed (at 100% AW) | Self-employed (at top marginal rate threshold) | None | | Employee |
| Australia | 34 | 47 | 46 | 42 | 47 |
| Austria | 49 | 50 | 44 | 39 | 50 |
| Belgium | 64 | 67 | 44 | 25 | 59 |
| Canada | 40 | 50 | 49 | 30 | 50 |
| Chile | 0 | 40 | 40 | 21 | 40 |
| Czech Republic | 30 | 30 | 31 | 19 | 26 |
| Denmark | 34 | 56 | 56 | 48 | 56 |
| Estonia | 54 | 54 | 21 | 33 | 23 |
| Finland | 53 | 62 | 42 | 39 | 57 |
| France | 58 | 54 | 52 | 40 | 55 |
| Germany | 41 | 47 | 49 | 44 | 47 |
| Greece | 35 | 46 | 33 | 26 | 46 |
| Hungary | 62 | 62 | 24 | 10 | 35 |

Table 2.7. **Marginal tax rates on different forms of business income, 2014** *(continued)*

| | **Single-level taxation** | | **Double-level taxation (typically, for incorporated SMEs)** | | |
|---|---|---|---|---|---|
| Nature of income | Labour or business | | Dividends | Capital gains | Labour |
| Corporate tax | None | | Basic or small business rates | | Deductible against corporate income |
| Personal tax | Labour (at 100% AW) | Labour (at top marginal rate threshold)[a] | Dividend, incl. integration (at top marginal rate) | Capital gains,[b] incl. integration (at top marginal rate) | Labour (at top marginal rate) |
| SSCs | Self-employed (at 100% AW) | Self-employed (at top marginal rate threshold) | None | | Employee |
| Iceland | 38 | 44 | 36 | 32 | 44 |
| Ireland | 52 | 55 | 55 | 44 | 55 |
| Israel | 33 | 50 | 49 | 38 | 50 |
| Italy[c] | 54 | 48 | 46 | 42 | 48 |
| Japan | 27 | 51 | 39 | 29 | 51 |
| Korea | 17 | 39 | 43 | 11 | 43 |
| Luxembourg | 53 | 44 | 43 | 28 | 45 |
| Mexico | 25 | 35 | 42 | 30 | 35 |
| Netherlands[d] | 39 | 39 | 40 | 35 | 53 |
| New Zealand | 30 | 33 | 33 | 28 | 33 |
| Norway | 47 | 50 | 47 | 37 | 47 |
| Poland | 36 | 44 | 34 | 31 | 39 |
| Portugal | 32 | 50 | 51 | 44 | 61 |
| Slovak Republic[e] | 30 | 22 | 33 | 33 | 35 |
| Slovenia | 21 | 39 | 38 | 20 | 61 |
| Spain | 50 | 52 | 45 | 40 | 52 |
| Sweden | 47 | 69 | 45 | 40 | 57 |
| Switzerland | 30 | 42 | 37 | 21 | 42 |
| Turkey | 18 | 36 | 34 | 20 | 36 |
| United Kingdom | 39 | 47 | 44 | 37 | 47 |
| United States | 45 | 49 | 60 | 48 | 49 |
| Unweighted mean | 40 | 56 | 42 | 32 | 49 |
| Median | 39 | 58 | 43 | 33 | 50 |

*Notes:* a. This is the marginal rate at the earnings level where the top statutory personal income tax rate first applies and is taken from Table I.7 of the OECD Tax Database (OECD, 2015b)

b. Personal tax rates on capital gains have been reduced by 25% to approximate the impact of deferral of taxation until realisation.

c. In Italy, the taxation of non-qualified dividends and capital gains at the personal level was increased from 20% to 26% from 1 July 2014. The combined rates shown here include the new rate of 26%.

d. Figures for the Netherlands include the impact of the SME profit exemption (which exempts 14% of the profits of single-taxed entities from taxation). They therefore differ from the figures shown in Tables 2.2 and 2.3.

e. The combined statutory rate on dividends in the Slovak Republic includes health contributions of 14% which are levied at the personal level, but the maximum effective assessment base is not taken into account.

*Source:* OECD calculations based on OECD (2015b), *OECD Tax Database*, www.oecd.org/tax/tax-policy/tax-database.htm. Capital gains rates are for long-held dividends and were taken from Harding, M. (2013), *Taxation of Dividend, Interest and Capital Gain Income*, OECD Taxation Working Paper, and from information provided by national governments. The combined personal tax and SSC rates on labour income may differ from the sum of the individual components (presented earlier in this chapter) due to rounding.

Comparing these five cases provides some insights into a number of different economic margins faced by the owners of SMEs, summarised in Figure 2.4. In considering the tax rates shown in the tables in this chapter, three important caveats should be kept in mind. The first is that these show the situation only for personal taxpayers paying the top marginal rate and do not capture incentives applying to lower rate taxpayers. Secondly, these are statutory rather than effective tax rates; differences in the calculation of tax bases between different forms of entity will also affect these incentives. Thirdly, in countries with small business rates, combined tax rates will increase if the amount of SME income exceeds the top small business threshold.

Figure 2.4. **Influence of taxation on SME economic margins**

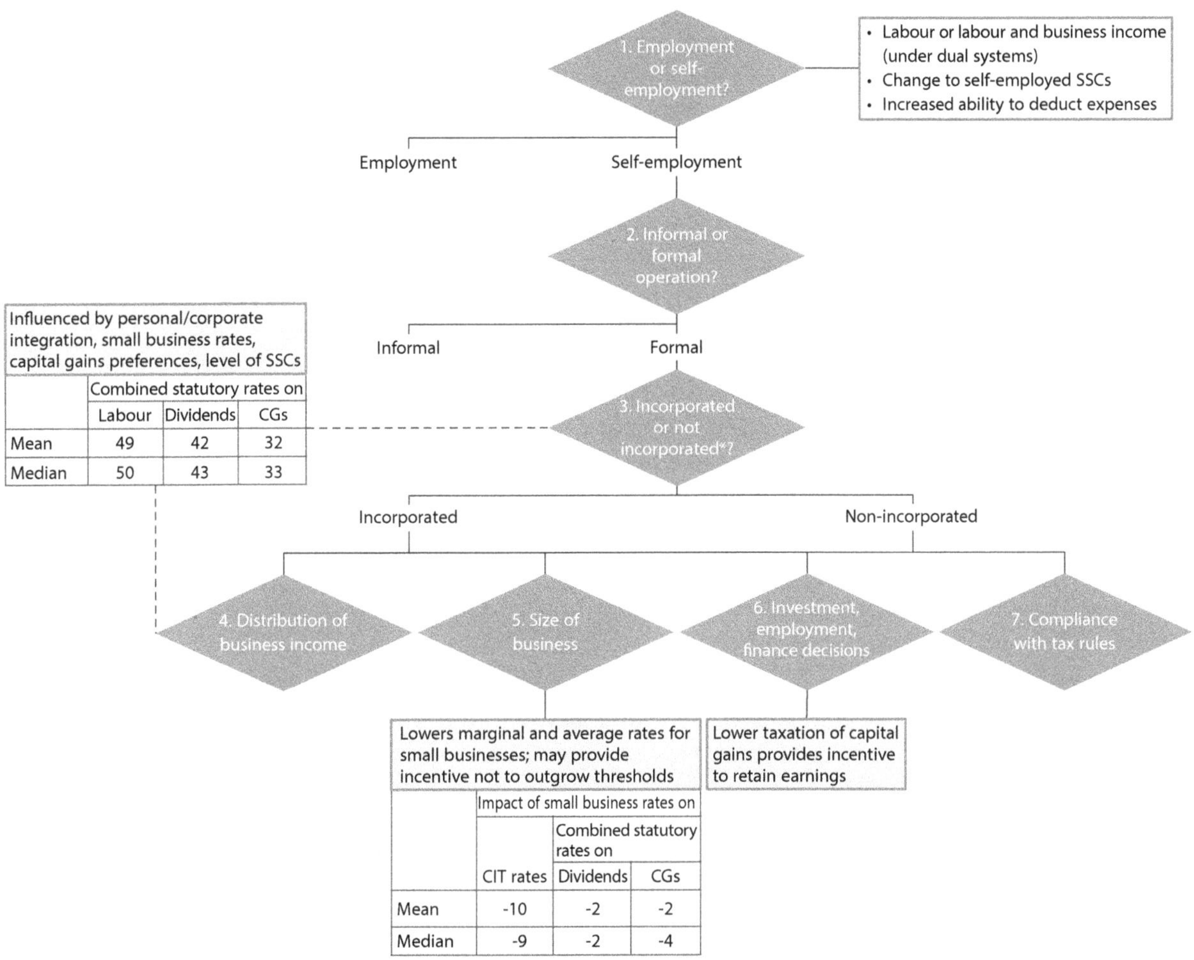


| | Combined statutory rates on | | |
|---|---|---|---|
| | Labour | Dividends | CGs |
| Mean | 49 | 42 | 32 |
| Median | 50 | 43 | 33 |

| | Impact of small business rates on | | |
|---|---|---|---|
| | | Combined statutory rates on | |
| | CIT rates | Dividends | CGs |
| Mean | -10 | -2 | -2 |
| Median | -9 | -2 | -4 |

* This assumes that the tax consequences of incorporation are to add a layer of taxation at the entity level. This may not be the case for all entities as in some countries, some incorporated entities are taxed only at the personal level, or some unincorporated entities may be subject to taxation at both the entity and personal level. Table 2.1 provides a brief description of these exceptions.

The income taxation of SMEs is most relevant to decisions 1, 3, 4, 5 and 6 of this schematic. In respect of the first, when facing the decision of whether to leave employment for self-employment, the resulting changes in taxation will depend on the respective levels of income in each form of activity, together with the form of entity used to conduct the business. If the decision is narrowed to a choice between employment or self-employment in an unincorporated SME, the difference in tax rates applicable will be a change in SSC contributions from employee and employer contributions to self-employed contributions, and the application of lower rates to business income from capital in a dual income tax system. In addition, the self-employed may have more flexibility in deducting personal expenses from income for tax purposes. Finally, self-employed individuals may benefit from tax preferences available to SMEs, discussed more fully in Chapter 3.

In respect of the decision to incorporate, incorporation typically introduces another level of taxation at the entity level, which could have the impact of increasing taxes relative to income from an unincorporated entity. However, this is not necessarily the case, for two reasons. Firstly, if income from an incorporated entity is distributed to the owner through dividends or capital gains,[6] SSCs, which can be a significant part of the tax burden even at lower levels of SME income, typically no longer apply. Secondly, a combination of corporate tax rates that are generally lower than top personal tax rates (particularly where small business rates are used), together with integration at the personal level and preferential taxation of dividend or capital gains income, may mean that the combined statutory tax rate on dividends or capital gains from small business are in fact lower than tax rates on unincorporated business income.

As a general result, incorporation does not necessarily place a higher income tax burden on a top PIT rate investor. Although it typically leads to some degree of double taxation of SME profits, small business rates and the form of integration between the personal and shareholder levels of taxation, together with the removal of SSCs on dividend or capital gains, often result in lower tax rates for entities subject to double taxation.[7] For firms reinvesting their earnings (generally a cheaper source of finance than new equity), the taxation of corporate profits at a low rate, compared with a top PIT rate on personal business income, combined with the ability to defer shareholder taxation of profits, tends to increase the relative attractiveness of incorporation as a choice of business form to profitable SMEs, at least for a top personal tax rate investor, and in particular where small business tax rates apply.

For SMEs in a loss-making position, the impact of the loss on marginal effective tax rates on profits in future years (assuming the SME survives to make a profit) will depend on whether the loss is able to be used to offset other income or whether it must be carried through to offset future income. For double-taxed entities where losses cannot be passed through to be used against other income of the owner, or for single-taxed entities where the owner has no other income, a carried-forward loss will be worth less in present value terms than if it were able to be used in the year in which it was incurred, increasing the marginal effective tax rate on future profits. If losses are able to be deducted against other income, however, they may be able to be deducted at higher personal rates, giving a tax advantage. This can be a significant incentive to choose single-taxed status. The treatment of losses is discussed further in Chapter 3.

For SME owner-operators without other sources of income, the average statutory tax rates on business income will be less than the top personal income tax rate and will be determined by the level of business income and the structure of the tiered personal tax rate schedule. For relatively low levels of business income, the average personal tax rate on business income may be below the basic corporate tax rate (and possibly zero). Thus, for relatively small firms, incorporation may involve a higher tax rate being applied to business profits even for growth-oriented firms reinvesting their earnings, making it a less attractive choice for small sole proprietorships and partnerships. This is consistent with the information on rates of double-taxation for microenterprises shown in Chapter 1.

Tax may also influence the decision to incorporate in other ways, including through the use of tax preferences described in Chapter 3. In addition, it may be easier for unincorporated businesses to characterise personal expenses as business expenses, an informal form of tax relief that will lower the average effective tax rate on income earned through an unincorporated SME relative to employment or incorporated SME income.

Taxes also influence the way in which income is distributed, again within the framework provided by other business considerations and anti-avoidance provisions of the tax code. Income that is retained and distributed in the form of capital gains generally has the lowest marginal statutory tax rate, in part due to lower taxation at the personal level and in part due to the deferral of taxation until realisation. Countries also report a number of tax preferences for capital gains on SME shares that increase the attractiveness of this option. A lower tax rate on retained corporate earnings than the combined tax rate on distributed earnings can also provide a deferral advantage that favours retention of earnings within a corporation. However, particularly among the SME population, many taxpayers may not be able to defer realisation of their earnings.

Finally, taxation can also impact decisions about the size of the business. Small business corporate tax rate thresholds may provide a disincentive to grow past a particular income threshold, particularly where the change in the marginal or average rate is steep. Tiered SSCs may also provide a disincentive to grow income past a particular threshold in a SME subject only to single-level taxation. Finally, many tax preferences and simplification measures (for example, presumptive taxes) are also based on size criteria.

Therefore, there are three main influences income taxation has on the economic margins faced by owners of SMEs. Firstly, the main tax difference in non-dual tax systems between the treatment of employment and self-employment will be determined by the respective levels of social SSCs. The increased ability of self-employed persons to determine the amount of labour income earned as well as to deduct expenses may also be relevant. Secondly, while incorporation typically adds a second layer of taxation at the entity level, this does not necessarily result in a higher level of taxation. This is for several reasons, including the availability of small business tax rates at the corporate level, preferential treatment of capital income (particularly capital gains, but to a lesser extent dividends) at the personal level and the removal of SSCs on business income. However, incorporation may restrict the usefulness of SME losses. Finally, SME income that is received in the form of capital gains is very often taxed at considerably lower combined statutory rates than income earned in other forms, even before the impact of further SME-specific exemptions and reductions (described in Chapter 3) are taken into account, providing a tax-incentive to distribute income in this form.

## Notes

1. Many countries are reforming or considering reforming their tax rules, including changes under consideration as part of the OECD/G20 project on base erosion and profit shifting (OECD, 2013).

2. In Finland, employee and employer SSCs are based on gross wages, whereas the base of (most) self-employed SSCs is YEL-income (defined as gross wage that would be paid to an equally competent person). The YEL is determined by the self-employed person, but the level of the contribution affects future entitlements.

3. The United States is an exception in that the SSC rate is lower above the USD 117 000 social security threshold.

4. For most countries, this is done at the first step of the applicable small business rate. For the United States, the small business rate used is the rate that applies at the top personal income tax threshold.
5. Reducing the personal tax rate on capital gains to reflect the benefit of deferral in decreasing effective tax rates was also the approach followed, for example, in King and Fullerton (1984) and Jorgenson and Yun (1987).
6. The ability of the taxpayer to defer receipt of income is also relevant. If the taxpayer needs current distributions of SME income for living expenses, which is particularly likely at lower levels of SME income, the capital gains rate may be less relevant to the incorporation decision.
7. However, the removal of social security contributions may also reduce a SME owner's entitlement to future benefits.

## References

Devereux, M. and L. Liu (2014), *Incorporation for Investment,* www.sbs.ox.ac.uk/sites/default/files/Business_Taxation/Events/conferences/symposia/2014/liu-v2.pdf.

European Commission (2015), *SME Taxation in Europe: An Empirical Study of Applied Corporate Income Taxation for SMEs compared to Large Enterprises,* European Union, Brussels.

Harding, M. (2013), *Taxation of Dividend, Interest and Capital Gain Income,* OECD Taxation Working Paper.

IBFD (2015), *IBFD Tax Research Platform,* accessed at http://online.ibfd.org/kbase.

Jorgenson, D. and K. Yun (1991), *Tax Reform and the Cost of Capital,* Oxford University Press, Oxford.

King, M. and D. Fullerton (1984), *The Taxation of Income from Capital: A Comparative Study of the United States, the United Kingdom, Sweden, and Germany,* http://econpapers.repec.org/bookchap/nbrnberbk/king84-1.htm.

Knittel, M., S. Nelson, J. DeBacker, J. Kitchen, J. Pearce and R. Prisinzano (2011), *Methodology to Identify Small Businesses and Their Owners,* Office of Tax Analysis, United States Department of the Treasury Technical Paper 4. August 2011.

OECD (2015a), *Taxing Wages 2015,* OECD Publishing, Paris, http://dx.doi.org/10.1787/tax_wages-2015-en.

OECD (2015b), *OECD Tax Database,* www.oecd.org/tax/tax-policy/tax-database.htm.

OECD (2013), *Action Plan on Base Erosion and Profit Shifting, OECD Publishing,* Paris, http://dx.doi.org/10.1787/9789264202719-en.

OECD (2009), *Taxation of SMEs: Key Issues and Policy Considerations,* OECD Tax Policy Studies, No. 18, OECD Publishing, Paris, http://dx.doi.org/10.1787/9789264024748-en.

Poterba, J. (1986), "How Burdensome are Capital Gains Taxes", *NBER Working Paper 1871.*

United States Internal Revenue Service (2015), *Independent Contractor Defined,* www.irs.gov/Businesses/Small-Businesses-&-Self-Employed/Independent-Contractor-Defined.

# *Chapter 3*

# Tax preferences for SMEs

*This chapter discusses tax preferences that are available to SMEs. It begins with an assessment of the case for the provision of tax preferences for SMEs, before discussing tax preferences provided to SMEs in 38 OECD and G20 countries. Tax preferences are divided into preferences provided at the entity level (e.g. enhanced deductions, tax credits and exemptions targeted at SMEs) and those provided to owners (e.g. incentives for investment, preferential treatment of income or losses from SMEs, and preferences on disposal of SME assets). The chapter concludes by discussing the impact of tax preferences on the decisions of SMEs, outlining principles to guide the implementation of these measures. Finally, it provides a summary table of preferences reported by the 38 countries.*

## 3.1. Introduction

The case for SME tax preferences is often justified by the special place of SMEs in the economy, particularly in terms of their contribution to employment, job creation and innovation. In assessing the need for tax preferences for SMEs, the case in favour is generally based on arguments related to market failure and the positive externalities associated with SMEs. A second rationale for intervention is based upon the argument that the tax system may inherently disadvantage SMEs due to their size and, in the absence of intervention, will unfairly disadvantage them against their larger competitors and may have distortive impacts on commercial decisions and between different business forms and different business activities.

Where a clear rationale for intervening exists, the advantages of doing so through the tax system as against other interventions should also be considered. If tax preferences are provided, they should be considered against the revenue and efficiency costs of doing so, including the risk of creating further distortions or barriers to growth, or increasing complexity. Any tax preferences should, therefore, clearly identify the problem they seek to address and the SMEs to which the measure should be targeted, and should seek to avoid introducing new distortions or adverse consequences.

Tax preferences provided to SMEs act to lower the amount of tax payable by the SME or by an investor or owner of a SME. They can take many forms, including additional deductions, credits or exemptions targeted to SMEs, or tax reductions and exemptions provided for SME owners and investors that are linked to their investment in SMEs. Most countries that replied to the questionnaire, report some form of tax preferences targeted to SMEs. These seek to address a range of different goals, most commonly to encourage SME investment, promote expenditure on research and development (R&D) and innovation, support employment, and encourage financing of SMEs by investors. They therefore directly affect a number of the economic margins outlined in the second chapter of this study.

This chapter is structured as follows. Section 3.2 assesses the case for providing tax preferences to SMEs, considering the rationale for intervention as well as some of the difficulties and risks of doing so. Sections 3.3 and 3.4 draw on responses from the questionnaires to discuss the tax preferences applied to SMEs in OECD and G20 countries. Of these sections, section 3.3 focuses on tax preferences provided at the entity level (whether incorporated or unincorporated), considering deductions, tax credits and exemptions, while section 3.4 considers tax preferences at the investor level (considering preferences for initial investment, for income received from the investment, and on the disposal of SME assets). Section 3.5 provides an overview in table form of the tax preferences reported by the countries that replied to the questionnaire and links these to the framework outlined in Chapter 2.

## 3.2. Assessing the case for tax preferences for SMEs

There are two main rationales put forward in support of tax preferences for SMEs. The first rationale argues that there are market failures that particularly affect SMEs due to their small size or age. The second rationale is that the tax system has a disproportionately adverse impact on SMEs, due to their small size, disadvantaging them relative to larger enterprises. As seen in Chapter 1, SMEs account for a large share of employment and taxable business income. They also contribute significantly to value-added and to exports, both directly and indirectly.

One market failure argument in support of SME incentives is that SMEs generate benefits over and above those accruing privately to investors. These benefits may include innovation that can be applied elsewhere, with positive growth consequences. Other potential benefits include labour training and skills development. As these benefits are not realised by SME owners or investors, under-investment in SMEs will result, relative to the socially optimal level. Therefore, tax incentives targeted at SMEs, and particularly at these activities, may encourage higher levels of investment in these activities. However, there is a question of whether it is only SMEs that generate these positive spillover benefits. There is a lack of empirical analysis of whether SMEs are more likely than large companies to upskill workers or to innovate.

Another market failure argument for providing tax preferences is that SMEs are affected by asymmetric information on markets or products, barriers to entry posed by incumbent firms, or difficulties in raising finance (Freedman, 2009). In particular, SMEs are seen as more vulnerable to capital market imperfections, making it more difficult for a new business or SME to obtain access to credit, or requiring them to pay higher interest rates (OECD, 2015). At the same time, their small size may make it more difficult for them to attract and retain equity finance. Difficulties for SMEs in accessing finance have been exacerbated by the recent financial crisis (OECD, 2009b). In these circumstances, it is argued that tax preferences supporting SME finance are justified. However, except where information asymmetries affect access to finance, the more restricted access to credit, or a higher risk premium, of SMEs may not be due to market failures but rather be related to the inherently riskier and less profitable nature of some SMEs as set out in Chapter 1, or it may be related to a general lack of investment.

The second rationale used to support tax preferences for SMEs is that the tax system is inherently disadvantageous for SMEs due to their small size. This is a specific instance of the more general issue of higher fixed costs for SMEs. Underlying this argument is the principle that the tax treatment of businesses, including SMEs, should not distort their commercial decisions and should be neutral between different business forms and activities, unless for considered policy reasons (Freedman, 2009). Some of the disadvantages posed by the tax system to SMEs include:

- The asymmetric treatment of profit and losses under the tax system: profits are taxed when they occur, however, losses typically are not refunded at the time they occur, but are carried forward to be used against future income. This may disproportionately affect SMEs who are more likely to have losses in their early stages of development, posing cash flow problems at a critical stage in the firm's growth. For firms that do not recover (particularly relevant for younger enterprises, as seen in Chapter 1) the deferred loss is not able to be utilised. Under this argument, the ability to refund losses at the time they occur or to use them to offset other income may be justified; as are refunds for tax credits provided to SMEs.
- Greater reliance on equity finance may result in higher tax for some SMEs subject to entity level tax. Corporate income tax systems generally provide deductions for interest expense which result in that capital income being subject to tax only at the lender level. To the extent that SMEs rely more heavily on equity finance, they have more of the SMEs capital income subject to entity level tax.
- The tax system imposes compliance burdens on taxpayers who must comply with record keeping, filing and payment processes. These burdens involve a large fixed component and are typically larger (in relative terms) for SMEs than for larger enterprises. This issue is considered further in Chapter 4.

- Taxes on the sale or inheritance of SMEs and SME assets may also disproportionately affect SMEs. Payment of capital gains or inheritance taxes on disposal of these assets could threaten the viability of the business in a way that would not apply to a larger enterprise.

Where a case for special SME tax rules exists, the use of tax preferences to redress the perceived market failure or size disadvantage should also be carefully considered against other options to address the difficulty, such as targeted intervention, broader changes to the tax system or processes, or information campaigns.

The design of any tax preference should also be carefully considered. Addressing tax incentives to correct market failures is in practice difficult, requiring careful identification and quantification of the degree of market failure and the firms which are affected. As the population of SMEs is heterogeneous, identifying the SMEs that should benefit from a tax incentive is also important. Size alone does not necessarily warrant intervention: many of the market failure arguments above do not apply to all SMEs, but rather to subsets of the SME population. For example, only a subset of SMEs may innovate, meaning that tax preferences relating to innovation should be carefully targeted to benefit SMEs most responsive to innovation incentives and that create the most spillover benefits. Similarly, younger SMEs are more likely to be affected by the asymmetric treatment of profits and losses under the tax system than more established SMEs. Freedman (2009) concludes that assistance with compliance costs is the only intervention that "is clearly justified on a size basis as opposed to some other test".

Tax preferences, whether targeted at SMEs or other groups of taxpayers, may also pose a risk to the revenue and integrity of the tax system. One challenge is that even when carefully targeted, caution must be exercised to ensure that taxpayers not intended to benefit from the preference are not able to reorganise their affairs, whether in terms of expenditure or business structure, in such a way as to benefit from the provision. Tax preferences that are initially extended only to SMEs may give rise to pressure for such preferences to be extended to all businesses, particularly if there is no clear rationale for limiting the incentive only to SMEs.

Finally, the creation of tax preferences can introduce additional complexity and distortions into the tax system. Thresholds limiting tax preferences to entities under a certain size can create barriers to SME growth. The introduction of tax preferences can also introduce complexity by requiring additional record-keeping, monitoring, or application and registration processes, particularly where anti-avoidance rules must also be complied with. This burden is exacerbated when multiple thresholds or benefits potentially apply.

## 3.3. Business-level preferences for SMEs

The discussion in this section reports business-level tax preferences available to SMEs drawing on the questionnaire responses provided by 38 OECD and G20 countries. It discusses preferences provided at the entity level to both incorporated and unincorporated SMEs, recognising that in the case of unincorporated SMEs, the distinction between the entity and the owner may be less clear. The section discusses three broad groups of preferences: enhanced deductions for SMEs; tax credits available to SMEs; and exemptions from tax liabilities. Reduced corporate tax rates for SMEs are discussed in Chapter 2.

## *Preferences for tax deductions of SMEs*

Deductions operate to reduce the amount of taxable income of a business to take into account expenses incurred in generating that income. While the nature and extent of deductions will vary between countries, common deductions include deductions for business expenses, employment expenses, interest and those related to the depreciation of assets. Special deduction provisions for SMEs may enhance the value of existing deductions, or provide new deductions that do not apply to other businesses.

The extent to which deductions reduce the tax liability of a taxpayer will depend on the marginal effective tax rate of the entity. For SMEs with a higher tax rate, the value of enhanced deductions will be higher than for a SME subject to a lower tax rate. For SMEs in a tax loss position, the value of special deductions will depend on whether the loss is able to be used against other income of the owner, or whether it can be used to offset profits in other time periods.

The impact of preferential tax deductions for SMEs is to increase the amount of after tax profit available for reinvestment into the company, lowering the cost of equity finance. They can also act to lower the post-tax cost of the expenditure to which they apply; making them comparatively more attractive. Deductions also increase the cash flow of businesses, which may be particularly helpful for those at an early stage or during a financial crisis.

### *Depreciation and investment allowances*

A channel through which investment incentives may be provided is via special tax provisions that lower the effective price of acquiring capital. One such measure is an investment allowance (e.g. accelerated and enhanced depreciation allowances), which are deductions against taxable income.

Accelerated depreciation allowances allow firms to depreciate capital costs over a shorter time period relative to the estimated useful economic life of the asset. This increases the present value of the depreciation deductions by shifting them forward, closer to the time of the investment. The present value of depreciation allowances is the greatest where the full cost of the capital asset can be deducted in the year the expenditure is made (i.e. immediate expensing). Where immediate expensing applies, the normal return on that investment is effectively untaxed and will give rise to a negative effective tax rate on that investment when the SME is financed by debt. Where a firm is in a "tax loss" position, depreciation allowances only provide value to the investor if the additional tax loss can be carried forward (or backward) to offset tax liabilities in other periods, or if they are able to be transferred to offset against the owner's income. Enhanced depreciation allowances permit firms to claim total deductions for the cost of qualifying capital that exceed the price at which it is acquired.

Tax incentives based on investment expenditures, such as accelerated or enhanced depreciation, immediate expensing of some proportion of capital costs and investment tax credits, provide a larger investment response for each dollar of tax revenue foregone, compared to a corporate tax rate reduction. Unlike a corporate tax rate reduction, tax preferences tied to the cost of purchasing capital benefit only new investment and therefore may provide a larger reduction in the effective tax rate on investment at a lower revenue cost. In contrast, a reduction in the statutory corporate tax rate benefits "new" as well as "old" capital, providing existing investors with a windfall gain by increasing the present value of the future stream of after-tax earnings from existing capital. In addition, the effect of investment tax preferences is higher for less profitable investments than a lower corporate tax rate, as the benefit of the lower corporate tax rate is tied to the level of the return on the investment.

Tax preferences in the form of immediate expensing or accelerated depreciation are the most commonly reported form of deduction preference available to SMEs. Table 3.1 summarises the depreciation preferences available to SMEs, drawing on the questionnaire responses.

Table 3.1. **Summary of depreciation preferences for SMEs**

| Country | Nature of preference for SMEs |
|---|---|
| Australia | • **Simplified rules:** SMEs are able to pool their assets and depreciate these (on a diminishing value basis) as a single asset. This is aimed to reduce compliance cost for small businesses.<br>• **Immediate expensing:** SMEs can write-off assets costing less than AUD 1 000 (AUD 300 for other businesses). Following its announcement in the 2015 Budget, the Government has introduced a temporary increase in this limit to AUD 20 000 until 30 June 2017 for SMEs. |
| Belgium | • **More flexible rules:** No requirement to pro rata depreciation in the year of acquisition for the proportion of the year they have owned the asset.<br>• **Immediate expensing:** Ability to expense acquisition costs related to the purchase of the asset. |
| Chile | If operating business income over a three year period prior to the purchase of the fixed asset (or the actual business operation period, provided the SME has been operating for less than three years) is:<br>• Less than or equal to UF 25 000, **immediate expensing**, applicable to new or used fixed assets.<br>• Over UF 25 000 and up to UF 100 000, **accelerated depreciation**, applicable to new or imported fixed assets, which can be depreciated in a period equal to a tenth of the useful life established by the Chilean Internal Revenue Service, provided it is no less than a year. |
| France | • **Accelerated depreciation:** Investments in robotics for use in industrial automation between 1 October 2013 and 31 December 2015 can be depreciated over a two-year period rather than across the duration of their useful life.<br>• **Accelerated depreciation:** Buildings for commercial and industrial use in rural development zones benefit from exceptional depreciation of 25% in the first year of the asset's use, if built or renovated before 1 January 2016 2004. The remainder of the property value is depreciated against its normal useful life basis.<br>• **Accelerated depreciation**: France exempts SMEs from the requirement to include in their taxable income a proportion of rent paid in cases where they, as lessees, acquire a leased property at the end of the lease period, if the total amount of deducted rent is higher than the total amount of depreciation the SMEs could have deducted if they had been the legal owner. This exemption only applies to SMEs in rural development zone. |
| Germany | **Accelerated depreciation** for SME business assets costing less than EUR 235 000 (125 000 for agriculture and forestry) |
| Hungary | • **Immediate expensing:** Reduction of pre-tax profit with payments on account for the acquisition of land and buildings and of tangible assets such as technical equipment, machinery and vehicles, as well as remodelling. The payments must be made for the purpose of putting the assets into service, remodelling to increase their value (in the case of real estate) or acquiring new software use rights or intellectual property<br>• **Immediate expensing:** Ability to expense investment in machinery, equipment and accessories (excluding passenger cars) if the assets are to be used in certain defined underprivileged areas.<br>• **Immediate expensing:** The KIVA small business tax (see Chapter 4) allows investment to be immediately deducted. |
| Japan | • **Accelerated depreciation:** For investments in machinery, depreciation of up to 30% of the acquisition cost is allowed in addition to the normal depreciation rate, meaning that the period of depreciation is shorter than for other assets.<br>• **Immediate expensing:** Japan allows low value assets (of up to JPY 300 000) purchased by SMEs to be immediately expensed, up to a limit of JPY 3 million per year. |
| Korea | • **Accelerated depreciation** for facility investment by SMEs, at a 50% rate rather than 25% as prescribed for other entities |
| Mexico | • **Immediate expensing:** The *Régimen de Incorporación Fiscal* (RIF) allows SMEs to calculate taxes on a cash basis, allowing investments to be expensed immediately.<br>• **Immediate expensing:** Incorporated and unincorporated SMEs in the primary sector (agriculture, livestock, forestry and fishery) can expense payments made for the acquisition of fixed assets, deferred charges and expenditures, if their income is less than 423 annual minimum wages. |

Table 3.1. **Summary of depreciation preferences for SMEs** *(continued)*

| Country | Nature of preference for SMEs |
|---|---|
| Netherlands | **Accelerated depreciation:** Enterprises are able to depreciate all their assets without limitation in the first three years of the business' operation. |
| Poland | **Immediate expensing:** SMEs with turnover of less than EUR 1.2 million or in the first year of activity can make one-off write-downs in the value of tangible assets (excluding passenger cars) purchased in that year of up to EUR 50 000 per year |
| South Africa | **Accelerated depreciation:** where turnover is less than ZAR 20 million, capital can be written off over three years (at 50%, 30% and 20% in each year) instead of over five years. Manufacturing SMEs can depreciate capital over one year |
| Spain | • **Immediate expensing:** If turnover is below EUR 10 million, immediate expensing is allowed of fixed assets and investment properties provided that the staff level is kept the same relative to previous years.<br>• **Accelerated amortisation:** SMEs can amortise new equipment, buildings and intangible assets, at twice the normal rate. |
| United Kingdom | • **Immediate expensing**: The Annual Investment Allowance allows businesses to deduct the full value of capital expenditure (with certain exclusions, primarily motor vehicles) in the year of purchase, up to a temporary limit of GBP 500 000 (for expenditure from 1 April 2014 to 31 December 2015). The temporary limit was set to provide an incentive for small and medium-sized businesses to bring forward capital expenditure, particularly for larger SMEs. In 2015, the permanent limit was set to GBP 200 000 from 1 January 2016. |
| United States | **Immediate expensing:** Businesses with less than USD 200 000 of qualifying investment can choose to expense up to USD 25 000 of the cost, which is phased out dollar for dollar starting at USD 200 000 of investment. The deduction is allowable up to the limit of business income, with excess being available to be carried over to future years. Qualifying investment is defined as depreciable tangible personal property purchased for use in a trade or business. (Limits in effect as of 1/01/2015) |

*Source:* Responses to an OECD questionnaire, *Survey on the Taxation of Small and Medium-Sized Enterprises*, 2015.

Belgium allows SMEs to benefit from the investment allowance with an increased deduction rate for security investments (at 20.5%). They can also apply a temporary allowance of 4% for ordinary investments that do not benefit from the normal or special investment deduction. This temporary deduction cannot be combined with the benefit of the Allowance for Corporate Equity (ACE), discussed below.

### *Other deduction preferences for SMEs*

SMEs, particularly newly-formed SMEs, may be more likely to be in a loss position than larger enterprises and less likely to have cash flow or asset reserves on which they can draw. For this reason, countries may choose to apply more flexible treatment of losses for SMEs than of other enterprises, for example, by allowing a greater amount of the loss to be carried over to be offset against the SMEs income in other years, or by allowing a longer carry-over period, relative to larger entities. Other preferences may allow losses to be used by the owner of the entity (discussed further in section 3.4).

Japan, Korea and Spain report more flexible loss provisions for SMEs than for larger entities. Japan allows SMEs to carry forward up to 100% of income, whereas a large corporation can only use losses to offset up to 65% of income before the loss deduction in 2015 and 2016, reducing to 50% in 2017. Korea allows SMEs to carry back losses to apply against income in the previous year. This provision applies to SMEs under the Special Tax Treatment Control Act, who are able to claim a refundable tax offset for losses in that year against the prior year's income. Spain allows entities with turnover of less than EUR 6.01 million to use all losses in previous periods to offset future tax liabilities, rather than limiting them.

Under the allowance for corporate equity (ACE) in Belgium, SMEs benefit from an increased notional deduction for equity which is 0.5 percentage points higher than the general rate (i.e. the SME rate is 2.13% in 2015). The ACE system operates to reduce the cost of equity finance, increasing the attractiveness of equity, including retained earnings, as a source of finance and reducing the tax system bias in favour of (deductible) debt finance. This also serves to minimise the disadvantage faced by SMES to the extent that they are less able to access debt finance than larger firms. The allowance for corporate equity available for small firms is not refundable and, therefore, cannot be used by firms in a loss making position. The increased rate of the allowance for the equity of a SME may make the tax system more neutral when SMEs are less able to access debt finance or must pay a higher interest rate than larger firms.

Other deductions are intended to promote employment by SMEs. In Hungary, SMEs are able to reduce their pre-tax profit by increasing the number of staff they employ. The deduction is calculated as the average wage paid on the first day of the tax year by the increase in the number of employees relative to the previous year (or the last year of the predecessor in the event of transformation, merger or division), or for new entities, from zero. This deduction only applies to companies that did not employ more than five persons in the previous tax year and which do not have any outstanding local or government tax obligations.

Japan and Korea provide preferential deductions for the entertainment expenses of SMEs by increasing the amount of entertainment expenses that are able to be deducted relative to larger enterprises. In Japan, SMEs defined as enterprises with less than JPY 100 million in capital, are able to deduct the greater of 50% of their entertainment expenses for eating and drinking or a fixed amount of JPY 8 million per year. Entities with more than JPY 100 million in capital are able to deduct only 50% of their entertainment expenses for eating and drinking. In Korea, the limit applied to entertainment deductions of SMEs is increased relative to the limit applied to larger firms. SMEs are able to deduct up to KRW 18 million (24 million in 2015-2016) of their entertainment expenses, relative to KRW 12 million for other enterprises.

The United Kingdom provides R&D relief against corporate tax for SMEs, allowing them to claim an additional deduction above the normal R&D deduction. SMEs for the purposes of this deduction are entities which fall under two times the level of the EU definition: i.e. companies with fewer than 500 employees and either an annual turnover of less than EUR 100 million or a balance sheet of under EUR 86 million. These entities qualify for an additional R&D deduction of 130%, of R&D expenditure, meaning that a SME gets a total deduction of 230% on qualifying expenditure. Qualifying expenditure is defined by the Department of Business Innovation and Skills. The purpose of the R& D deduction is to encourage innovation and therefore to promote economic growth.

A range of other deductions were also reported in the questionnaire responses:

- Belgium provides a fiscal incentive for the hiring of additional staff. For each low-income staff member employed in Belgium, EUR 5 660 (in 2014) is deductible from the taxable income of the SME. Entities considered to be SMEs are companies declaring profits or proceeds and employing less than eleven wage or salary earners on 31 December 1997 (or where the company started activity after that date, on 31 December of the year the company started its activity).
- Hungary exempts SMEs from making a correction to Prices Applied Among Affiliated Companies with regard to long-term contracts concluded with affiliated companies in the case of joint purchases and sales. The exemption applies only if the voting rights of the SME in the affiliate company exceed 50%. The measure is designed to reduce the competitive disadvantage faced by SMEs compared to larger businesses.

- Spain allows a tax deduction of 1% of accounts receivable, to allow for potential bad debts. Spain also allows a tax base reduction of up to 10% for setting up a non-distributable reserve for offsetting tax losses. This reserve is limited to a maximum of EUR 1 million for five years.
- In the Netherlands, entrepreneurs are allowed to make a fixed deduction of EUR 7 280 from taxable profits, lowering their average tax rate and increasing the effective threshold for the application of marginal rates.
- The United States allows taxpayers with less than USD 50 000 of start-up or organisational expenditure to deduct (rather than amortise) up to USD 5 000 of each type of expense in the first year of business. The amount of the deduction is phased out if these expenses exceed USD 50 000. The purpose of the provision is to lower the tax cost of investigating new business opportunities and investing in new business activities and also to simplify tax administration and reduce the compliance burden.
- France provides an allowance against the profits of SMEs located in Guadeloupe, Guyana, Martinique, Mayotte and Reunion. Corporate profits of SMEs in eligible sectors (accounting, business advice, or engineering) are able to deduct 40% of taxable profits in 2015, 35% in 2016 and 30% in 2017. The deduction is capped at EUR 150 000 per year. Both the amount of the reduction and the cap can be increased for certain areas or industries.

### *Tax credits targeted at SMEs*

The second type of tax preference that may be provided for SMEs are tax credits that serve to reduce the amount of tax payable on taxable income. These include tax credits for R&D or innovation, investment tax credits, credits for employment, health, or other forms of expense. Unlike a deduction, tax credits directly reduce the tax liability of the SME and so their value is not dependent on the SME's rate of tax.

Whether a tax credit is refundable or transferable will be of particular importance for firms in a tax loss situation. As for deductions, tax credits are generally of no immediate use to firms in a "tax loss" position. Governments may allow firms in a temporary loss position (e.g. start-up firms) to carry forward balances of earned but unused investment tax credits. This avoids placing them at a competitive disadvantage relative to profitable firms, although even with carryover provisions, a timing disadvantage still persists. An alternative is to allow for tax credit "refundability". Where a credit is refundable, taxpayers are provided with cash relief for that portion of the credit that cannot be used to offset income tax liability in the year the credit is earned. Refundability can boost cash-flow and address possible liquidity constraints inhibiting investment plans.

However, from the government's perspective, care must be exercised in introducing refundable tax credit provisions. Refundability increases the cost of an investment tax credit programme by shifting forward tax expenditures that would be delayed under tax credit carryover provisions. It also extends support to firms that may eventually fail and may never report taxable profits as well as increasing incentives to re-characterise non-targeted activities as qualifying ones. Carryover provisions limit programme costs by extending assistance only to firms that will eventually be profitable, in effect targeting them to surviving firms.

The most common forms of tax credit are investment tax credits and tax credits for R&D or innovation. The remainder of this subsection discusses each before considering other reported tax credit preferences for SMEs.

### *Investment tax credits*

Like investment allowances, investment tax credits also alter investment incentives by lowering the effective price of acquiring capital. Investment tax credits are typically earned as a percentage of qualifying expenditures. Investment tax credits may be flat or incremental. A flat investment tax credit is earned as a fixed percentage of qualifying investment expenditures. An incremental investment tax credit is calculated on the excess against a moving-average base (e.g. the average investment expenditure by the taxpayer over the previous three years). One rationale for an incremental tax credit is to improve the targeting of the relief to investment expenditure that would not have occurred in the absence of the tax relief.

A range of tax credit preferences were reported by OECD and G20 countries. These are summarised in Table 3.2. Tax credits include measures targeted at SME investment in particular geographical areas (the Atlantic region in Canada, or in Corsica in the case of France), as well as investment in particular forms of assets (for example facility investment in Korea or machinery in Japan). In many cases, the credit is specifically aimed at SMEs, whereas in others, SMEs benefit from more favourable rates (as in the case of Chile) or entry criteria (as in Portugal).

Table 3.2. **Summary of investment allowance preferences for SMEs**

| Country | Rate of credit | Eligible expenditures | Comment |
|---|---|---|---|
| Canada | 10% | New buildings, machinery and equipment for farming, fishing, logging, manufacturing and processing, by corporations in the Atlantic region (Newfoundland and Labrador, New Brunswick, Nova Scotia, Prince Edward Island, the Gaspé Peninsula in Quebec). | For larger corporations, the credit is non-refundable. Forty per cent of the credit is refundable for Canadian-controlled private corporations (CCPCs) that have taxable income below the qualified income limit. The qualified income limit is equal to CAD 500 000 for CCPCs with prior-year taxable capital of less than CAD 10 million. The limit is phased out on a straight-line basis for CCPCs with prior-year taxable capital between CAD 10 and 50 million. |
| Chile | 6%[a] | Physical assets acquired, built or held under a lease with a purchase option. | The annual maximum amount of the credit cannot exceed UTM 500.<br>The different rates apply depending on the average annual sale of the taxpayer (6% in case of taxpayers who have average annual sales that do not exceed UF 25 000; 6% by the result of dividing 100 000 minus annual earning over 75 000 in case of taxpayers who have average annual sales greater than UF 25 000 but which do not exceed UF100 000; 4% in case of taxpayers who have average annual sales greater than UF 100 000) |
| France | 1. 20%<br>2. 20% | 1. Tangible or intangible property that is not yet available on the market and differs from existing or previous products, having superior technical performance, ergonomics, functionality or eco-design.<br>2. Depreciable capital goods, fixtures and commercial facilities, related software, hotel renovations in Corsica. | 1. Limited to EUR 400 000 per year. The tax credit is able to be carried forward for up to three years or can be refunded. This is an extension of the research tax credit.<br>2. Applies to enterprises with less than 250 employees and turnover of less than EUR 40 million or assets under 27 million The investments must be operated in Corsica, have been acquired between 2002 and 2020, and be funded without public aid for at least 25% of their cost. The tax credit can be carried forward for nine years or is refundable. |

Table 3.2. **Summary of investment allowance preferences for SMEs** *(continued)*

| Country | Rate of credit | Eligible expenditures | Comment |
|---|---|---|---|
| Germany | 40% | Estimated acquisition costs of a depreciable tangible asset up to three years prior to the acquisition | SMEs with business assets costing less than EUR 235 000. After the acquisition, the amount of the credit reduces the base for depreciation of the asset. This instrument, together with the accelerated depreciation described above, is intended to boost SME competitiveness, improve their liquidity and support investment. |
| Hungary | 60% | Interest paid on a loan for a tangible asset. | Limited to HUF 6 million per year. |
| Japan | 7% | Acquisition cost of machinery. | Non-refundable, but able to be carried forward for one year. Taxpayers must choose between the special depreciation rate described above and this tax credit. |
| Korea | 1. 3-9%<br>2. 7-10% | 1. Facility investment (investment in tangible assets for business purposes).<br>2. Investment in R&D facilities, productivity enhancement facilities, safety facilities, energy-saving facilities, environmental conservation facilities and facilities designed to promote employees' welfare. | 1&2. Other criteria are used to determine the applicable rate within this range. |
| Netherlands | 28% | Investments | SMEs can deduct 28% (maximum) from their investments, up to a value of EUR 15 609 of their taxable income. |
| Portugal | 10-25% | Investment expenses. | SMEs must remain in the same region for three years (as opposed to five years for larger entities). The amount of the credit is limited to 100% of the SME's tax liability in the first three years of business activities and 50% for the next 10. |

*Note:* a. The percentage resulting from multiplying 6% by the result of dividing 100 000 minus annual earning over 75 000, provided the resulting rate is not lower than 4%.

*Source:* Responses to an OECD questionnaire, *Survey on the Taxation of Small and Medium-Sized Enterprises*, 2015.

## *Research & development and innovation*

Tax credits for research and development reduce the cost of R&D expenditure relative to the cost of other forms of expenditure. They therefore increase the net present value of prospective research projects, making them more attractive. Unlike subsidies for R&D they do not require the government to "pick winners", but correspondingly also allow reduced scope for governments to target the support and direct the nature of R&D. Like investment tax credits, they can be applied either on the total amount of R&D expenditure, or on the incremental increase in R&D expenditure. Incremental tax credits may help to avoid windfall gains to R&D expenditure that would have taken place even in the absence of the credit, but are more complex to administer and comply with than volume-based credits. They may also change the timing of investment plans (European Commission, 2014). In value terms, most R&D tax benefits are claimed by larger enterprises; while measures for SMEs may encourage innovative expenditures at the margin. For this reason, countries may choose to target tax incentives (whether volume-based or incremental) to smaller firms, who are less likely to make investments in R&D due to financial or other constraints.

A recent European Commission report (2014) found that in some countries, SMEs were more responsive to R&D credits than larger firms, although this did not hold for all countries. However, the spillover benefits associated with R&D tax credits were typically greater for larger enterprises than for SMEs, weakening the case for targeting R&D tax credits towards SMEs. However, the report found that the benefit from targeting R&D incentives at new firms was typically greater than for SMEs generally and that targeting credits at younger firms was good practice. Other elements of good practice highlighted by the report include:

- R&D tax schemes should be volume-based rather than incremental, to avoid higher administrative and compliance costs as well as distorting the timing of a firm's R&D investment;
- R&D schemes should clearly target activities that advance the worldwide stock of knowledge rather than the firm's knowledge base;
- Tax incentives should target expenditures that lead to strong knowledge spillovers, particularly those based on the wage bill paid to researchers;
- Carry-over or refunds of R&D tax credits are useful to ensure that firms, particularly young firms, can benefit from the tax credits even when not profitable.

Countries reported a number of R&D preferences for SMEs or young enterprises in their responses to the questionnaire. These measures include credits that are specific only to young or new enterprises as well as more generous application of generally-available credits to SMEs.[1] In some cases, R&D tax preferences fall under more than one category:

- R&D credits may be targeted only to SMEs or to young enterprises;
  - France offers a tax credit targeted to SMEs (*Credit d'impôt innovation*) which is an extension of the general research credit. Under this credit, SMEs can benefit from a tax credit in respect of certain expenses relating to prototypes or pilot trials of new products. Eligible expenses are capped at EUR 400 000 per year and the rate of the credit applied to the expenses is 20%. Any unused amount of the credit can be carried over for up to three years or refunded under certain conditions. In addition, France provides a credit for young innovative enterprises (*Jeunes Entreprises Innovantes*), when their R&D expenditure reaches at least 15% of the total costs. This scheme was recommended as best practice by the European Commission (European Commission, 2014) due to its targeting toward new innovation, immediate refund option and short response time.
  - Denmark also allows tax credits for R&D, which are most commonly used by new SMEs, although they are not restricted by firm size. For entities that have a tax loss of up to DKK 25 million that results from R&D expenditure, the company can have the tax value of the deficit (up to DKK 5.87 million) paid out. The loss that is able to be carried forward is reduced by the loss that forms the basis of the amount paid out.
- SMEs may benefit from a greater tax credit rate, or be able to use a greater proportion of, eligible expenditure than larger enterprises. For example:
  - Canada provides small Canadian-controlled private corporations (CCPCs) with an enhanced credit under the Scientific Research and Experimental Development programme, at a 35% rate on the first CAD 3 million of eligible expenditures rather than at the general 15% rate.

  - In the Netherlands, SMEs or start-ups undertaking R&D activities can benefit from the *Wet Bevordering Speur- en Ontwikkelingswerk* (WBSO), a wage tax credit that provides higher deduction rates for the first EUR 200 000 of the business' wages.
  - Under the *SkatteFUNN* R&D tax credit in Norway, SMEs benefit from a higher tax credit rate of 20% than the 18% rate that applies to larger enterprises.
  - Portugal provides a tax credit for R&D undertaken between 2014 and 2020 with a basic deduction rate of 47.5% for SMEs relative to the 32.5% rate applying to firms generally.
- SMEs may be eligible for a refund in respect of unused R&D tax credits, when the firm is in a loss position, for example, in:
  - Australia, where the concessional R&D tax credit applies to entities who have at least AUD 20 000 of notional R&D deductions, up to a limit of AUD 100 million. SMEs may be able to receive their unused R&D tax credits in monetary terms, when the firm is in a loss position, whereas for entities over this threshold the tax credit is not refundable.
  - Canada, under the Scientific Research and Experimental Development (SR&ED) programme, where unused credits at 35% on the first CAD 3 million of expenditure are refundable to CCPCs with a prior-year taxable income of less than CAD 500 000 and capital of less than CAD 10 million. For these entities, SR&ED expenses above CAD 3 million are eligible for a 15% credit which is 40% refundable. When income increases between CAD 500 000 and 800 000 or capital between CAD 10 and 50 million, the CAD 3 million limit is reduced so that firms with income above CAD 800 000 or capital of more than CAD 50 million do not qualify for the enhanced refundable credit.
  - New Zealand, where the tax benefit from R&D expenditures can be refunded if the company is in a tax loss position. This will apply mostly to start-ups and SMEs, allowing them to cash out losses up to a limit of NZD 500 000, with this cap rising by NZD 300 000 per year until it reaches NZD 2 million. To be eligible for the credit the company must carry out eligible research and 20% of its wage and salary expenditure must be in relation to R&D.
  - The United Kingdom where any unused R&D deductions, including those provided at the enhanced rate for SMEs, are able to be refunded to SMEs in a tax-loss position.

Iceland also has more generous rules under its R&D tax credit for SMEs than for larger firms. Iceland allows a tax credit at 20% of expenditure on R&D projects. The tax credit applies to all firms, but small and medium-sized enterprises have more favourable deduction rights than large enterprises.

In the Netherlands, provisions are made for SMEs that are not available to large firms to make access easier to the innovation box – a tax regime under which a 5% tax rate is applied to the income generated by a qualifying intangible asset to the extent the income from the intangible asset exceeds the related R&D expenses. The provision allows SMEs improved access to the innovation box as they are not obliged to prove the amount of eligible income for the intellectual property regime up to EUR 25 000 per year.

*Employment preferences*

Another common form of preference provided to SMEs involves reduced obligations under employment taxes. These take the form of exemptions from certain payroll deductions, as well as reduced tax rates or bases on which these obligations are assessed.

Germany exempts self-employed individuals from mandatory pension contributions. These individuals can apply to enter the statutory pension insurance scheme within 5 years of becoming self-employed. If so, new businesses are able to make payments based on half the monthly reference value (EUR 2 345 or 2 765, depending on the region), although their pension benefits will be reduced accordingly. However, all self-employed individuals can apply to make contributions based on their actual income, with a minimum payment of at least EUR 85.05 per month.

Reduced rates apply to payroll deductions in several countries. In Argentina, employers with a turnover of less than ARD 48 000 000 and those who perform industrial, agricultural, livestock or mining activities benefit from a reduced social security contributions (SSC) rate of 17%. Belgium allows firms to reduce their SSCs by up to 1.71 percentage points depending on the number of workers in the firm. In Spain, the self-employed benefit from several rebates and reduced rates according to their current status (e.g. young entrepreneurs, self-employed, disabled). Finally, Sweden allows firms with employees between 26 and 65 years of age who work 75% or more with R&D to reduce the social security fees in respect of these employees from 31.42% to 21.42%. This reduction is limited to a maximum of SEK 230 000 per month and per company group.

Other preferences provide credits or rebates against employment taxes. For example, in Austria, SMEs benefit from a tax allowance of EUR 1 095 for a wage sum of less than EUR 1 460 for local authority taxes on the sum of wages and the same allowance of the employer's contribution to the family burden equalisation fund.

Canada provides support to small businesses through the Small Business Job Credit. The credit applies to Employment Insurance (EI) premiums paid by small businesses in 2015 and 2016. Any firm that pays employer EI premiums equal to or less than CAD 15 000 in those years will be eligible for the credit. The credit will be calculated as the difference between premiums paid at the legislated rate of CAD 1.88 per CAD 100 of insurable earnings and the reduced small business rate of CAD 1.60 per CAD 100. Employers must pay 1.4 times the legislated rate, meaning that the credit is worth CAD 0.39 per CAD 100 of earnings. This applies in addition to the Quebec Parental Insurance plan. Almost 90% of premium paying businesses in Canada will receive the credit and it is estimated that the credit will save small employers more than CAD 550 million over the two year period, reducing their payroll taxes by nearly 15%.

In Poland, self-employed persons pay SSCs according to a lower basis for assessment. The basis is the declared amount that is not less than 60% of the projected average monthly wage. The minimum amount in 2015 is PLN 2 375 and the limit of the annual basis for pension and disability contributions is PLN 118 770. Self-employed persons also pay health care contributions against a lower assessment basis. This is also the declared amount which is not lower than 75% of the average monthly wage in the business sector in the fourth quarter of the previous year. The minimum amount in 2015 is equal to PLN 3 105.

Finally, the United States provides a small employer health credit. This credit applies to employers with less than 25 full-time equivalent staff, with average wages of less than USD 50 000, and which make non-elective uniform contributions of at least 50% of the premium. The credit is set at a specified percentage of premiums paid during the taxable year. It is applied in full until the number of employees reaches 10 or the average salary is above USD 25 000 up to the limits mentioned earlier. It is available only for health insurance purchased through an Affordable Insurance Exchange for up to two years.

### *Other tax credits*

In Chile, SME taxpayers subject to VAT can use payments against the Stamp Tax as a VAT tax credit. To do this, they must declare the VAT electronically or in a non-electronic form determined by the SII, have an income not over UTM 60 000 in each of the three previous calendar years, and have paid the stamp tax without any right to recover it from third parties.

France offers a tax credit for marketing expenditure by SMEs. Regardless of their form, SMEs are able to obtain a tax credit for business development spending for export purposes. The tax credit requires that a person or volunteer company be assigned to the development of exports. Eligible expenses include expenses for 24 months after the person's recruitment (provided they are deductible from taxable income). These include fees and travelling expenses, market research, participation in fairs and trade fairs, publicity in relation to exportable goods and services, monthly allowances and benefits, consulting activities, or demonstrations outside of France. The tax credit is equal to 50% of eligible expenditure and is capped at EUR 40 000 over the two year period.

## ***Tax exemptions targeted at SMEs***

The third main category of tax preferences that may be available to SMEs are exemptions from the requirement to pay a particular kind of tax. These may be standalone exemptions or may apply as a component of a replacement tax system, which provides a simplified tax regime for SMEs that replaces one or several other taxes, including income taxes, VAT, excise taxes and/or payroll deductions. These are discussed in Chapter 4. This subsection discusses only exemptions from existing taxes that are not replaced by another tax.

Exemptions may be temporary in nature, designed to ease the burden of the tax system in the first year of existence. Examples of this include an exemption in France for young innovative companies, who are able to obtain a full exemption from income tax in their first year of operation and a 50% exemption in their second year, under certain conditions, including restrictions on ownership and minimum levels of R&D expenditure. Similarly, in Ireland, companies incorporated after 14 October 2008 that have commenced a new trade are eligible for relief from income tax liability. Full relief is available for a corporate tax liability of under EUR 40 000 and marginal relief is available when corporate tax liability is between EUR 40 000 and 60 000. This relief is linked to the amount of employers' Pay Related Social Insurance contributions, subject to a maximum of EUR 5 000 per employee and up to eight employees per company. The policy rationale for both measures is the stimulation of new activities and the creation of jobs.

China offers a number of exemptions for small and micro-sized enterprises relating to different time periods. Monthly sales of small micro enterprises of less than CNY 30 000 are exempt from VAT and business tax between 1 October 2014 and 31 December 2015. From 1 January 2015 to 31 December 2017, these businesses will also be exempt from additional educational fees, water conservancy construction fund, the local additional educational fees, cultural construction fees. Furthermore, from 1 November 2014 to 31 December 2017, loan contracts signed by financial institutions and small and micro enterprises are exempt from stamp tax. In addition, from 1 January 2015, small and micro-sized enterprises (including individual business) are exempted from 42 administrative fees including land registration fees, housing registration fees and housing transaction fees. Small and micro-enterprises with 20 or less staff are also exempt from the disabled employment security payment within three years from the date of industrial and commercial registration.

Mexico provides another example, under its *Régimen de Incorporación Fiscal*, described more fully in Box 3.1. This tax regime provides for a simplified cash flow calculation of taxes

### Box 3.1. The Régimen de Incorporación Fiscal (RIF) in Mexico

In January 2014, the Mexican government introduced a new tax regime for small taxpayers (i.e. individuals who carry out business activities selling goods or services) for which no professional qualification is required, provided that their incomes do not exceed MXN 2 million. This tax regime, named the *Régimen de Incorporación Fiscal* (RIF), replaced the former small taxpayers' regime the *Régimen de Pequeños Contribuyentes* (REPECOs) and the intermediate regime (*Régimen Intermedio*).

This tax scheme is part of a comprehensive strategy (known as "growing together") that aims to reduce informality among small enterprises, which is a pervasive problem in the Mexican economy. By significantly lowering their personal, social security, VAT and excise tax obligations in the first ten years of operation, the new tax regime creates incentives for informal enterprises to switch to the formal sector.

Income tax is calculated on a cash-flow basis, with similar tax rates to those that apply in the general tax regime. For VAT and excise taxes purposes, there is an optional regime based on a simplified schedule of tax rates, which vary by economic activity and the type of product and is applied according to the enterprise's turnover level. This reduces the administrative burden of calculating VAT and excise tax liabilities. Taxpayers also benefit from a number of exemptions during the first ten years of participation, as is outlined in the table in this box. Further, taxpayers with an income of less than MXN 100 000 can apply for 100% VAT and excise tax reductions for a ten year period of participation in the regime. The RIF regime provides a gradually elimination of the tax reductions for over a ten-year period.

**Exemptions and reductions in taxes under the RIF in Mexico**

| | Year | | | | | | | | | |
|---|---|---|---|---|---|---|---|---|---|---|
| **Reduction in Tax Liability** | **1** | **2** | **3** | **4** | **5** | **6** | **7** | **8** | **9** | **10** |
| Income, VAT and excise tax | 100% | 90% | 80% | 70% | 60% | 50% | 40% | 30% | 20% | 10% |
| SSC (up to maximum income of 3 minimum wages. | 50% | 50% | 40% | 40% | 30% | 30% | 20% | 20% | 10% | 10% |

RIF taxpayers fill out two-monthly tax returns and their payments are considered final. This contrasts with the general regime which requires taxpayers to calculate their tax monthly and make provisional payments.

To be beneficiaries, entities must enrol in the Federal Taxpayer Registry (RFC), record revenues and expenses, invoice clients upon request and deliver sales notes otherwise and submit bimonthly statements. This scheme is complemented by a range of services to help small, often informal, businesses expand and professionalise as further encouragement to join the formal economy. These services include access to special government-backed credit lines and training programmes, as well as a special internet tool that facilitates tax compliance. This tool, provided by the Tax Administration, is named "My Accounts" (*Mis cuentas*) and further reduces SME compliance costs. The tool allows SMEs in the RIF regime to issue electronic invoices, simplify their tax accounting, keep registers of income and expenditure and use that information to present their simplified tax returns. RIF taxpayers are also able to buy a tablet at reduced price to give them access to this tool and to receive payments with bank cards.

together with exemptions from income taxes, VAT, excise taxes and SSCs that gradually reduce to zero over a period of ten years. The regime is intended to ease the transition of SMEs into the tax system and to simplify their compliance costs.

Mexico also provides benefits to taxpayers in the primary sectors. Incorporated enterprises with an income up to 20 AMW per associate (with a total limit of 200 AMW) are exempted from the corporate income tax, while those with an income over this threshold benefit from a 30% reduction until their income reaches 423 AMW. Companies or associations of producers with an income up to 4 230 AMW receive a 30% income tax reduction.

In the Netherlands, unincorporated SMEs benefit from the SME profit exemption (*MKB- winstvrijstelling*), which exempts 14% of all profits, lowering the marginal effective tax rates in each tax bracket at the personal level. Entrepreneurs also benefit from the fixed deduction of EUR 7 280 under the *Zelfstandigenaftrek*, described earlier in this study.

Several countries offer exemptions from particular taxes or from income taxes on particular activities. For example, Australia offers a fringe-benefits tax (FBT) concession for small businesses, whereby employers do not have to pay FBT for car parking if it is a SME or has income of less than AUD 10 million. Another example is found in Greece, where microenterprises (EU definition) are exempt from income tax on profits from the disposal of generated electricity if they are included in the Special Programme for the Development of Photovoltaic Systems up to 10 KW). In Chile, payments remitted abroad by Chilean taxpayers that have an average annual business income not exceeding UF 100 000 in the last three business years, to a non-Chilean resident or domiciled service provider for advertising services or for the subscription to a technological services internet platform, are exempt from withholding tax.

Finally, in some countries, reduced VAT rates or exemptions may apply to sectors that are in practice largely comprised of SMEs. For example, in Belgium the reduced VAT rate for catering services (from the standard rate of 21% to 12%) was designed to counter high labour tax rates in this sector. Other European countries have also introduced reduced VAT rates for labour intensive services.

## 3.4. Investor level preferences

This section discusses tax preferences that apply to investors in SMEs, rather than to the SME itself. Preferences which apply to SME investors lower the effective tax rate on the returns to investors, increasing their post-tax return on investment. This may operate to increase investment by lowering the rate of return that a firm needs to earn in order to pay investors their expected rate of return. Tax preferences for investors can therefore be seen as SME financing incentives.

For financing incentives to operate effectively, the incentive should result in investors lowering their expected pre-personal tax rate of return by an amount reflecting in full the amount of tax relief that they are provided. This will result in a reduction in the SME's cost of capital. The incentive should also be directed at the marginal investor. Ideally, unless a specific policy choice is made to the contrary, they should also be neutral as regards risk; if losses are deductible against higher rate personal income, but profits are taxed at lower small business rates, the tax system may encourage excessive risk taking.

There are three broad groups of financing incentives delivered through the tax system. Firstly, preferences may be provided for the initial investment in a SME by providing up-front personal tax relief on the cost of equity investments in or loans to targeted entities. Secondly, preferences for income received from a SME ownership interest (tax deductions or credits including imputation credits and dividend tax credits) can provide shareholders with income tax relief in respect of the return (i.e. dividends or capital gains) from their investments in targeted entities. This includes flow-through tax incentives which allow businesses to transfer unused tax deductions or tax credits earned on qualifying expenditures to investors, to be used to offset shareholder-level rather than business-level taxation. Finally, tax systems may provide preferences on the sale or disposal of SME assets, such as relief from capital gains, inheritance, or gift taxes. The section discusses each of these in turn.

## *Preferences for initial investments in SMEs*

### *Incentives for direct investment in SMEs*

A number of countries provide up-front tax preferences for investment in SMEs at the level of the investor or owner. These typically take the form of up-front deductions against personal taxes on the other income of the investor and are often limited to investment in new or very small SMEs. The intention of these provisions is to increase the available finance to firms in start-up phases. They are, therefore, often intended to encourage entrepreneurship by reducing the cost of initial investment and by promoting the development of highly innovative young firms.

Finland offers a business angel deduction which allows natural persons investing in small Finnish businesses to deduct 50% of their investment against their income taxes. The SME must be in its first six years of operation, be unlisted and have fewer than 50 employees and turnover and total assets of less than EUR 10 million. Certain sectors are excluded. To qualify for the deduction, the amount of the investment must be at least EUR 5 000 with a maximum per company of EUR 75 000 and per person of EUR 150 000. The investment must be less than 50% of the capital of the company after the investment is made and the target company may not have more than EUR 2.5 million of these investments per year. The amount deducted against income taxes is subtracted from the acquisition cost of the shares when they are disposed of.

In France, a reduction in income taxes of 18 percentage points is available to taxpayers who invest in SMEs, being defined as businesses with less than 50 employees and with a turnover or balance sheet of less than EUR 10 million. Eligible entities must be less than five years old, unlisted, taxed at the corporate level, and carry out commercial, industrial, or agricultural activities; however, some financial and wealth management activities are not eligible. The investor must subscribe in cash. The reduction in tax liability is granted up to EUR 50 000 per year (EUR 100 000 if married) and can be carried over to future years' income.

Ireland provides an Employment and Investment Incentive. This is an income tax incentive for private investors who invest in medium-term equity in qualifying companies, which provides for a tax relief of 30% in respect of investments of up to EUR 150 000 per year, after they hold their investment for a minimum of 3 years. If additional jobs were created or the company has used the investment for R&D expenditure, an additional relief of 11% is available at the end of the holding period. The rationale for this incentive is to support the development of SMEs and their importance in the economy, by encouraging private investors to invest in companies which would otherwise find it difficult to secure finance.

Ireland also provides a seed capital scheme, which allows relief from income tax for investments in a business of up to EUR 100 000 in any year and can be claimed back as a refund for up to 6 prior years. It is intended for employees, unemployed persons, or individuals who have been made redundant and who start their own business. It, therefore, applies only to new ventures, and the money must be used for trading activities, or research and development. The use of the money must directly contribute to the creation or maintenance of employment and the individual must be employed by the company within 6 months of the date of the last investment, owning at least 15% of the SME's capital and holding the ownership interest for at least three years. The seed capital scheme is designed to provide support for entrepreneurs and to improve SME access to finance.

Italy provides specific tax incentives for investing in innovative start-ups. These incentives apply from 2013-2016 to investment in new, non-listed companies and co-operatives that focus on research, development and innovation. Under this incentive, Italian personal income taxpayers receive a credit of 19% of the amount invested in innovative start-ups up to a maximum of EUR 500 000, while corporate taxpayers receive a tax allowance of 20% of the amount invested, up to a limit of EUR 1.8 million. The investor must maintain their investment for at least 2 years. The relief was recently extended to Innovative SMEs (EU definition) which meet one of the following three requirements: 3% of sales or costs must be attributable to R&D activities, one-third of employees have a degree (or one-fifth have or are doing a doctorate); and the company owns a patent. The aim of these provisions is to recognise that Innovative Start-ups and SMEs are important to promote sustainable growth, technological development and employment, particularly for youth. Also they are to develop a new business culture which is favourable to innovation, increase social mobility and attract investment and skilled labour to Italy.

Sweden provides a tax deduction for natural persons who invest in small firms (firms with a turnover of less than SEK 80 million and fewer than 50 employees). The tax credit applies against the capital income for the investor and reduces tax payments by 15% of the amount of the investment. The deduction is limited to SEK 195 000 per year and to a maximum level of investment of SEK 20 million per firm. The purpose of this tax credit is to promote access to capital for small firms.

### *Tax preferences for investments in venture capital funds*

Venture capital can be an important source of finance for start-up firms and small businesses, particularly where these firms do not have access to capital markets. To encourage equity investment in companies which might struggle to raise capital through conventional bank finance and to stimulate entrepreneurship, several countries have introduced schemes to promote investment in venture capital funds.

Australia has two programmes to promote investment in venture capital funds. Under the Venture Capital Limited Partnership (VCLP) and the Early Stage Venture Capital Limited Partnership programmes, venture capital funds structured as limited partnerships can be eligible for flow-through tax treatment and other tax concessions for gains or refunds from investments made by the fund. To qualify as a venture capital limited partnership, the fund must have at least AUD 10 million of committed capital and all foreign partners of the fund must be residents of a country with which Australia has a double tax agreement. Eligible investments must be at-risk and must be held for at least twelve months. The Venture Capital Limited Partnership must invest in unlisted Australian businesses with a total asset value of less than AUD 250 million with at least 50% of both employees and assets located in Australia. Certain sectors are excluded, including property or land development, finance, insurance, construction or infrastructure. The Early Stage Venture Capital Limited Partnerships are limited to total investment of between AUD 10 and 100 million and must have an investment plan with a focus on making early stage venture capital investments approved by Innovation Australia. The requirements for eligible investments are similar to those required under a VCLP, except that the total level of the investment cannot exceed AUD 50 million.

In Japan, investors in specific SMEs are able to deduct the amount of their investment from the taxable capital gains on shares. Capital losses at the time the shares are sold are deductible from the taxable capital gains on shares and the remainder of losses after deduction can be carried forward. For specific newly-established SMEs, the amount of their investment can be deducted from the investor's income subject to certain limitations.

In Korea, venture capital companies investing in newly organised SMEs do not pay corporate tax on the gains from the sale of their equity interests in SMEs.

Turkey allows amounts reserved as venture capital funds to be deducted from the income of investors on the condition that they do not exceed 10% of the taxpayer's declared income. Turkey also has a business angel system, which allows 75% of investments in early stage companies to be deducted against individual income, with the ratio increasing to 100% for companies with projects that fall within the scope of programmes determined by the Science, Industry and Technology Ministry, TUBITAK (Scientific and Technological Research Council of Turkey) and KOSGEB (Small and Medium Enterprises Development Organization). More details on this scheme are found in Box 3.2.

### Box 3.2. Licenced business angel investors in Turkey

Turkey introduced a tax deduction for licensed business investors as part of a wider law regarding the regulation and promotion of business angel investments. This law was enacted in 2012 and secondary legislation came into force on 15 February 2013. It provides a legal framework for licensing business angels, with the aim to increase the availability of equity financing for SMEs for which traditional debt financing is not well suited. It hopes to institutionalise business angel investments and to improve business culture and ethics in the angel investment market. Further, licensing will improve the data collection regarding business angel operations in Turkey.

Licensed business angel investors can deduct 75% of the capital that they invest in innovative and high growth SMEs from their annual personal income tax base. The annual deduction is capped at TRY 1 000 000. However, licenced business angel investors can co-invest in the venture capital firms. The amount of investment that is eligible for tax support in those co-investments is TRY 2 000 000. In order to be accredited as a business angel by the Treasury, certain qualifications are required, pertaining to the wealth and income of the investor as well as his or her experience as fund manager of a financial institution, manager of a business or member of a business angel network. The 75% deduction rate will be increased to 100% for those investors investing in SMEs whose projects are supported by Ministry of Science, Industry and Technology, the Scientific and Technological Research Council of Turkey (TÜBİTAK) and Small and Medium Enterprises Development Organization (KOSGEB) in the last five years. The given licenses will be valid for 5 years and the tax deduction will be applied until 2017 with the option to extend it for another five years.

Certain conditions have to apply in order to be eligible for this tax deduction. The SMEs' shares are not traded at stock market and the acquired shares must be held for at least two years. Moreover, it only applies investments in businesses with annual net sales of TRY 5 million or less and 50 employees or fewer. Between 15 February 2013 and 1 July 2015, 313 business angels have been licensed out of 321 applicants. In the same period 6 investments benefitting from the tax incentive have been made for a total amount of TRY 2 650 882.

In South Africa, a venture capital company regime is in place to encourage equity investors to invest in SMEs. Taxpayers investing in a venture capital company generate an upfront deduction for the investment and there is no recoupment on withdrawal if the investment is held for more than 5 years. The legislation does not permit any excess deduction to be carried forward to apply against future income. The venture capital company receiving the investment must invest in qualifying SME companies. Qualifying SME companies are those that have assets of less than ZAR 50 million (ZAR 500 million for junior mining companies).

The United Kingdom offers three venture capital schemes to provide tax preferences to equity investors in SMEs to encourage investment in small and growing higher-risk businesses. Under the Enterprise Investment Scheme (EIS), direct investment in qualifying SMEs is eligible for 30% relief against the income tax of the owner up to a limit of GBP 1 million. The company is limited to investment of GBP 5 million per year and the investment must be held for three years. The SME into which the investment is made must have less than GBP 15 million of assets pre-investment (and no more than GBP 16 million post-investment) and have less than 250 employees. The Seed Enterprise Investment Scheme (SEIS) is available to investments in very small SMEs; allowing 50% relief on investments of up to GBP 100 000 in qualifying SMEs. Qualifying SMEs are those with less than GBP 200 000 of investment and less than 25 employees, and are restricted to SEIS investment of GBP 150 000 per year. Finally, the Venture Capital Trust (VCT) scheme allows a relief of 30% of investments in listed venture capital firms of up to GBP 200 000, that are held for 5 years, provided the venture capital fund has less than GBP 15 million in assets, less than 250 employees and invests at least 70% of its holdings in eligible SMEs. Dividends paid by venture capital firms are exempt from taxation. For each of these schemes, further preferences apply on the capital gains realised on these investments. The aim of these schemes is to encourage equity investment in smaller unquoted trading companies.

### *Investor-level preferences for income or losses from SMEs*

Another type of tax preference that may be available to SME investors relates to the treatment of capital income or losses derived from SMEs. Tax preferences that lower the amount of tax payable on income received from an investment in SMEs decrease the pre-tax required rate of return on the investment, increasing the attractiveness of SMEs relative to other investments generating the same pre-tax rate of return.

By comparison, the treatment of losses may relax "ring-fencing" provisions applicable to larger entities, increasing the ability of losses from SMEs to be offset against personal income. Strict ring-fencing would allow losses incurred on investments in entities taxed only at the personal level to be used only against other capital income; and losses of double-taxed enterprises would be quarantined at the entity level (and may be able to be carried into other time periods to offset future or past tax liabilities). Countries differ in the degree to which losses are ring-fenced under general tax provisions. However, some countries choose to relax their loss offset rules further for SMEs, allowing losses on single-taxed entities to be offset against the personal income of the owner (whether capital or labour-based) or allowing the flow-through of losses at the entity level to offset the personal income of the investor, in the case of double-taxed entities. This can increase the symmetry of the tax treatment of business profits and business losses. However, if the effect of the provisions is to allow loss deductions at a higher personal rate, the system is not neutral in its treatment of risk and implicitly encourages greater risk-taking.

Canada allows losses from small business investments to offset the ordinary income of the investor, which is not possible for other capital losses. Fifty per cent of a capital loss from an arm's length disposition of a share or debt of the small business can be deducted against any other income of the investor and any excess will be able to be carried back for three years or forward for ten years, to apply to other personal income, whether from capital or labour. At the end of the ten-year period, it becomes a net capital loss, applicable only against other capital income.

In Canada flow-through shares are available for the mining, and oil and gas sectors to finance exploration and development expenses as well as certain intangible start-up expenses for clean energy generation projects. Flow-through shares are primarily used by SMEs, but are not explicitly limited to corporations of a particular size. The shares allow a corporation to transfer unused tax deductions in respect of eligible expenses to shareholders.

France allows the losses of some companies to be applied to the owners' income for anonymous companies, close corporations and limited liability companies with less than 50 employees and turnover of assets of less than EUR 10 million. The entity must have been operating for less than 5 years. Under this regime, the entities are taxed as partnerships, provided that at least 50% of capital and voting rights are held by natural persons, with at least 34% held by a managing director or member of the board. The measure applies for five years and is intended to allow losses from the development stage of the company to be applied against the personal income of the investors.

Switzerland taxes only 60% of dividends from qualifying investments at the federal level if the investment is part of the taxpayer's private assets (the shareholder must own 10% or more of the company). If the investment is held as part of the taxpayer's business assets, only 50% of the dividend income is taxable at the federal level.

## *Preferences on sale or disposal of SMEs*

For many owners of SMEs the business constitutes a significant proportion of their total assets. Selling a closely held business is often required for the owners of SMEs to fund their retirement, which may result in substantial tax consequences. For example, capital gains accrued over many years, but taxed only on realisation will incur a greater tax liability where taxed at progressive rates, than if they had been taxed as the gains accrued. Similar concerns may arise when SME assets are transferred to other family members, or on the death of a SME owner, with resultant capital gains tax as well as gift and inheritance tax consequences. In some cases, general preferences are offered for taxes on sales or inheritances, which can remove the need to support SMEs by providing further preferential treatment. Moreover, the introduction of preferences on the disposal of SME assets can create distortions, for example by discriminating against transfers of private wealth relative to transitions of business ownership. This section reviews the preferences provided to the owners of SME assets on sale or disposal, including preferences under capital gains taxes and under gift and inheritance taxes.

### *Capital gains tax preferences*

Capital gains preferences for SMEs are typically intended to take into account the disadvantages faced by SMEs due to their small size, recognising that capital gains taxes, particularly when imposed on the death or retirement of a sole-proprietor, can have a significant impact on the viability of the business. Relief from capital gains taxes on the sale of SME assets also acts to increase the attractiveness of retained earnings as a source of SME finance and maximises the amount of capital available to buy a new business.

Finally, capital gains preferences may be provided to avoid adverse tax consequences on retirement savings or intergenerational transfers of assets. Table 3.3 summarises capital gains preferences reported in the questionnaire.

Table 3.3. **Capital gains tax preferences for SMEs**

| Country | Nature of preference for SMEs |
|---|---|
| Australia | Concessions for SMEs with an aggregate turnover of less than AUD 2 million or assets of less than AUD 6 million:<br>• Small business retirement exemption, allowing a capital gains tax exemption on active assets up to a lifetime limit of AUD 500 000 per individual;<br>• Rollover relief, allowing deferral of tax payable on the proceeds from active assets if they are reinvested within two years in another business asset.; and/or<br>• 50% reduction available for capital gains on active SME assets (this includes assets used in the course of carrying on business, but not assets used to derive rent, as well as interests in companies or trusts in certain circumstances).<br>• Finally, if a business has owned an asset for 15 years, the capital gain on the asset is not assessable on sale if the sale is due to the owner's incapacitation, or if the owner is aged over 55 years and is retiring. |
| Austria | • Realised capital gains on SME assets in the case of closing down a business may either be:<br>- reduced by EUR 7 300 in the year of sale; or<br>- spread and taxed across three years.<br>• In the case of the death or early retirement of the SME owner, only half of the average tax rate must be paid on the revenue from sale. In this case, no other deductions apply. |
| Belgium | • The 0.4% separate tax that must be paid by gains on shares of companies does not apply to SMEs. |
| Canada | • Lifetime capital gains tax exemption on the disposition of qualified small business shares (CCPCs whose assets are used in active business) of CAD 813 600 in 2015 per individual (indexed to inflation).<br>• Deferral of taxation of capital gains that are realised on the disposition of an individual's common shares in an incorporated SME, if the proceeds are reinvested into another small corporation within 120 days after the end of the year of the disposition, provided that the total value of the corporation and related corporations is less than CAD 50 million.<br>• If proceeds from the sale of a capital property are not all receivable in the year of the sale, realisation of a portion of the capital gain may be deferred until the year in which the proceeds are received. A minimum of 20% of the gain must be brought into income each year, creating a maximum five-year reserve period. However, if the proceeds derive from the sale of small business shares to children, grandchildren or great-grandchildren, only 10% of the gain need be included in income each year (creating a maximum 10-year reserve period). |
| Czech Republic | Gains in relation to agricultural corporates are exempt from taxation when the property is transferred between close relatives and the relative carries on the business for at least three periods after the property transfer. |
| France | Greater exemption (up to 85%) for capital gains tax on shares in SMEs if held for eight years prior to sale, provided the shares were acquired within 10 years of the creation of the SME. |
| South Africa | Increased capital gains tax exclusion (at ZAR 1.8 million) for SME owners aged 55 years or more. |
| United Kingdom | • Gains on disposal of shares in the Enterprise Investment Scheme and the Seed Enterprise Investment Scheme are exempt from capital gains taxation if held for more than three years. Rollover relief applies to gains reinvested into these shares; in full for EIS shares and at 50% for SIES shares (up to a maximum reinvestment of GBP 100 000);<br>• Gains on the disposal of Venture Capital Trust shares are exempt, regardless of holding period;<br>• Gains on the disposal of shares acquired on exercise of an Enterprise Management Incentive option are taxed at a reduced rate of 10%. |
| United States | • Lower taxation for stock in certain C-corporations with gross assets under USD 50 million, where realised gains, are subject to an exclusion of 50% and are taxed at a maximum rate of 28%, up to the greater of USD 10 million or ten times the investor's basis. Certain businesses, such as professional services or finance are excluded.<br>• A related provision allows investors that sell qualified small business stock held for over 6 months prior to sale to defer recognition of capital gains by reinvesting the proceeds in new qualified stock within 60 days. The investor's basis in the new stock is reduced by the amount of the deferred gain. |

*Source:* Responses to an OECD questionnaire, *Survey on the Taxation of Small and Medium-Sized Enterprises*, 2015.

### *Gift and inheritance tax preferences*

For similar reasons, several countries report preferences targeted at SMEs under gift and inheritance taxes:

- Germany provides an exemption from gift and inheritance taxes if the successor continues to hold the business and keeps the wage bill steady. This requirement is relaxed for SMEs so that they only need to continue to hold the business. This is because the separation of owner from the company has a different impact in a small business than a large business; and it reduces the compliance burden for SMEs.
- Hungary exempts the inheritor or donee of the SME's assets from stamp duties or gift taxes, depending on the number of employees and net sales revenue.
- Italy allows transfers of firms or shares to the spouse or descendant to be exempt for inheritance tax if the activity is carried on (or for shares, if control is retained) for five years.
- In Japan, there are various measures to ease the transition of the business, including reducing the taxable value of sites for business under the inheritance tax by 80%, up to a limit of 400m$^2$, deferment of inheritance tax payments and gift tax on unlisted shares.
- The Netherlands provides a provisional exemption for inheritance taxes of businesses that are continued for at least five years. This exemption applies at 100% up to a going concern value of EUR 1 045 611 (in 2014) and at 83% for values above this amount.
- In respect of closely-held businesses, the United States allows estate tax to be paid over a 10 year period if the value of the business exceeds 35% of the estate and the owner had an interest of at least 20% in the business. Only the tax relating to the interest in the business may be deferred. The United States also allows a special use valuation for real property used as a farm or in another trade or business, allowing them to be valued for estate tax purposes at actual use rather than highest and best use. This can decrease the value of the asset by up to a maximum of USD 750 000, which is adjusted for inflation since 1997.
- Belgium also provides preferences under gift taxes, although these are levied at the regional level.

## 3.5. Conclusions and recommendations

A range of tax preferences are provided to SMEs in OECD and G20 countries. These include measures targeted to SMEs, through more generous tax deductions, tax credits or tax exemptions, as well as preferences that apply directly to the owner or investor of the SME, providing relief for initial investment, ongoing income, or on disposal of the SME's assets.

Most countries who replied to the questionnaire report one or more preferences targeted at SMEs. Common preferences include more generous depreciation allowances or credits and R&D incentives, most usually in the form of more generous R&D tax credits for SMEs. At the level of the investor, measures allowing deductions for initial investment and investment in venture capital funds, relaxed treatment of losses, and preferences on the disposal of assets are commonly used in respect of investments in SMEs. Table 3.4 provides an overview of the preferences reported in each country.

Different types of preferences will affect the economic margins described in the framework set out in Chapter 2 in various ways, as summarised in Figure 3.1, and may often be explicitly intended to do so. For example, where preferences are meant to address market failures, these preferences may be explicitly targeted in such a way as to affect business decisions relating to investment (notably R&D investment), employment or finance. Preferences provided to mitigate size disadvantages of SMEs may affect decisions about the distribution of business income, or compliance. Some preferences may also inadvertently affect other economic margins set out in this framework.

Figure 3.1. **Influence of tax preferences on economic margins of SME owners and investors**

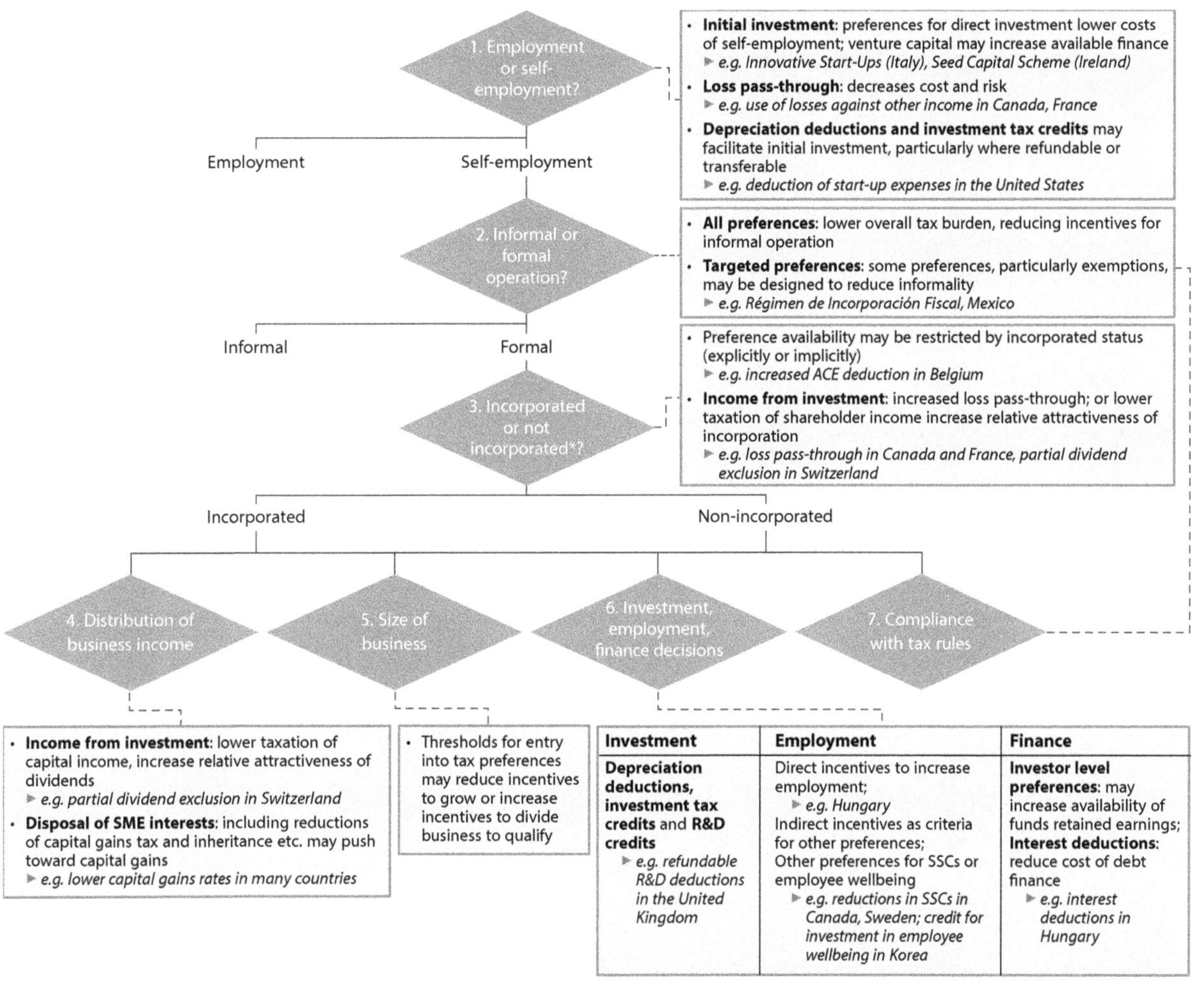


At the outset, some preferences can influence the decisions of a potential owner to enter into self-employment. Allowing the owners or investors in SMEs an offset against their personal income for their investment in a SME may, for example, lower the costs of entering into self-employment as well as increase available funding for new enterprises. Preferences which allow greater use of business losses against other income of the investor may also affect the decision to enter self-employment as it reduces the asymmetry of the tax system with regards to losses and reduces the risk associated with business creation. Such preferences may also increase the attractiveness of incorporation for smaller enterprises. Depreciation deductions and investment tax credits also facilitate initial investment by lowering the cost of investment, and particularly so when refundable or transferable to future years.

Some tax preferences may also provide a means of easing transition into the formal economy and encouraging compliance with tax rules, by lowering the overall tax and compliance burden. In addition, certain preferences may be explicitly provided in order to address informality, such as the *Régimen de Incorporación Fiscal* in Mexico, which provides a graduated introduction to the tax system as income tax, VAT, excise tax and SSC exemptions are gradually phased out over ten years.

Both double-taxed and single-taxed SMEs face a number of decisions about how to distribute their income. Tax preferences that reduce the tax rates on the income received by owners in respect of their investments in SMEs increase the attractiveness of distributing income in the form of returns on capital rather than labour. The preferences available to SMEs on disposal of SME assets, in addition to the generally observed lower tax rates on capital gains income described in Chapter 2, provide further tax incentives towards earning income in the form of capital.

As mentioned, tax preferences are often intended to have direct impacts on business decisions, including decisions on investment (including investment in R&D), employment and finance. These decisions, particularly in relation to innovation and employment are often the ones argued to have the most spillover benefits and therefore sought to be encouraged through the use of tax preferences. A range of tax preferences are observed in these areas in OECD and G20 countries. Investment preferences are most commonly related to depreciation, allowing immediate expensing or accelerated depreciation for certain forms of investment, reducing the cost of the initial investment and increasing the cash flow of the SME. Like investment tax credits, they target new investment. Special SME R&D incentives are predominantly provided in the form of tax credits, rather than as a deduction. These tax credits may be tailored to SMEs as a result of their greater responsiveness, or particularly to younger firms, including SMEs, due to their greater potential to generate spillover benefits. Other R&D preferences tailored to SMEs provide more generous incentives to overcome barriers faced by new or younger SMEs, providing a higher rate of credit or offering SMEs in a loss-making position the ability to have the R&D tax credit refunded.

Indirectly, tax preferences may also affect different margins set out in the framework. This can occur through the creation of distortions or complexities in the system due to the nature of the preference or the threshold under which it is applied. Tax preferences that apply only to double-taxed entities may influence decisions about incorporation, for example. More significantly, the introduction of multiple preferences may increase complexity and the compliance burden faced by small businesses. Finally, thresholds below which tax preferences are provided can reduce incentives to grow or create incentives to divide or artificially reduce business income to continue to qualify for the preference.

The case for providing tax preferences to SMEs is often based on the role of SMEs in the economy, particularly in terms of their contribution to employment, job creation and innovation. In assessing the case for tax preferences, rationales for providing tax preferences for SMEs are often based on market failure arguments related to these positive externalities. A second rationale for intervention is that the tax system may inherently disadvantage SMEs due to their size and is therefore not neutral in terms of its impact on commercial decisions or between different business forms and activities.

Table 3.4. **Summary of tax preferences for SMEs**

| | Business level preferences for SMEs | | | | | | | Investor level preferences for SME investment | | | |
|---|---|---|---|---|---|---|---|---|---|---|---|
| | Deductions | | Tax credits | | | | | | | Disposal of SME interests | |
| | Depreciation | Other | Investment | R&D | Employment | Other | Exemptions | Initial investment (incl. venture capital funds) | Income from investment | Capital gains | Gift and inheritance |
| Argentina | | | | | Y | | | | | | |
| Australia | Y | | Y | Y | | | Y | Y | | Y | |
| Austria | | | | | Y | | | | | Y | |
| Belgium | Y | Y | | | Y | Y | | | | Y | Y |
| Brazil | | | | | | | | | | | |
| Canada | | | Y | Y | Y | | | | Y | Y | |
| Chile | Y | | Y | | | Y | Y | | | | |
| China | | | | | | | Y | | | | |
| Czech Republic | | | | | | | | | | Y | |
| Denmark | | | | Y | | | | | | | |
| Estonia | | | | | | | | | | | |
| Finland | | | | | | | | Y | | | |
| France | Y | Y | Y | Y | | Y | Y | Y | Y | Y | |
| Germany | Y | | Y | | Y | | | | | | Y |
| Greece | | | | | | | Y | | | | |
| Hungary | Y | Y | Y | | | | | | | | Y |
| Iceland | | | | Y | | | | | | | |
| India | | | | | | | | | | | |
| Ireland | | | | | | | Y | Y | | | |
| Italy | | | | | | | | Y | | | Y |
| Japan | Y | Y | Y | | | | | Y | | | Y |
| Korea | Y | Y | Y | | | | | Y | | | |
| Luxembourg | | | | | | | | | | | |
| Mexico | Y | | | | | | Y | | | | |
| Netherlands | Y | Y | Y | Y | Y | | Y | | | Y | Y |
| New Zealand | | | | Y | | | | | | | |
| Norway | | | | Y | | | | | | | |
| Poland | Y | | | | Y | | | | | | |
| Portugal | | | Y | Y | | | | | | | |
| Slovak Republic | | | | | | | | | | | |
| Slovenia | | | | | | | | | | | |
| South Africa | Y | | | | | | | Y | | Y | |
| Spain | Y | Y | | | Y | | | | | | |
| Sweden | | | | | Y | | | Y | | | |
| Switzerland | | | | | | | | | Y | | |
| Turkey | | | | | | | | Y | | | |
| United Kingdom | | Y | | Y | | | | Y | | | |
| United States | Y | Y | | | Y | | | | | Y | Y |

*Source:* Responses to an OECD questionnaire, *Survey on the Taxation of Small and Medium-Sized Enterprises*, 2015.

Where a clear rationale for special rules exists, the advantages of intervening through the tax system as against other interventions should be considered. If tax preferences are provided, they should be considered against the revenue and efficiency costs of doing so, including the risk of creating further distortions or barriers to growth, or increasing complexity. Tax preferences should clearly identify the problem being addressed and the SMEs to which the measure should be targeted, and should seek to avoid introducing new distortions or adverse consequences.

## Note

1. The generosity of R&D incentives for SMEs and for larger enterprises, whether in a profit-making or loss-making position, is estimated in the OECD's R&D Tax Incentives Indicators (OECD, 2013).

## *References*

An Roinn Airgeadais Department of Finance (2015), *Review of the Employment And Investment Incentive And Seed Capital Scheme*, http://budget.gov.ie/Budgets/2015/Documents/EII_Report_finalrev.pdf.

Brouwer, E., P. den Hertog, T. Grosfeld, and T. Poot (2005), *Evaluation of a major Dutch Tax Credit Scheme (WBSO) aimed at promoting R&D*, ftp://ftp.zew.de/pub/zew-docs/evaluationR%26D/EBrouwer.pdf.

Canadian Department of Finance (2012), *Tax Expenditures and Evaluations 2012: Part 2 – Taxation of Small Businesses in Canada,* Canadian Government, Ottawa, www.fin.gc.ca/taxexp-depfisc/2013/taxexp1303-eng.asp.

Conseil Superieur des Finances (2014), *Un Tax Shifting en Faveur du Travail, et des Bases Imposables plus Larges Scenarios pour une Reforme Fiscale Globale et Significative,* http://finances.belgium.be/fr/binaries/csf_fisc_rapport_2014_08_tcm307-255311.pdf.

Crawford, C. and J. Freedman (2010), "Small Business Taxation" in *Dimensions of Tax Design* (ed. Adam, S., Besly, T., Blundell, R., Bond, S., Chote, R., Gammie, M., Johnson, P., Myles, G., and Poterba, J.) Oxford University Press, www.ifs.org.uk/uploads/mirrleesreview/dimensions/ch11.pdf.

Davis Tax Committee (2014), *Small & Medium Enterprises: Taxation Considerations, Interim Report,* www.treasury.gov.za/TaxReviewCommittee/DTC%20SME%20Report%20for%20Public%20Comment%2014%20July%202014.pdf.

European Commission (2014), *A Study on R&D Tax Incentives: Final Report,* http://ec.europa.eu/taxation_customs/resources/documents/taxation/gen_info/economic_analysis/tax_papers/taxation_paper_52.pdf.

Fowkes, R., J. Sousa and N. Duncan (2015), "Evaluation of Research and Development Tax Credit", *HMRC Working Paper 17*, https://www.gov.uk/government/uploads/system/uploads/attachment_data/file/413629/HMRC_WorkingPaper_17_R_D_Evaluation_Final.pdf.

Freedman, J. (2009), *Reforming the Business Tax System: Does Size Matter? Fundamental Issues in Small Business Taxation,* www.law.ox.ac.uk/themes/tax/documents/Ref.Bus.Tax.03.09.09.pdf.

Gale, W., and S. Brown. "Small Business, Innovation, and Tax Policy: A Review", *Tax Policy Center Urban Institute & Brookings Institution,* http://mpra.ub.uni-muenchen.de/57384/1/1001675-Small-Business-Innovation-and-Tax-Policy-A-Review.pdf.

IBFD (2015), *IBFD Tax Research Platform,* accessed at http://online.ibfd.org/kbase.

International Tax Dialogue (2013), *A Decade of Sharing Tax Experiences and Knowledge, Key Issues and Debates in VAT, SME Taxation and the Tax Treatment of the Financial Sector,* International Tax Dialogue, Paris.

Jorgenson, D. and K. Yun (1991), *Tax Reform and the Cost of Capital,* Oxford University Press, Oxford.

Marron, D., and J. Rosenberg (2015), "Tax Policy and Investment by Startups and Innovative Firms", *Tax Policy Center Urban Institute & Brookings Institution*, www.taxpolicycenter.org/publications/url.cfm?ID=2000103.

Mintz, J. and D. Chen (2011), *Small Business Taxation: Revamping Incentives to Encourage Growth*, SPP Research Paper No. 4-7, http://papers.ssrn.com/sol3/papers.cfm?abstract_id=1920866.

Mirrlees, J., S. Adam, T. Besly, R. Blundell, S. Bond, R. Chote, M. Gammie, P. Johnson, G. Myles, and J. Poterba (eds) (2011), "Small Business Taxation" in *Tax by Design,* Oxford University Press, www.ifs.org.uk/uploads/mirrleesreview/design/ch19.pdf.

OECD (2015), *Financing SMEs and Entrepreneurs 2015: An OECD Scoreboard*, OECD Publishing, Paris.

OECD (2013), *R&D Tax Incentives Indicators,* www.oecd.org/sti/rd-tax-stats.htm.

OECD (2011), Supporting the Development of More Effective Tax Systems, *a report to the G-20 Development Working Group by the IMF, OECD, UN and World Bank.*

OECD (2009), *Taxation of SMEs: Key Issues & Policy Considerations.* OECD Tax Policy Studies, No. 18, OECD, Paris.

OECD (2009b), *The Impact of the Global Crisis on SME and Entrepreneurship Financing and Policy Responses*, OECD Publishing, Paris.

President's Advisory Panel on Federal Tax Reform (2005), *Simple, Fair and Pro-Growth: Proposals to Fix America's Tax System.* Available at: www.treasury.gov/resource-center/tax-policy/Documents/Simple-Fair-and-Pro-Growth-Proposals-to-Fix-Americas-Tax-System-11-2005.pdf.

Verhoeven, W., A. van Stel and N. Timmermans (2012), *Evaluatie WBSO 2006-2010*, www.rijksoverheid.nl/documenten-en-publicaties/rapporten/2012/04/02/hoofdrapport-evaluatie-wbso-2006-2010.html.

The World Bank Group (2007), *Designing a Tax System for Micro and Small Businesses: Guide for Practitioners*, World Bank, Washington.

# *Chapter 4*

# Tax compliance and SMEs

*This chapter considers SMEs and tax compliance. It first considers tax simplification measures reported by OECD and G20 countries in relation to income, value-added, and other taxes. It includes a description of replacement taxes implemented in these countries and a summary of presumptive taxes that apply. It then considers process simplifications which can reduce the compliance burden for SME taxpayers and enhance compliance. The chapter concludes by summarising the impact of simplification measures on the decisions of SME owners, outlining principles to guide the implementation of these measures. Finally, it provides a summary table of simplification measures reported by the 38 countries.*

## 4.1. Introduction and framework

In addition to the direct cost of taxes, the tax system also imposes a burden on all taxpayers, including SMEs, in terms of the costs of complying with tax laws. These form part of the broader regulatory compliance costs faced by SMEs, which also encompass compliance with other regulations, for example labour, environmental or safety regulations. Tax compliance costs typically have a significant fixed cost component, tending to impose a relatively higher burden on SMEs than on larger enterprises which can benefit from returns to scale in complying. Tax compliance costs may affect a number of economic margins faced by the owners and operators of SMEs, notably, whether to become self-employed, whether to employ others and whether to operate in the formal economy.

A number of factors influence tax compliance costs. These include the number of taxes that must be complied with, the frequency of changes to the tax laws, the complexity of the tax system, the existence of different tax administrations (including national and subnational jurisdictions), the difficulty associated with interpreting unclear tax laws, multiple deadlines for tax payments throughout the year, costs of external tax service providers as well as internal staff or owner time spent complying, and tax registration procedures (European Commission, 2007). SMEs are subject to a number of taxes not filed or paid by an employee, notably obligations related to VAT and social security contributions.

While total business tax compliance costs tend to be higher for large companies, the relative compliance burden tends to be regressive with regard to firm size, with SMEs subject to higher costs than large enterprises when measured as a percentage of turnover or income. A 2007 European Commission study, drawing on a number of European studies of compliance costs, found that the compliance burden, measured as a proportion of revenue, is greater for smaller sized firms, despite the impact of simplification measures available to SMEs. The study stated that "on average, a company with fewer than ten employees has to face a regulatory burden that is roughly twice as high as the burden of a company with more than ten but fewer than twenty employees and about three times as high as the burden of companies with more than twenty but fewer than fifty employees. For larger companies, the burden per employee is only one fifth or one tenth of that of small enterprises".[1] A survey of businesses in Canada found that the compliance costs of small businesses are higher than that of large businesses when measured as a proportion of revenue, initially increasing when the first employees are hired, before decreasing steadily with firm size, on average (Canadian Department of Industry, 2013). Similar conclusions are found in other surveys of SME tax compliance costs.[2] However, tax compliance may also bring with it managerial benefits through improved record-keeping (Lignier and Evans, 2012).

To reduce the disproportionate compliance burden posed by the tax system on SMEs and to reduce its impact on SME formation, business decisions and growth potential, many countries have tax provisions designed to reduce SME compliance costs. Simplification provisions of various types can be expected to impact small businesses differently, given the heterogeneity of the small business population. Certain measures may directly encourage business creation and tax compliance for some small businesses, but not others. For example, allowing simplified accounting or less frequent filing of tax returns may operate to encourage the creation of small or medium-sized businesses and their compliance with tax obligations. However, micro or small businesses with very low turnover may regard the tax compliance burden of a simpler tax system as too costly, thus discouraging participation in the formal economy. For these businesses, a simple replacement tax, for example a presumptive tax, may be more helpful.

This chapter discusses measures that may be used to reduce the compliance burden on SMEs. Section 4.2 considers first various approaches to the simplification of tax rules as they apply to SMEs, considering simplified single replacement tax regimes as well as simplification measures applying to particular taxes, including income taxes and VAT. Section 4.3 considers how administrative measures can support policy measures to improve compliance outcomes. Section 4.4 concludes, presenting an overview of the various simplifications measures considered.

## 4.2. Simplification measures

### *Single replacement tax regimes for SMEs*

To assist very small taxpayers, and in some cases to encourage compliance, several countries report simplified tax schemes for SMEs that replace a number of other taxes. These single replacement taxes typically include three main elements: a) a simplified method of tax calculation (often on a presumptive or cash flow basis); b) simplified reporting and filing requirements; and c) exemption from all or several other taxes. This section discusses only taxes which meet these three criteria and specifically, only those that replace more than one of the tax obligations of a small business. Cash flow or presumptive systems that replace only one form of tax (typically VAT or income tax) are discussed in those respective sections.

Single replacement taxes may be introduced with more than one goal in mind. They may be introduced as a means of encouraging formalisation of small businesses as well as simplifying compliance. In this respect, country experience differs.

Brazil uses a single replacement tax to simplify tax compliance for SMEs. Entities with gross revenues of up to BRL 3.6 million can choose the *Simples Nacional* regime, subject to some restrictions. This scheme replaces several other taxes, including Contribution for the Financing of the Social Security (COFINS), Social Contribution on Net Profit (CSLL), Tax on the Circulation of Goods and Transportation and Communication Services (ICMS), Tax on Industrialized Products (IPI), Tax on Services (ISS), Corporate Income Tax (IRPJ), Social Integration Program or Civil Servants Savings Program Contribution (PIS or PASEP) and social security contributions (CPP). Under this scheme, taxes are calculated against gross revenue, with progressive rates applying at different levels of gross revenue. These rates encompass a component for each of the taxes that are replaced, generating the single rate applied. Different schedules of rates are applied for different sectors. In the trade sector, for example, rates range from 4% for entities with revenue of less than BRL 180 000 to 11.61% for entities with turnover of between BRL 3.4 and 3.6 million. Under the *Simples Nacional*, companies are only required to file a single annual tax declaration, replacing several other declarations that were previously required at the national, subnational and local levels. They are also exempt for traditional bookkeeping requirements but must maintain certain records as required by the legislation of the particular taxes.

A related regime in Brazil, the *Microempreendedor Individual*, applies to self-employed natural persons, with up to one employee (who is remunerated at the minimum wage). The entity must have an income that is less than BRL 60 million per year. Under the *Microempreendedor Individual*, the taxpayer is exempt from federal taxes (IRPJ, CSLL, PIS, COFINS and IPI) and pays a fixed monthly amount toward social security contributions, ICMS and ISS. This fixed amount is BRL 40.4 per month for the commercial or industrial sector, BRL 44.4 for the service sector and BRL 45.4 for commerce and services.

In Hungary, two simplified tax regimes exist for small businesses. The first, KIVA, is a cash-flow based tax which replaces corporate income tax, social contribution taxes and vocational training contributions. This tax applies at a rate of 16% of the tax base, which is based on the taxpayer's cash-flow profit and is increased by staff costs. The tax is available to entities with less than 25 staff and where the revenue and balance sheet for the previous tax year were less than HUF 500 million. The intention of this tax is to provide a simple framework to favour fast-growing and labour-intensive businesses, and to ensure that wage payments are neutral with regard to an employer's tax liability.

A second simplified regime in Hungary, KATA, is a lump-sum tax for the self-employed. Under this regime, full-time entrepreneurs registered as small business taxpayers pay tax of HUF 50 000 per month. Taxpayers may elect to pay HUF 75 000 per month in return for higher social security service eligibility. Part-time entrepreneurs pay HUF 25 000. The lump sum tax is payable separately for each person registered as a small business taxpayer. This applies up to a revenue limit of HUF 6 million. Once revenues exceed this amount, tax is payable at 40% on the part of the revenue exceeding HUF 6 million. Payment of KATA releases the taxpayer from corporate income tax, personal income tax, social contributions tax, and healthcare, pension, employment and vocational contributions. It does not, however, provide an exemption from VAT obligations, although the taxpayer may apply for the tax exemption detailed in the VAT section. KATA was designed to counter informality and also allows simplified obligations for bookkeeping purposes.

In Italy, a presumptive tax is used to replace personal income tax, regional and municipal surcharges and regional production taxes for small businesses. Further, those eligible for this scheme are not required to pay VAT, but also cannot deduct input VAT payments. Businesses eligible for this tax must be natural persons with annual revenue under thresholds which vary by business, as set out in Table 4.1. Taxable income is calculated as 15% of the tax base, which is determined by the application of a profitability ratio to gross revenues. The scheme can be continued indefinitely for firms that are under the thresholds. For example, a retail trade SME at the revenue threshold of EUR 40 000 would have taxable income of EUR 2 400, being 15% of the tax base calculated based on a notional profitability ratio of 40% of gross revenues (i.e. EUR 16 000).

Table 4.1. **Thresholds and profitability ratio for simplified taxes in Italy**

| | Revenue threshold | Notional Profitability Ratio |
|---|---|---|
| Food and beverage industry | 35 000 | 0.4 |
| Wholesale and retail trade | 40 000 | 0.4 |
| Itinerant food and beverage trade | 30 000 | 0.4 |
| Itinerant trade | 20 000 | 0.54 |
| Constructions and real estate | 15 000 | 0.86 |
| Trade intermediaries | 15 000 | 0.62 |
| Restaurant and accommodation services | 40 000 | 0.4 |
| Professionals | 15 000 | 0.78 |
| Other | 20 000 | 0.67 |

*Source:* Responses to an OECD questionnaire, *Survey on the Taxation of Small and Medium-Sized Enterprises*, 2015.

The *Régimen de Incorporación Fiscal* (RIF) was introduced in 2014 in Mexico for small taxpayers, replacing the previous regimes for small and intermediate taxpayers. It is applicable to individuals with entrepreneurial activities that do not require a professional graduate degree and that have an annual income of less than MXN 2 million. Under this regime, income is calculated on a cash-flow basis, with investments being fully deductible in the year they are made. Simplified reporting requirements also exist, requiring taxpayers to provide the revenue administration with information on their income, expenditures, purchases and investments in fixed assets. RIF taxpayers also benefit from a number of tax exemptions which gradually phase out during the first ten years after they register with the Tax Administration Service. Box 3.1 in Chapter 3 provides further information on this simplified tax scheme.

In South Africa, a simplified presumptive tax regime replaces SMEs' income tax, VAT, provisional tax, capital gains tax and dividends tax liability. The simplified presumptive tax is able to be used by entities with annual revenue of less than ZAR 1 million. Under this regime, taxable income is equal to annual revenue, with the applicable tax rate determined by the tax authority according to a scale that increases as turnover increases.

Turkey has a simplified business activity tax (*basit usul vergi*) aimed at micro businesses, which are defined as very small firms, traders and craftsman. Under this regime, most of these units declare only some of their workers for social security purposes. They must comply with the Tax Procedure Law with regard to notifications, recordkeeping, other obligations and punitive measures, but are exempted from bookkeeping. Personal income tax is paid on the difference between revenues and expenses with the purchase price of goods in the accounting year.[3]

### *Income tax simplifications*

Various measures are also observed in countries to reduce the compliance requirements for SMEs of regular income taxes and to support the creation, growth and compliance of SMEs. This section reviews a number of simplification measures identified in questionnaire responses, including the use of presumptive taxes, the possibility to use cash accounting to calculate taxable income, other simplified accounting procedures and less frequent interim filing requirements for SMEs.

#### *Presumptive taxes*

Under a presumptive tax scheme, firms under a small business threshold are exempted from regular income tax. Regular income tax is replaced by a presumptive tax, which presumes a different tax base than income in the calculation of the firm's tax liability. As a presumptive tax base replaces income, it therefore does not vary directly with income but with a selected proxy, such as annual revenue or a firm characteristic serving as an indicator. While presumptive taxes usually refer to an adjusted tax base where regular income tax rates apply, in some cases tax rates are prescribed based on the type of business activity (e.g. Brazil and France).

Eligibility is generally determined by an annual revenue threshold. Some countries also specify a maximum number of employees (e.g. Brazil, Czech Republic, Poland and Slovenia). However, as discussed in Chapter 1, the definition of SMEs can vary substantially, as can presumptive tax eligibility. Eligibility requirements determining which small businesses benefit from presumptive tax schemes require careful consideration to ensure that the appropriate segment of the economy benefits. In addition, some presumptive tax regimes are voluntary, with the decision to opt in (and thus out of the regular income tax system) binding for a certain number of years (e.g. Denmark). Beyond the careful design and as with any guidance from tax authorities, the eligibility requirements, the calculation of the tax liability and the potential for optional participation, must be clear.

Allowing firms with turnover below some threshold level to opt out of the regular income tax system may be an effective means of reducing tax compliance costs and the costs of tax administration. Small businesses may be freed from bookkeeping requirements that are not essential to their operational success (particularly as small businesses are less likely to employ staff resources dedicated to tax preparation). Calculation according to a presumptive tax scheme may also provide taxpayers with greater certainty regarding their tax liabilities. Aside from contributing to tax revenues and supporting good governance by aiming to have all firms, including the very small, participate in the tax system, replacement tax schemes may ease firms' transitions into a country's regular income tax regime when a small business turnover threshold is crossed, thereby encouraging continued participation in the formal economy.

In some cases, presumptive taxes are explicitly designed to counter non-compliance, as in the case of China, where a presumptive tax applies to businesses that do not keep financial statement records, have not filed a tax return by the appropriate deadlines even though they have a tax obligation, or have underreported their tax liability without justification.

To the extent that the economic incidence of regular income tax falls on business owners, an income tax exemption for firms under a small business turnover threshold represents a breach of horizontal equity. Small businesses able to take advantage of their presumptive tax eligibility may have a competitive advantage relative to firms just over the same threshold. Moreover, such an advantage may dis-incentivise growth, particularly if the foreseen increase in income tax is sharp (i.e. high marginal tax rate).

As taxable profits are not linked to income, highly profitable firms will, in effect, pay less tax than less profitable firms. In addition, firms are incentivised to substitute away from the replacement tax base, causing distortions to economic activity. There is also a risk of fraud, as a presumptive tax may create incentives to artificially remain below the designated threshold, or for larger firms to create or outsource work to smaller firms with the intention of benefiting from the presumptive tax.

As reviewed below, presumptive tax bases and tax burdens may differ significantly from those under a regular income tax, to a greater or lesser extent depending on the type of presumptive tax, its design features and the taxpayer's profit position. The following types of presumptive taxes may be used as a proxy for a regular income tax: a lump-sum tax, an indicator-based tax and a turnover tax.

## Lump-sum tax

The simplest presumptive tax is a lump-sum tax, levying a uniform amount on firms below a certain size threshold. In practice, a lump sum may indirectly target small businesses when imposed on types of activities that typically involve relatively low levels of turnover (e.g. hairdressers, mechanics or fishermen). The main advantage of a lump-sum tax is its simplicity, implying lower tax compliance and administration costs.

However, being a fixed amount, a lump-sum tax imposes a relatively higher tax burden on firms with relatively lower income, tending to distort competition amongst firms of different sizes subject to the lump sum amount. For the same reason, it imposes a relatively high tax rate on profits during downturns in business activity when profits are low or negative (tending to reinforce rather than counter business cycles) and may thus create cash-flow problems for firms. A lump-sum tax scheme requires periodic review of the lump-sum amount to ensure that it remains appropriate (both at various points of the business cycle and over time).

Lump-sum schemes are often used for the very smallest firms and the self-employed, where compliance costs are likely to be heaviest and revenue considerations are minimal. For example, Brazil maintains the *Microempreendedor Individual* programme for very small entrepreneurs with annual revenue less than BRL 60 000 and employing not more than one person at the minimum wage.

In addition, Hungary maintains the lump-sum tax scheme, KATA, for self-employed entrepreneurs registered as small taxpayers, which also applies a reduced lump sum for entrepreneurs qualifying as part-time (i.e. working fewer than 36 hours per week). See Table 4.2 for more information.

## Indicator-based tax

Another relatively simple presumptive tax is one based on indicators of firm size, other than turnover or income. Examples of such indicators include total number of employees, floor space, inventory values, electricity consumption and other variables that may be correlated with income. The base of an indicator-based tax is generally less easy to misreport than turnover or income, and may offer significant savings in tax compliance and tax administration costs.

A particular feature of this type of tax is that it is effectively a tax on the indicators that form the base. Accordingly, an indicator-based tax that is increasing in the amount of floor space and/or total employment would tend to discourage investment in buildings and/or the hiring of additional workers by taxing these factor inputs. On the other hand, unlike an income tax, an indicator-based tax does not tax revenue and thereby discourage income growth accompanying increased work effort, or more generally, does not discourage increased utilisation of factors of production falling outside the tax base (i.e. the marginal tax rate on revenue is zero). An indicator can only seek to correlate as highly as possible with income, however, depending on the business activity, an indicator may still be a superior proxy to turnover.

Indicator-based taxes are often used to target specific types of business activity. For example, Denmark applies an indicator-based presumptive tax scheme to shipping enterprises, where taxable income is based on individual vessel tonnage (with tax rates increasing with tonnage). India has an indicator-based presumptive tax on transport businesses, where taxable income is computed as INR 7 500 per goods carriage.

Indicator-based taxes can also be used to target businesses operating in specific geographic locations. For example, Poland's tax for micro-entrepreneurs relies on, among other indicators, the number of inhabitants in the city in which the business is located. In addition, an indicator-based tax in Austria relies on, among other indicators, whether the business is in an Alpine region. See Table 4.2 for more information.

## Turnover tax

A common form of presumptive tax is a turnover tax, levied on gross revenue. Unlike a lump-sum or indicator-based tax, a turnover tax varies directly with firm size measured by turnover and thus goes some way towards avoiding the competitive distortions of entirely profit-insensitive taxes. However, a fixed turnover tax rate imposes a relatively high effective tax rate on businesses that have lower profit margins as a percentage of sales. Thus a turnover tax, in addition to imposing a higher tax burden on less efficient firms, would tend to discourage the allocation of capital to business activities where profit margins are below average.

Turnover taxes may be applied to the gross revenue firms below a small business threshold to determine the tax base. Once determined, tax rates may be the same as for other forms of income or may be specific to the turnover tax. Specific rates may be set at a single flat rate or a tiered rate schedule, and may be uniformly applied or vary by type of business sector (e.g. Brazil, Chile and France). While introducing some degree of complexity, one potential advantage of a tiered rate structure that applies a relatively low rate on low turnover, is encouraging tax compliance amongst young start-up firms. Low compliance costs under a turnover tax, together with a relatively low tax rate on low turnover in the initial years, may provide an effective combination to encourage participation in the tax system. Once in the system, firms may be more likely to remain operating in the formal economy, particularly where a tiered rate structure is set to avoid large upward adjustments in tax burden when the small business threshold is crossed.

Alternatively, reduced tax rates may be applied to the turnover of businesses in sectors where profit rates on average are relatively low. With sector differentiation, complexity may be contained by applying a flat rate rather than tiered rate schedule, with the rate set lower (or higher) in sectors where profit margins on average are lower (or higher). Under a system with varying flat rates across sectors, a degree of graduation may be introduced to encourage tax compliance amongst start-ups by relying on standard deductions from the turnover base.

As mentioned, turnover tax schemes often apply to certain business sectors. An interesting example is Chile, where the tax liability of small artisanal miners varies with the price of copper (if the metal mined is copper, gold or silver), due to the increase of the tax rate applied to the net value of sales of mining products. In the case of medium-sized mining companies subject to the presumptive tax, the price of copper determines the tax base.

In addition to providing a better proxy for income than lump-sum and indicator-based taxes, turnover taxes also facilitate the adjustment of firms to a regular income tax system by requiring the maintenance of cash accounts measuring turnover. As with other presumptive taxes, small business creation and compliance with the tax system is encouraged through reduced tax compliance costs.

Closer in design and effect to a regular income tax are presumptive taxes that adjust the turnover tax base (gross revenues) for business costs. Given the goal of replacement taxes to contain tax compliance costs, the cost adjustments tend to be ones that can be readily measured. Rather than capitalise capital costs, for example, firms may be allowed to expense capital costs (i.e. full and immediate deduction). Similarly, rather than require that firms track inventory costs, a simple fixed deduction may be provided to reflect input costs, determined as a percentage of turnover. Deductions representing wages (and possibly other costs and taxes) may also be included in the calculation, on the presumption that the relevant information is required for other purposes (e.g. calculation of employee social security contributions) and therefore available for presumptive tax purposes.

Table 4.2. **Presumptive income taxes**

| | Eligibility | Calculation of tax payable |
|---|---|---|
| Austria | 1. Small business: Annual revenue less than EUR 220 000<br>2. Agriculture and forestry: Natural persons within the agriculture and forestry sector and assessed business value below EUR 130 000 (in 2015) | 1. Taxable income calculated as 88% of annual revenue; normal tax rates apply<br>2. Taxable income calculated as annual revenue (including VAT) minus a percentage of annual expenditures (70-80%) depending upon the type of activity, land size, location, and how (and where) products are sold. Taxable income for smaller (or less profitable) businesses is calculated based on the assessed tax value of land |
| Brazil | 1. *Simples Nacional*: Annual revenue less than BRL 3 600 000<br>2. *Microempreendedor Individual*: Natural person owner of a small business and annual revenue less than BRL 60 000 and employing not more than one person at minimum wage<br>3. *Lucro Presumido*: Annual revenue less than BRL 78 million | 1. Taxable income = annual revenue, with tax rates increasing in annual revenue and varying by activity (trade, industry or services)<br>2. Monthly tax payable in lump-sum calculated by activity, as follows: BRL 40.4 (commercial or industrial), BRL 44.4 (service) or BRL 45.4 (commerce and services); exemption from federal taxes (state and municipal still apply, which are covered by the lump-sum payments described)<br>3. Taxable income under corporate income tax calculated by applying a tax rate to annual revenue, where rates vary by activity |
| Chile | Agricultural property:<br>1A. Owners or beneficiaries of agricultural property with annual revenue less than UTM 8 000 (including revenue from related parties)<br>1B. Taxpayers that make use of the agricultural property under any other title (e.g. lessee, sub-lessee, gratuitous bailee) with annual revenue less than UTM 8 000 (including revenue from related parties)<br>1C. Taxpayers with annual revenue less than UTM 1 000 (including agricultural annual sales carried out by related societies, communities or co-operatives, in proportion to the taxpayer participation in their capital, income or profits)<br>2. Non-agricultural property: Owners or beneficiaries of non-agricultural property (no corporations, joint stock companies or foreign agencies) and effective income from property less than 11% of its fiscal property appraisal<br>3. Mining: Sales of less than 36 000 tons of non-ferrous metal or UTA 2 000 of any mineral (provided that taxpayer is not a small-scale miner)<br>Land transport:<br>4A. Passenger: Annual revenue from passenger transport services less than UTM 3 000 (including revenue from related parties)<br>4B. Freight: Annual revenue from passenger transport services less than UTM 3 000 (including revenue from related parties)<br>5. Small taxpayers: Very small taxpayers in certain sectors (e.g. employment as a small-scale miner, trader selling on sidewalks, news vendor, fisherman or owner of a workshop) | 1A&B. Taxable income calculated as 10% (A&B) or 4% (C) of the fiscal property appraisal; normal tax rates apply<br>2. Taxable income calculated as 7% of the fiscal property appraisal; normal tax rates apply<br>3. Taxable income calculated as a 4-20 % of net sales, based on the price of copper (even if the metal is gold or silver). If products do not contain copper, taxable income is calculated as 6% of the net value of their sale<br>4A&B. Taxable income calculated as 10% of the vehicle value as determined by the tax authority<br>5. Taxable income is subject to a single small taxpayer tax, which replaces all other income tax law taxes. For small-scale miners, taxable income calculated as the net value of the price received by the miner on sales of mining products, less rental income or royalties, where the tax rate depends on the variety of metal and its market price. For traders selling on sidewalks, tax payable is 0.5 UTM, paid annually. For news vendors, taxable income calculated as the total revenue from sales of newspapers, magazines, brochures and leaflets, with a 0.5% tax rate. For fishermen owning 1-2 ships, the annual tax payable depends on the gross tonnage: 0.5 UTM for gross tonnage less than 4 tons; 1.0 UTM for gross tonnage 4-8 tons; and 2.0 UTM for gross tonnage 8-15 tons. For owners of a workshop, tax payable is the higher of two values: 2.0 UTM or the sum of monthly advanced income payments of 3.0% of monthly gross income.<br><br>Note: The presumptive tax schemes described here are active in 2015, but will be amended as of 1 January 2016. |
| China | Eligibility is determined by the following criteria:<br>a. Taxpayers who do not keep books; b. Taxpayers who have a tax obligation but have not filed by the deadline; or c. Taxpayers who have underreported their tax liability without justification. | Tax payable calculated according to a certain tax rate, where the rate varies with the taxpayer's sector or firm characteristics, such as business location, size and other factors. |
| Czech Republic | Small businesses owned by natural persons, no employees and with taxable income less than CZK 5 million in any of the three previous tax periods | Taxable income determined by tax authority |

Table 4.2. **Presumptive income taxes** *(continued)*

| | Eligibility | Calculation of tax payable |
|---|---|---|
| Denmark | Danish Tonnage Tax: Applies to shipping enterprises | Calculation of taxable income based on individual vessel tonnage, where the rate used to calculate taxable income increases with tonnage |
| France | Micro enterprises: VAT exempt and annual revenue less than:<br>1A. EUR 82 200 (sales of goods)<br>1B. EUR 32 900 (provision of services)<br>2. Self-employed micro enterprise: In addition to the micro enterprise rules above, household income tax ceiling of EUR 26 631 (in 2014) and contribution to a social security system | Taxable income calculated as:<br>1A. 29% of annual revenue; normal tax rates apply<br>1B. 50% of annual revenue; normal tax rates apply<br>2. Monthly tax payable calculated as a percentage of monthly revenue by business activity, as follows: 1% for sales of goods; 1.7 % for provision of services; and 2.2% for provision of professional services |
| Hungary | 1. Simplified entrepreneurial tax (EVA): Annual revenue in the year preceding the previous year less than HUF 30 million and previous year annual revenue estimated at less than HUF 30 million<br>2.Tax for the self-employed (KATA): Registration as a small taxpayer | 1.Tax payable is calculated by applying a tax rate of 37%to annual revenue<br>2. Flat tax scheme, as follows: Tax payable equal to HUF 50 000 per month for each full-time entrepreneur or HUF 75 000 per month per full-time entrepreneur if the taxpayer elects for a higher social security service base. HUF 25 000 per month for each part-time entrepreneur (fewer than 36 hours per week) |
| India | 1. Transport business: Ownership of fewer than 10 goods carriages<br>2. Non-transport business: Annual revenue of less than INR 1 crore and status as a resident individual, Hindu undivided family or partnership firm | 1. Taxable income computed at the rate of INR 7 500 per goods carriage, per month; normal tax rate applies<br>2. Taxable income equal to 8% of annual revenue, where normal tax rates apply; eligible small businesses are not required to maintain books of accounts |
| Italy | 1. Natural persons with annual revenue less than EUR 40000, where the threshold varies by sector<br>2. Natural persons and partnerships engaged in agricultural activity | 1. Taxable income calculated by applying a ratio to annual revenue; a reduced, flat tax rate of 15% applies<br>2. Taxable income calculated by cadastral criteria with reference to PIT and VAT |
| Japan | Taxation by estimation method: Incorporated or unincorporated businesses | Taxable income calculated using indirect information from tax audits |
| Poland | 1. Natural persons or civil partnership with annual revenue in previous year less than EUR 150 000<br>2. Micro-entrepreneurs: Small services businesses employing fewer than five employees | 1. Tax payable is a flat amount determined by the tax authority<br>2. Tax payable calculated using a tax card, where the tax liability depends on the activity and its scope, the number of employees and number of inhabitants in the city where business is located |
| Portugal | Annual revenue less than EUR 200 000 or net assets less than EUR 500 000 | Taxable income calculated by applying coefficients for each type of income to annual revenue |
| Slovak Republic | Self-employed unincorporated business owners | 40% of taxable income can be deducted to represent expenses, with a maximum deduction of EUR 5 040. Taxable income is calculated as the difference between annual revenue and the sum of the lump sum deduction and mandatory social and health contributions. |
| Spain | Annual revenue less than EUR 450000 and engagement in certain business activities | Taxable income for unincorporated businesses calculated by applying certain coefficients (based on the number of employees, business site surface, etc.) to annual revenue; normal tax rates apply |
| Slovenia | Annual revenue less than EUR 50000 in the previous tax year or less than EUR 100 000 in the previous tax year and taxpayer employs one full-time person for at least 5 months | Taxable income calculated as 80% of annual revenue (including expenses) |
| South Africa | Annual revenue less than ZAR 1 million (EUR 77 000) | Tax rate determined by the tax authority according to a scale, where the rate applies to annual revenue and is increasing in annual revenue |

*Source:* Responses to an OECD questionnaire, *Survey on the Taxation of Small and Medium-Sized Enterprises*, 2015.

No countries reported a turnover based tax that was adjusted for expenses, although Austria provides a partial example of this type of presumptive tax, applied to businesses with annual revenue less than EUR 220 000. The tax base is measured as turnover, with 12% of turnover being deducted to represent wages, cost of goods (inputs) and related taxes (including VAT on inputs).

Instead of deducting actual expenses, individual entrepreneurs in the Slovak Republic who are not registered as VAT payers (taxable persons) or are so registered for only part of the taxable period, may elect to deduct a lump sum, equal to 40% of their income but may not exceed an amount of EUR 5 040 per year. This measure is applicable to craftsmen, sole proprietors holding a trade licence, experts and interpreters, as well as from certain professional services and leasing. If a lump-sum deduction is claimed, no other expenses may be deducted, except for mandatory social security and health insurance contributions. See Table 4.2 for more information.

### *Cash accounting*

Income tax systems in most countries are accrual based, requiring businesses to pay tax against their net income on an accrual basis. Accrual accounting requires SMEs to recognise revenues and expenditures at the time where the transaction occurs, rather than when the cash payment is received or made. For SMEs, this process can be complex, as they will be required to account for expenses related to long-term assets (e.g. depreciation), inventory and pension liabilities on an accrual basis. Accrual taxation can also pose cash flow problems for SMEs, as they could be required to pay tax on income that has accrued but has not yet been received.

To simplify compliance requirements and to reduce any cash flow disadvantages, many jurisdictions allow SMEs to calculate their income on a cash flow basis in full or in part. Under cash accounting, income tax is paid on revenues only when cash is received and input costs are claimed only when cash is paid out. Cash accounting systems targeted at SMEs, determining taxable profit based on entries of revenues actually received and costs actually paid, including immediate expensing of capital purchases may significantly reduce compliance costs, although this may depend on the type and extent of additional supporting documentation that taxpayers are required to assemble and maintain. They also have the advantage that they allow investment and reinvested income to automatically be deducted from the tax base.

Cash flow taxes differ from presumptive taxes in that they still use income as the tax base – albeit measured in a different way – and the amount of the tax base does vary with the amount of income. While simplified accounting requirements may assist with cash flow when income is not received in the same tax year, in some cases it may delay a deduction of an accrued expense that will not be paid until a future year.

Turnover is the most common threshold used to determine eligibility for cash accounting. In many cases, a fixed turnover threshold is used to determine eligibility, as in Poland, where entrepreneurs with revenues under EUR 1.2 million are able to use cash accounting. To avoid creating incentives for SMEs to remain under the threshold, flexible thresholds may be used which permit businesses to temporarily exceed the threshold and retain the ability to use cash accounting. For example, in the United Kingdom, a business using cash accounting may exceed the turnover threshold – up until twice the threshold – within a tax year without losing its ability to use cash accounting. Other eligibility tests consider turnover across more than one year to avoid volatility in taxable income affecting eligibility. For example, Chile uses a threshold of UF 50 000 for average turnover over the past three years, but requires that the amount of turnover does not exceed UF 60 000 in any one of those years.

Other eligibility criteria also apply, based on the characteristics of the SME. For example in Austria, unregulated self-employed individuals do not have to use double bookkeeping, whereas the ability of regulated self-employed individuals and commercial businesses to use cash accounting is limited to businesses under a turnover threshold. Cash accounting is also limited to sole proprietors in Sweden and to unincorporated businesses in the United Kingdom. Finally, different requirements may apply to different sectors, as seen in Austria, or in Canada, where farming and fishing corporations can use cash accounting.

Table 4.3 summarises cash accounting provisions reported for SMEs.

Table 4.3. **Cash accounting for SMEs**

| Country | Threshold (annual turnover) | Comment |
|---|---|---|
| Australia | | SMEs are able to immediately deduct prepaid expenses where they incur expenditure for something to be done in a later income year. |
| Austria | 1. No threshold<br>2. EUR 700 000 in two consecutive years, or EUR 1 million in one year<br>3. EUR 400 000 in two consecutive years | 1. Unregulated self-employed people do not have to use double bookkeeping<br>2. regulated self-employed and commercial businesses<br>3. Agricultural businesses |
| Canada | - | Farming and fishing corporations are able to use cash accounting for income tax purposes. |
| Chile | Average annual income over the past three years of less than or equal to UF 50 000 provided that in none of these years, their income exceeded UF 60 000 | Applies to small business in the simplified tax regime and which pay the First Category Income Tax. These businesses are able to calculate their tax payable on cash basis, adding certain forms of allowed accrual income. |
| Poland | EUR 1.2 million in the previous year | Able to choose simplified accounting requirements (a tax book of revenues and expenditures) rather than full accounting books. |
| Sweden | SEK 3 million | Sole proprietors can apply simplified financial accounting for income tax purposes, including possibilities for cash accounting. Simplified calculation of inventory, machinery and long-term contracts also applies. |
| Turkey | - | Taxpayers with annual purchases below a certain threshold based on purchases, sales or gross turnover, are able to opt for the business account method which requires them only to keep a record of their purchases and sales used to calculated their commercial income. Commercial income is calculated as the positive difference between their cash proceeds and their expenses |
| United Kingdom | GBP 82 000 (the VAT registration threshold) | Unincorporated businesses under this threshold may use cash accounting. If a business using a cash basis grows within the year it can continue to use cash accounting until income reaches GBP 164 000 after which it must use accrual accounting. |
| United States | USD 5 million or 10 million, depending on the legal status and business activity of the taxpayer | Able to use cash accounting. |

*Source:* Responses to an OECD questionnaire, *Survey on the Taxation of Small and Medium-Sized Enterprises*, 2015.

In 2005, the President's Advisory Panel on Federal Tax Reform in the United States recommended adopting a Simplified Income Tax Plan for SMEs which would have required the use of a separate business account for all SME transactions. The aim of the plan was to both reduce compliance costs and to ensure compliance. This plan would exempt businesses with less than USD 1 million in receipts from the requirement to maintain books and allow them to report income and expenditures on a cash basis for all items excluding the purchase of real property. Medium-sized businesses (less than USD 10 million in receipts) would also be able to use cash accounting but would be required to depreciate the cost of equipment and other capital expenditures. Under this scheme, small and medium-sized enterprises would have been required to use designated business bank accounts for all business receipts and expenditures and would be prohibited from making personal transactions in these accounts. If adopted, banks would be required to provide a summary of the inflows and outflows of these accounts, to further simplify compliance, which would also be reported directly to the IRS (President's Advisory Panel on Federal Tax Reform, 2005). This proposal presents an innovative approach that would combine simplifications with a requirement (the separate bank account) intended to enhance compliance.

### *Other simplified accounting measures for SMEs*

To further reduce tax compliance costs related to tax accounting procedures, countries use a range of other simplification measures. These include simplified rules for the calculation of inventory, bad debts and long-term contracts, relaxation of the requirement to keep financial accounting books for tax purposes, and simplified accounting regimes.

Several countries report simplifications to the calculation of inventory for SMEs. Eligibility for these simplified rules is typically based on the value of the inventory rather than the level of turnover of the business. For example, Australia has simpler trading stock rules for SMEs, which are not required to value each item of trading stock at the end of the year or account for changes to the value of the stock if the difference between the value at the start and end of the year is less than AUD 5 000. New Zealand also allows taxpayers with a low turnover of trading stock to use simplified valuation methods.

Other simplified inventory calculations apply to firms below a certain level of turnover. This includes simplified inventory requirements in Sweden and the United States. Simplified valuation of inventory is allowed in Sweden for sole proprietors with an annual turnover of less than SEK 3 million. In the United States, a Simplified Last-In First-Out accounting method is allowed for firms with average gross receipts under USD 5 million. Also in the United States, uniform capitalisation rules in inventory accounting do not require taxpayers with less than USD 10 million in average annual gross receipts to capitalise costs in the production of real or personal property or in the purchase of inventory. Other exceptions to standard inventory accounting rules are available to certain SMEs that meet size and activity conditions.

Another simplification measure applied to SMEs is simplified bookkeeping requirements for tax purposes. For example, Germany allows traders, farmers and foresters to be exempted from the requirement for bookkeeping for tax purposes if their turnover was under EUR 500 000 (or if they had gains from trade of less than EUR 50 000). India requires businesses to maintain books of accounts only if the amount of business income exceeds INR 120 000 or the business has had gross receipts in excess of INR 1 million in any of the last three years.

Under the simplified tax regime in Chile (noted in Table 4.2), taxpayers are also exempted from the requirement to keep complete accounting, balance sheets, inventory records, asset depreciation, and to keep information on the taxable profits fund. However, they are required to keep a chronological cash register, and if subject to VAT, a purchases and sales ledger (if not, they must keep an income ledger for received or accrued revenue and expenses).

Other countries allow simplified accounting systems for SMEs under a certain size threshold. For example, Italy allows individuals and partnerships not exceeding a revenue limit to opt for a simplified accounting system to determine the PIT base. For services, the threshold is EUR 400 000, while for goods, it is EUR 700 000. Another example is seen in Spain, which has a general accounting plan for companies that meet at least two out of three requirements in two consecutive years: firstly, the total assets cannot exceed

Table 4.4. **Simplified filing requirements for SMEs**

| Country | Threshold | Comment |
|---|---|---|
| Canada | 1. < CAD 3 000 of corporate income tax payable<br>2. CCPCs<br>3. Other corporations | Remittance of corporate income tax:<br>1. Annual<br>2. Quarterly<br>3. Monthly |
| Denmark | 1. < DKK 300 000 (single-taxed entities)<br>2. < DKK 500 000 (double-taxed entities)<br>3. DKK 25 million (single-taxed)<br>4. DKK 100 million (double-taxed) | 1&2. Exempt from the requirement to provide financial information on their tax return, whereas companies above this limit (up to a threshold of DKK 25 million for single-taxed entities and DKK 100 million for double-taxed entities) must return this information.<br>3&4. Exempt from the requirement to provide tax accounts with the tax return |
| Hungary | Tax payable of less than HUF 5 million in the previous year | Advance payments of income taxes may be made in quarterly instalments |
| India | | India allows unincorporated SMEs under the presumptive tax regime to file a separate and specific simplified tax return form. |
| Japan | The number of employees must be always less than or equal to 9 | Japan allows those SMEs to pay withholding tax on income twice a year rather than each month. |
| Poland | | Poland allows small taxpayers to make quarterly advance payments that are equal to the difference between the tax due on the income from the beginning of the fiscal year and the sum of advances for previous quarters, rather than doing this on a monthly basis, as for other CIT and PIT taxpayers. |
| Turkey | | In Turkey, taxpayers under the simple method file on annual tax returns and are not required to file withholding tax, pre-paid tax and VAT returns. |
| United Kingdom | Turnover from self-employment or income from UK property of less than GBP 82 000 | The United Kingdom allows businesses under this threshold to fill in a simplified return showing only turnover, total expenses and net profit or loss, for tax purposes. |
| United States | Less than USD 10 million in assets | In the United States, firms with less than 10 million in assets and less than 250 returns (or partnerships with 100 or fewer partners) are exempted from the requirement to file electronically. |

*Source:* Responses to an OECD questionnaire, *Survey on the Taxation of Small and Medium-Sized Enterprises*, 2015.

EUR 2.85 million; secondly the net annual turnover cannot exceed EUR 5.7 million, and thirdly, the average number of staff should not exceed fifty persons. Self-employed individuals in the Slovak Republic are allowed to follow single-entry bookkeeping accounting, while micro accounting units may opt for simplified financial reporting if they meet two of the following criteria *(i)* an asset value of less than EUR 350 000; *(ii)* turnover of less than EUR 700 000; or *(iii)* an average number of employees of less than 10.

Finally, the United States provides a simplified treatment of bad debts for banks and thrifts with less than USD 500 million in assets. These institutions are allowed to use a reserve method to calculate bad debts (deducting an increase to its financial statement reserve) rather than having to apply the specific charge-off method which requires them to identify the worthlessness of debt on a debt-by-debt basis.

### *Reduced filing requirements*

Another approach that reduces tax compliance costs, while at the same time providing firms with a cash-flow advantage, is allowing firms to make less frequent advance instalments of income tax and to meet interim reporting requirements. Many countries require larger firms to make advance instalments of income tax, often on a quarterly or even more frequent basis. Where small firms are allowed to remit less frequently, for example semi-annually or annually, compliance costs may be reduced and cash flow improved.

### *Other income tax simplification measures*

Countries report a range of other tax simplification measures for SMEs. These include:

- Australia reduces the period within which a notice of assessment can be issued by the Commissioner of Taxation, whereas this compares to four years for other taxpayers. Australia also has pay-as-you-go instalments based on gross domestic product adjusted notional tax. SMEs that are full self-assessment taxpayers are eligible for the GDP adjusted notional tax method of calculating instalment liabilities. This removes the requirement to calculate instalment income themselves, reducing compliance costs.
- Canada provides a shorter reassessment period for the income returns of SMEs that are individuals or CCPCs, limiting the assessment period to three rather than the four years that applies to certain other taxpayers.
- India does not have audit requirements under the income tax law for SMEs with turnover of less than INR 10 million.
- In the Slovak Republic unincorporated self-employed business owners are not subject to the minimum tax regime (tax licence).
- Other countries simplify compliance obligations for SMEs for transfer pricing documentation. For example, in Denmark, SMEs are only required to prepare and retain transfer pricing documentation for business with persons that are resident in a country that is not a member of the EU, the EEA and does not have a double taxation agreement with Denmark. SMEs that qualify for this preference must have less than 250 employees, a balance sheet of under DKK 125 million or turnover of less than DKK 250 million.

## *VAT[4] simplification measures*

Along with other taxes, VAT imposes compliance costs on businesses and administrative costs on tax authorities. Although VAT is designed to be neutral for business taxpayers, VAT is often classified as particularly difficult and burdensome for SMEs to collect and comply with.[5,6] Hence simplified VAT regimes for SMEs are often an efficient way to promote compliance.

This subsection draws on responses to the questionnaire to discuss VAT simplification approaches applied to SMEs in OECD and G20 countries. Countries that replied to the questionnaire follow a range of approaches for facilitating VAT compliance. These approaches can be grouped into three main categories: those that provide for an exemption from the VAT regime; those that facilitate the calculation of the VAT liability; and those that simplify accounting, filing or payment obligations. A number of less commonly used simplification schemes were also reported, including but not limited to those aiming at a direct compensation of SMEs for high compliance costs. In most cases countries use a combination of approaches, as set out in Table 4.8 at the end of this chapter.

### *Exemption thresholds (registration and collection)*

Exemption thresholds set a level of turnover below which there is no obligation to comply with VAT regulations. Entities under these thresholds do not account for output VAT and consequently are not entitled to deduct input tax incurred on purchases of goods and services. This is a commonly-used and straightforward option to address VAT compliance costs.

There are two kinds of exemption thresholds. Registration thresholds relieve suppliers from both the requirement to register for VAT and to collect the tax. Collection thresholds require taxpayers, even those below the threshold, to register for VAT, but relieve them from collecting VAT until they exceed the threshold. Different types of activities (e.g. supply of services vs supply of goods) or sectors (e.g. the non-profit sector) may be subject to different thresholds or even be excluded from their application (e.g. in Belgium, certain fraud sensitive sectors, such as the construction sector, are excluded). In most cases registration thresholds do not apply to foreign businesses and in some cases collection thresholds apply only to individuals or to businesses for which commercial accounting is not compulsory (e.g. Portugal).

Table 4.5 provides an overview of applicable collection and registration thresholds in OECD countries. In principle, the calculation of thresholds is based on annual turnover. In the Netherlands, however, the basis for calculation is the net annual VAT due. With some exceptions, in Japan businesses (companies and individuals) are not required to register and account for VAT during the first two years of establishment during which a threshold based on their capital (etc.) applies; a threshold based on an annual taxable turnover applies only after the first two years. (If turnover exceeds a certain amount in the first half of the previous year, it applies after the first one year.) It should be noted, however, that even in countries where the threshold is based on an annual turnover its application may be subject to additional requirements.

Threshold levels vary significantly between countries with a relatively high threshold (Australia, Austria, the Czech Republic, France, Hungary, Ireland, Italy, Japan, New Zealand, Poland, the Slovak Republic, Slovenia, South Africa, Switzerland and the United Kingdom) to those with a relatively low threshold (Belgium, Canada, Denmark, Estonia, Finland, Germany, Greece, Iceland, Israel, Luxembourg, Norway and Portugal). There are also countries (Chile, Mexico, Spain, Sweden and Turkey) which have no exemption threshold.

Table 4.5. **Annual turnover concessions for VAT or GST registration and collection, 2015 (domestic businesses)**

| | General Threshold | | | | | |
|---|---|---|---|---|---|---|
| | Registration or collection | Turnover, in national currency | In USD [a] | Voluntary registration or collection | Specific rules for the application of the threshold [b] | **Other thresholds** |
| Australia | R | 75 000 | 50 041 | Yes | Yes | Yes |
| Austria | R | 30 000 | 35 496 | Yes | Yes | No |
| Belgium | C | 15 000 | 17 828 | Yes | Yes | No |
| Canada | R | 30 000 | 23 911 | Yes | Yes | Yes |
| Chile | None | | | | | |
| Czech Republic | R | 1 000 000 | 73 885 | Yes | Yes | No |
| Denmark | R | 50 000 | 6 561 | Yes | Yes | Yes |
| Estonia | R | 16 000 | 28 996 | Yes | Yes | No |
| Finland | R | 8 500 | 9 145 | Yes | Yes | Yes |
| France | R | 82 200 | 96 934 | Yes | Yes | Yes |
| Germany | C | 17 500 | 21 946 | Yes | Yes | No |
| Greece | R | 10 000 | 16 099 | Yes | Yes | No |
| Hungary | C | 6 000 000 | 46 124 | Yes | Yes | No |
| Iceland | R | 1 000 000 | 7 293 | Yes | No | No |
| Ireland | R | 75 000 | 91 303 | Yes | Yes | No |
| Israel | R | 79 482 | 20 000 | No | Yes | No |
| Italy | R | 30 000 | 39 812 | Yes | Yes | No |
| Japan | R | 10 000 000 | 96 034 | Yes | Yes | No |
| Korea | R | 24 000 000 | 28 152 | Yes | No | No |
| Luxembourg | C | 25 000 | 27 565 | Yes | Yes | No |
| Mexico | None | | | Yes | | |
| Netherlands [c] | C | 1 345 | 1 632 | No | Yes | Yes |
| New Zealand | R | 60 000 | 40 809 | Yes | | No |
| Norway | R | 50 000 | 5 472 | Yes | Yes | Yes |
| Poland | R | 150 000 | 82 874 | Yes | Yes | No |
| Portugal | C | 10 000 | 17 094 | Yes | Yes | Yes |
| Slovak Republic | R | 49 790 | 98 979 | Yes | Yes | No |
| Slovenia | R | 50 000 | 83 349 | Yes | Yes | No |
| Spain | None | | | | | |
| Sweden | None | | | | | |
| Switzerland | R | 100 000 | 73 470 | Yes | Yes | Yes |
| Turkey | None | | | | | |
| United Kingdom | R | 81 000 | 115 626 | Yes | Yes | No |

*Notes:* a. Exchange rates for conversion into USD are Purchase Parity Rates (PPPs) for private consumption. Data is taken from OECD Dotstat http://stats.oecd.org/index.aspx?queryid=27286 accessed on 11 March 2014. For further detail see www.oecd.org/std/ppp.

b. Specific rules for the application of the threshold, including rules applicable to businesses reaching the threshold, calculation of the threshold, restrictions to some sectors or types of transactions (incl. restrictions under Directive 2006/112/EC for members states of the European Union. For detailed information please refer to OECD Tax Database (OECD, 2015).

c. Thresholds are in principle turnover thresholds. In the case of Netherlands however the threshold is determined with reference to the net annual VAT due.

*Source:* OECD (2015), *OECD Tax Database*, www.oecd.org/tax/tax-policy/tax-database.htm; position as at 1 January 2015.

The main reason for introducing a threshold is to reduce the disproportionately high VAT compliance costs, as a percentage of turnover, on SMEs. However, where some firms are part of the VAT system and others are not, this can affect their relative competitiveness. In particular, non-participating firms may be negatively impacted owing to their inability to claim input tax credits (i.e. credits in respect of VAT paid on inputs). One means of addressing this is to allow SMEs to register voluntarily. However, in some cases, non-participating firms may enjoy a competitive advantage since they are exempt from charging output VAT.

A relatively high VAT threshold can frustrate policy efforts to have all businesses actively participate in the formal economy. However, the latter may be at least partly addressed if firms below the VAT threshold and who do not elect to pay VAT are required to pay another, simpler, form of tax– and thus be part of the "formal" economy.

A relatively low VAT threshold, while encouraging participation by a greater number of firms in the regular tax system and avoiding distortions to competition, may be seen as a disincentive to growth. As pointed out in the context of presumptive tax schemes, a SME close to the threshold may keep the volume of its business artificially below it to continue benefiting from the simplified system.[7] This could be at least partly addressed by the use of flexible thresholds, discussed further below. Where the number of taxpayers in the system tends to grow with lower threshold values, tax administration challenges may also grow.

Whether to establish a threshold is an important issue for VAT design. The level of the threshold is often a trade-off between minimising compliance and administration costs and the need to avoid jeopardising revenue and/or distorting competition. Exempting small firms from the VAT system may forgo little revenue, however, the balance between cost savings and revenue losses shifts as thresholds increase and at some point the forgone revenue will exceed the compliance and administrative costs. At some intermediate point an optimal VAT threshold can be identified, at which the cost savings and revenue losses are equal.[8] Further, there are a number of other factors including distortionary effects inherent in the application of thresholds that should be taken into account. All these considerations make the identification of the optimal threshold for each country a difficult question to determine and one which may vary across the heterogeneous SME population.

Where voluntary thresholds are used, often intended to circumvent the disadvantages of non-registration, these increase tax administration costs and impose compliance costs on entities that elect to be in the system. Additionally, caution needs to be exercised to avoid VAT fraud by "fly-by-night" traders who may register and ask for refund claims on an ad hoc basis. For this reason, several countries impose a minimum period of time during which taxpayers that have registered voluntarily must remain registered. This period varies from one year (Australia, Canada, Czech Republic, Greece, Hungary, Slovak Republic, Switzerland) to two years (Denmark, France, Japan, Norway) or in some cases, up to five years (Austria, Germany, Luxembourg, Slovenia).

Another issue related to the adoption of a threshold is how to encourage borderline businesses to increase their turnover or at least to discourage them from underreporting turnover to remain below the exemption threshold. The adoption of a flexible threshold is one option. In this case SMEs that reach the regular exemption registration threshold are not obliged to register immediately but are allowed to continue to benefit from the exemption as long as their annual turnover does not exceed the threshold by a considerable percentage. The adoption of a flexible threshold could also be regarded as a convenient way to smooth the transition to a regular VAT regime.

One example of a flexible threshold is in France, where the regular thresholds of EUR 82 200 (for goods) and EUR 32 900 (for most services) are increased to EUR 90 300 and EUR 34 900 respectively, as long as the annual turnover of the SME exceeds the regular threshold during a year but remains under the second tier threshold. Another example of a flexible threshold is used in the United Kingdom, where a SME can apply for a registration exemption where their taxable turnover temporarily exceeds the regular threshold. Finally, the Netherlands provides a flexible collection threshold which is based on the net annual VAT due. If the net annual VAT due is less than EUR 1 345, no VAT is remitted to the tax authorities. If the net annual VAT due is between EUR 1 345 and EUR 1 883 the taxpayer gets a gradual tax reduction which ensures its smooth entry into a taxpaying position.

### *Simplification schemes for calculating VAT liability*

Under VAT regimes, taxable persons or entities have to remit to the tax authorities the proportion of tax corresponding to their margin, i.e. the difference between the VAT imposed on their taxed inputs and the VAT imposed on their taxed outputs. One route used in many countries to minimise compliance costs for SMEs is to apply simplified presumptive schemes to facilitate the calculation of the VAT liability. For example, certain SMEs may be allowed to apply a single flat rate to turnover for determining the amount of VAT to be remitted to tax authorities (instead of requiring a detailed VAT calculation). An alternative simplification scheme for calculating VAT liability relies on simplified input tax credit calculations, which as a consequence affect the amount of VAT to be paid.

#### (i) VAT and presumptive tax schemes

Under VAT presumptive tax schemes, SMEs charge the normal VAT on their outputs but they pay VAT at a single rate calculated on the basis of specific indicators. Those specific indicators may include: the *turnover* (for example in France, Korea, United Kingdom, Mexico, Brazil); *certain indicators* (e.g. electricity consumed, surface of facilities used for the business activity, rental or leasing costs paid, total number of employees) with each indicator having an associated monetary amount, the sum of which will result in the VAT due (this is the case for example in Argentina and Spain); *a combination of both turnover and certain indicators* (for example in Belgium); *a combination of turnover and amount of VAT due* as calculated according to the presumptive tax scheme (this is the case for example in Switzerland under the net tax rate scheme). Applicable rates vary not only among countries but also among sectors in the same country. Variable flat rates are intended in most cases to reflect the average VAT rate in that industry or sector after taking into account recovery of VAT on inputs, and zero- or reduced rating of some outputs.

In principle, under presumptive schemes SMEs give up the right to reclaim VAT on their inputs.[9] SMEs, therefore, keep the difference between what they have charged their customers and what they pay to the tax administration. In some cases, such presumptive approaches may result in the payment of a lump sum based solely on the type of activity without considering any other indicator such as the annual turnover or the nature of the activity. Eligibility for presumptive tax schemes may be based on the type of business activity performed as well as on an annual turnover threshold.

Variations of these schemes have been reported by Belgium, Chile, China and Spain. In Belgium, enterprises eligible for this scheme (also called flat rate enterprises), consisting of businesses dealing mainly with private individuals active in certain sectors (e.g. bakeries, butchers, hairdressers) with turnover not higher than EUR 750 000 have their annual turnover set under special regulations (on the basis of fixed specific factors such as the amount of hours worked, the purchases made etc.) with the deduction of inputs determined according to standard rules. In Chile, the VAT calculation under such a scheme is related to the declaration of a monthly fixed tax debit, according to the amount of the business' sales or services. After that, a VAT credit is deducted from the monthly fixed debit assessed. The tax credit is equal to 19% of all the purchases and services acquired, either taxed or exempt ones, excluding VAT. In China, qualifying small taxpayers (based on VAT amount and sector) pay VAT at a lower rate of 3% on turnover, without the right to deduct tax on their inputs. In Spain, two variations apply: "the simplified special scheme" and the "special compensatory charge scheme". Under "the simplified special scheme" the calculation of VAT is based on indicators (e.g. annual turnover) where the VAT arising from specific supplies (including the sale of immovable property, imports and supplies subject to reverse charge) is added. This is combined with the application of special input tax deduction rules (notably the possibility to also deduct an amount equivalent to 1% of the initial VAT due). The "special compensatory charge scheme" on the other hand, was reported by Spain as a mandatory scheme (the only one among countries that replied to the questionnaire) targeted to taxable persons that qualify as "retailers" independently of any annual turnover threshold (see Box 4.1 for further details).

### Box 4.1. Special compensatory charge scheme in Spain

This special compensatory charge scheme is set up as a simplification measure targeted at taxable persons that qualify as "retailers", i.e. taxable persons who predominantly sell goods – without any previous transformation process – to final consumers. Retailers are exempted from submitting any VAT return as well as from collecting and remitting any VAT amount on their outputs. However they are obliged for each purchase they make from a third party provider to pay apart from the consideration for the purchase itself an additional amount (special compensatory charge). This additional amount is collected and remitted to the tax authorities by the third party provider on behalf of the retailer while the retailer is relieved from any VAT reporting and filing obligations. This special compensatory charge is calculated on the basis of different rates applicable on the value of the purchased item. Those rates depend on the nature of the supplied item and may range from 0.5% to 5.2%. A special rate of 1.75% is applied in case of products subject to excise duties (e.g. manufactured tobacco). The scheme does not apply to specific business activities.

*Source:* Responses to an OECD questionnaire, *Survey on the Taxation of Small and Medium-Sized Enterprises*, 2015.

## (ii) Simplified input tax credit calculation schemes

In cases where a simplified input tax credit calculation scheme applies, SMEs are expected to impose VAT on their outputs (i.e. their sales of goods and services) in line with regular VAT provisions. SMEs, however, are granted a fixed input tax deduction from the amount of VAT due. Hence, the amount of VAT to be paid to tax authorities is calculated differently than the standard way (i.e. the difference between the VAT imposed on taxed inputs and the VAT imposed on its outputs). Such an approach reduces the VAT tax burden for SMEs as it is unnecessary to determine the recoverability of VAT on individual items of expenditure, or may even exempt SMEs with only a minor VAT liability from paying small amounts to the tax authorities. This approach also reduces the risk of administration and compliance costs exceeding the amount of VAT actually paid. It is often combined with simplified filing and reporting obligations.

Such a simplified input tax credit calculation scheme is available in Germany for specific taxable persons with an annual turnover that does not exceed EUR 61 356. The deductible input tax can be calculated on the basis of a fixed rate applicable to the overall turnover (e.g. 1.8% in Austria for SMEs with turnover under EUR 200 000). A variation of this scheme is applied in Japan where VAT calculations are simplified for businesses with turnover[10] of less than or equal to JPY 50 million, where a deemed input tax credit is calculated as a percentage of VAT payable on taxable sales (optional scheme). The deemed percentage depends on the particular industry or trade of the business and varies from 40 to 90%.

A variation of a simplified input tax credit calculation scheme is reported by Australia and relates to the annual apportioning of VAT credits between business and private purchases. In particular, in Australia businesses with a turnover of less than AUD 2 million per annum can choose to account for the private portion of business purchases annually rather than each time they file their GST return. This means that they can then claim the full GST credit for a business purchase and make an adjustment for the private portion of the purchase at the end of the income year. One of the main benefits of this scheme is the resulting interim cash flow benefit until the final adjustment is made at the end of the year.

Countries may provide for more than one form of simplified scheme for calculating VAT liability to be optionally implemented by SMEs depending on their specific situation. This is the case for example in Canada, as described in more detail in Box 4.2.

### Box 4.2. Simplified GST and HST calculation schemes for SMEs in Canada

Canada applies two simplified GST or HST calculations that benefit SMEs: the quick method and the simplified method for claiming input tax credits.

**The Quick Method**

Under the Quick Method, a registrant does not track the tax collected on most sales and the tax paid on most purchases under the regular GST/HST rules. Rather, the registrant's net tax remittance is calculated by simply multiplying total GST/HST-included taxable supplies made in Canada by a prescribed Quick Method remittance rate. The prescribed remittance rates, which depend on the type of business engaged in and the tax status of supplies made, are designed to take average input tax credits (ITCs) into account; therefore, actual ITCs generally cannot be claimed under this method. There is also a credit of 1% related to the first CAD 30 000 of supplies (including the GST/HST) for each fiscal year. Tax paid or collected on purchases and sales of real property and capital property, and improvements to the property, are accounted for in the normal manner (or, for capital personal property, using the Simplified Method for Claiming Input Tax Credits). Any business, whether incorporated or unincorporated, with annualised worldwide GST-included taxable sales and other revenues of CAD 400 000 or less, for itself and all associates, may be eligible to use the Quick Method. The reference to "worldwide" means that registrants must include supplies made outside Canada that would be taxable or zero-rated if the supplies were made in Canada. Some businesses, e.g. accountants and lawyers, cannot use the Quick Method.

**Simplified Method for Claiming Input Tax Credits**

Under the Simplified Method for Claiming Input Tax Credits, small businesses do not have to show GST or HST separately from purchases in their records. Instead, taxable purchases for which an ITC is being claimed must be totalled. The Simplified Method can be used by small businesses whose annual worldwide revenues from taxable supplies of goods and services (including those of associates) are CAD 1 million or less in the last fiscal year. The total taxable supplies (including those of associates) for all preceding fiscal quarters of the given fiscal year must also be CAD 1 million or less. This does not include zero-rated financial services, sales of capital real property, or goodwill. In addition, taxable purchases (excluding zero-rated purchases but including purchases imported into Canada or brought into a participating province) made in Canada by the small business must also not exceed CAD 4 million in the immediately preceding fiscal year.

*Source:* Responses to an OECD questionnaire, *Survey on the Taxation of Small and Medium-Sized Enterprises*, 2015.

These simplification schemes for calculating VAT liability may promote compliance to the extent that they capture the potential taxable base rather than the actual taxable base. Given that most simplification schemes are optional, eligible businesses have the opportunity to estimate their liability under both regimes (simplification and standard) and opt for the regime that results in the smallest liability.[11]

These simplification schemes may also make reporting less burdensome as it is not necessary to determine the recoverability of VAT on individual items of expenditure. However, the variation of flat tax rates among different categories of industry may create distortions and policing problems at the boundaries. Moreover, a standard assessment method may substitute away from the indicators on which liability is based. For example, an employment-related indicator may discourage formal employment.

### *Accounting, return filing and payment simplification schemes*

This subsection discusses accounting, filing and payment simplification schemes for VAT, drawing on the responses provided by countries to the questionnaire.

One simplification measure involves the use of VAT cash accounting schemes. VAT systems are generally accrual based, requiring that VAT be remitted on taxable sales where the cash has not yet been received. Under cash accounting, VAT is paid on sales only when the cash is received and, similarly, input tax credits are claimed only when cash is paid on a purchase. Accounting for output VAT on a cash basis is generally an option that enables designated businesses to make designated supplies to account for VAT at the time their customers pay the price for goods and services supplied to them. Prior notification of opting for this regime and for approval from tax authorities may be required (e.g. Greece, Hungary and Germany). Certain countries require businesses who choose to operate under the cash accounting regime to do so for a minimum period unless their turnover exceeds the relevant threshold (e.g. in Luxembourg, where SMEs that have opted for the accounting scheme must apply it for at least five years). The applicable threshold is calculated on the basis of the annual turnover of the last twelve months and businesses will not be able to use the cash accounting scheme after they have exceeded this threshold. In the case of New Zealand and Slovenia, the threshold is also calculated on the estimated value of supplies in any future twelve months.

In principle, SMEs that apply this scheme are bound by all the other obligations under the general VAT provisions (i.e. issue of invoices and keeping of books and records). In certain cases SMEs that choose to enter the scheme have to keep additional records of their collections and payments and provide electronically relevant information to the tax authorities (e.g. in Greece) or meet other specific conditions (e.g. in Hungary and Poland – see also Table 4.6).

As discussed, cash accounting systems may significantly reduce compliance costs for SMEs and assist with their cash flow by allowing them to defer tax payments until they have collected payment from their customers. They may also prevent the supplier from having to apply a refund of initially remitted VAT on bad debts. At the same time this option may be less attractive considering that the right to deduct input VAT can only be exercised in the tax period in which the taxable person pays the consideration (inclusive of VAT) to his supplier (e.g. in Greece, Hungary and Poland). There is significant variation among countries in terms of the amount of turnover under which the cash accounting system can be applied, as shown in Table 4.6.

Table 4.6. **Optional cash accounting schemes in OECD and non-OECD G20 countries**

| Country | Threshold (turnover as per previous year) | Notes |
|---|---|---|
| Australia | AUD 2 million | |
| Austria | EUR 700 000<br>EUR 110 000 | Company incomes<br>All other incomes |
| Estonia | EUR 200 000 | |
| Germany | EUR 500 000 | |
| Greece | EUR 500 000 | |
| Hungary | HUF 125 million | Under the condition that the claimant is not adjudicated in bankruptcy or liquidation proceedings |
| Ireland | EUR 2 million | |
| Italy | EUR 2 million | |
| Luxembourg | EUR 500 000 | |
| Mexico | - | The RIF regime has an annual income limit of up to MXN 2 million. If the income exceeds this amount the taxpayer must participate in the general regime. |
| New Zealand | NZD 2 million | Under the additional condition that the total value of their taxable supplies is not likely to exceed NZD 2 million in any future 12 months |
| Poland | EUR 1.2 million | The threshold of EUR 45 000 applies in the case of a taxable person that runs a brokerage enterprise, administers investment funds, is an agent, mandatory or another person that provides services of a similar character (except for sale on commission) |
| Portugal | EUR 500 000 | |
| Slovenia | EUR 400 000 | Under the additional condition that the total value of their taxable supplies is not likely to exceed EUR 400 000 in the next 12 months |
| South Africa | ZAR 2.5 million | The scope of this provision (currently applicable to taxable persons which are natural persons or incorporated bodies of which all members are natural persons), will be reviewed to increase the threshold and/or broaden the application to include incorporated businesses coupled with anti-avoidance measures. |
| Sweden | SEK 3 million | |
| Switzerland | | Primarily available for SMEs |
| United Kingdom | GBP 1.35 million | The scheme applies to retailers, regardless of turnover |

*Source:* Responses to an OECD questionnaire, *Survey on the Taxation of Small and Medium-Sized Enterprises*, 2015, and IBFD (2013), *EU VAT Compass 2013/2014*, IBFD Publications, Amsterdam.

Other accounting, filing and payment simplification schemes for VAT reported in the questionnaire responses include:

- ***Simplified reporting methods***: In Portugal, special accounting standards (i.e. "small or micro entities accounting standards") apply depending on the net turnover and average number of employers. In Australia, retailers that sell taxable and GST-free food, with a turnover of less than AUD 2 million, may use simplified accounting methods to avoid compliance difficulties associated with identifying and recording GST free sales. In cases where a special presumptive tax scheme applies based on specific indicators, SMEs may be permitted to keep only the information that provides evidence of the indicators used to calculate the final VAT payable amount (e.g. in Spain). Some VAT systems (e.g. South Africa, Japan and Spain) provide for simplified invoices for SMEs under certain conditions (the most common being the value of the transaction below a value threshold). These SMEs may, however, still be required to issue a normal invoice should the customer specifically ask for it, as is the case in Spain and South Africa. In Chile and Mexico technologically based simplified accounting systems for SMEs are available (see also Box 4.5 for further details on Chile's Electronic VAT Invoicing system).

- ***Less frequent filing requirements***: Most countries with VAT systems require firms to file VAT returns on a monthly basis. Where small firms are allowed to file and pay at less frequent intervals, compliance costs may be significantly reduced while also providing SMEs with a cash-flow advantage and savings in present value terms. These cash-flow savings may be viewed as a form of subsidy to help defray remaining compliance costs. Most commonly, SMEs are allowed to file VAT returns quarterly, semi-annually or annually, typically after passing a small business test based on taxable turnover in the prior year, as set out in Table 4.7.
- ***Payment flexibility schemes***: In some cases (e.g. in France, Spain and the United Kingdom) payment flexibility schemes providing for regular advance payments are available to SMEs on an optional basis. Under these schemes the taxpayer is obliged to make monthly or quarterly instalments based on an estimate of their total VAT liability. However a SME may not be required to make these advance payments if the estimate of its total VAT liability is below a certain threshold (e.g. in France no advance VAT payment is required if the estimate of total VAT liability is less than EUR 1 000). Among the main benefits of those payment flexibility schemes are *(i)* easier budgeting and cash flow planning because the timing and amount of instalments are known in advance and *(ii)* reduction of time needed to prepare returns as only one annual return is generally required under these schemes.

### Box 4.3. VAT Annual Accounting Scheme in the United Kingdom

Usually, VAT-registered businesses submit their VAT returns and payments to HM Revenue and Customs four times a year. With the Annual Accounting Scheme eligible businesses make advance VAT payments towards their VAT bill – based on their last return (or estimated if they are new to VAT) and submit one VAT return a year. When they submit their VAT return they either:

- Make a final payment – the difference between their advance payments and actual VAT bill; or
- Apply for a refund – if they have overpaid their VAT bill.

The scheme would not suit businesses that regularly reclaim VAT because they will only be able to get one refund a year (when they submit the VAT return). Businesses can join the scheme if their estimated VAT taxable turnover is GBP 1.35 million or less with some exceptions. SMEs that have opted for the scheme and reach the threshold are not obliged to quit immediately but they may remain in the system until their annual turnover exceeds a specific amount i.e. stay in the preferential regime as soon as the business turnover does not exceed the turnover threshold level of the scheme by a considerable percentage (i.e. their VAT taxable turnover is (or is likely to be) more than GBP 1.6 million at the end of the annual accounting year).

*Source:* https://www.gov.uk/vat-annual-accounting-scheme.

Other payment simplification schemes include the payment of VAT due in instalments. In Australia for instance, businesses with turnover of less than AUD 2 million per annum (up to date with their lodgements and not in a net refund position) may elect to pay their GST in instalments. In Italy, payments can be made (on an optional basis) on quarterly instead of monthly for firms under a turnover threshold (i.e. EUR 400 000 for the supply of services and EUR 700 000 in case of the supply of goods). In Chile, enterprises subject to the general or simplified accounting regime with an average annual business income not exceeding UF 100 000[12] in the last three business years, and those adhering to the Simplified Taxation System may defer their VAT payment for up to two months.

Table 4.7. **Return filing simplification provisions for SMEs in OECD and other non OECD G20 countries**

| Country | Eligibility (turnover per year, unless otherwise indicated) | Return filing frequency or simplification | Notes |
|---|---|---|---|
| Australia | < AUD 20 million per year | Quarterly | Applies only if electronic lodgement not compulsory. Concessions available, but not confined to SMEs |
| Belgium | < EUR 2.5 million | Quarterly | For some fraud sensitive sectors (such as mobile phones) turnover is reduced to EUR 250 000 |
| Brazil | | Annually | |
| Canada | < CAD 1.5 million<br>CAD 1.5-6 million<br>> CAD 6 million | Annually<br>Quarterly<br>monthly | SMEs may elect to make more frequent returns, up to a monthly-basis |
| Chile | | Quarterly | |
| Czech Republic | < CZK 10 million<br>> CZK 6 million | Quarterly<br>No obligation for e-filing | Conditions apply.<br>Firms must be natural persons. |
| Denmark | < DKK 5 million<br>DKK 5-50 million | Six-monthly<br>Quarterly | Taxable persons may opt for the quarterly period starting from their second year of registration if: their turnover in the previous calendar year was lower than CZK 10 million; they have not been identified as an unreliable payer; and they are not members of a VAT group. |
| Finland | < EUR 25 000<br>< EUR 50 000 | Annually<br>Quarterly | |
| France | < EUR 783 000 (goods)<br>< EUR 236 000 (services)<br>VAT < EUR 15 000 per year | Annually<br>Annually<br>Quarterly | Construction sector including cleaning, repairing, maintenance, demolition and transformation services excluded |
| Hungary | | No obligation for filing [see notes] | Full exemption from filing requirements if no VAT due, no intra-Community transaction to be declared in a recapitulative statement, and no right to exercise the right of deduction or does not exercise the right of deduction during a tax period. |
| Ireland | | Annually (otherwise two-monthly) | |
| Italy | < EUR 400 000 (services)<br>< EUR 700 000 (goods) | Quarterly<br>Quarterly | |
| Luxembourg | < EUR 620 000<br>< EUR 112 000<br>< EUR 25 000 | Quarterly<br>Annually<br>No return required | All taxpayers with turnover above EUR 112 000 have to file electronically. |
| Mexico | | Two-monthly | |
| New Zealand | < NZD 500 000<br>< NZD 24 million | Six-monthly<br>Two-monthly | Taxpayers over NZD 24 million have to file monthly |
| Norway | <NOK 1 million | Annually | Upon consent of the Tax Office |
| Poland | | Quarterly | SMEs under the cash accounting scheme and who have chosen to submit tax returns quarterly (in accordance with the principles defined in detail by legislation) |

Table 4.7. **Return filing simplification provisions for SMEs in OECD and other non OECD G20 countries** *(continued)*

| Country | Eligibility (turnover per year, unless otherwise indicated) | Return filing frequency or simplification | Notes |
|---|---|---|---|
| Portugal | < EUR 650 000 | Quarterly | |
| Slovak Republic | < EUR 100 000 | Quarterly | |
| South Africa | < ZAR 1.5 million | Four-monthly | This facilitating provision to be withdrawn as of 1st July 2015 due to low utilisation by enterprises. |
| Spain | SMEs under simplified scheme | Quarterly<br>Annually: the final vat return | |
| Sweden | < SEK 1 million | Annually | Not applicable to "*handelsbolag*" (limited partnerships) |
| Switzerland | SMEs under the net tax rate method | Six-monthly | |
| United Kingdom | < GBP 1.35 million + annual accounting scheme | Annually | |

*Source:* Responses to an OECD questionnaire, *Survey on the Taxation of Small and Medium-Sized Enterprises*, 2015. Unless otherwise indicated the standard filing period is monthly.

### *Other VAT simplification measures for SMEs*

This subsection considers a number of other less commonly used forms of VAT simplification measures, drawing on questionnaire responses. These include, but are not limited to, measures aimed at providing direct compensation to SMEs for high compliance costs:

- ***Standard deduction:*** As a means of compensating SMEs for their compliance costs, certain countries allow SMEs a fixed deduction from the amount of VAT due (when VAT due does not exceed a certain threshold). This is the case in the Netherlands where if the net annual VAT due is more than EUR 1 345 but less than EUR 1 883 the SME will get a VAT rebate and will have to pay only a part of the VAT due. Similarly, in Finland SMEs that have exceeded the exemption registration threshold of EUR 8 500, must register and are subject to VAT, but graduated relief is granted until they reach a second threshold of EUR 22 500.
- ***Flat-rate compensation:*** In cases where SMEs are exempt from VAT and are unable to deduct any input VAT, they may be granted a flat-rate compensation for their inputs depending on the sector and their annual turnover. This flat-rate compensation is not a VAT credit, but it acts as compensation for the loss of the right to recover input VAT. Such fixed rate compensation schemes apply for farmers in a number of European countries (e.g. Austria, Belgium, Denmark, Greece, Estonia, France, Hungary, Italy, Netherlands, Poland, Slovenia and United Kingdom).
- ***Reliance on a specific (simple) VAT rate structure for SMEs:*** Studies suggest that a multiple rate VAT structure contributes considerably to SME compliance costs. For example, a study of VAT compliance in Sweden estimates that compliance costs would be reduced on average by roughly 30% if a single rate system replaced a multiple rate system. While a multiple rate system may satisfy public demands for lower rates on specific products, for a variety of reasons, adhering to a single or simple rate structure can both limit tax distortions to consumption and production and at the same time reduce compliance costs. However, these

advantages, including those tied to reduced informality, are difficult to measure and to communicate to the public, implying considerable difficulty in imposing a simple VAT rate structure. This has often led policy makers to look for other means to reduce and alleviate the compliance costs of SMEs. Luxembourg reported the application of a special reduced rate to the agriculture and forestry sector. Even though the introduction of a special reduced rate for SMEs may appear to be a straightforward means of compensating businesses for high compliance costs, it presents significant disadvantages since at the same time it complicates the VAT system and increases compliance and administrative costs. In addition it creates additional tax evasion risks.

- ***Exempting supplies made to SMEs:*** Exempting supplies to SMEs from VAT could be another possible method of mitigating the tax burden on SMEs. However, these approaches have significant drawbacks since they complicate the VAT system, affect its integrity and increase compliance and administrative costs. In addition, it creates additional tax evasion risks. The application of such measures appears to be limited. Turkey reported the application of a special VAT exemption to supplies of goods and services to SMEs under specific circumstances, mainly in the context of investment projects.
- ***Special input tax refund procedures for SMEs:*** France reported that they apply special VAT refund procedures for SMEs. Under these procedures, eligible SMEs are entitled to ask for a VAT refund if upon filing of their annual VAT return there is a VAT credit of over EUR 150. They can also ask for a provisional VAT refund related to the acquisition of fixed assets if the relevant credit amount is at least EUR 760 or more.

### *Simplifications under other taxes*

Simplification measures may also be available with respect to a number of other taxes. These simplification provisions exist in relation to payroll deductions, where SMEs are required to withhold social security contributions and/or income tax on wages paid to employees; as well as simplification measures under excise tax provisions.

Several countries allow simplified calculation and remittance of payroll deductions and contributions. Studies of compliance costs have found that compliance costs initially increase as the business begins to hire staff, in part due to the increased compliance burden introduced by employee-related tax requirements, as well as other regulatory requirements.

Simplification measures related to payroll deductions reported by countries take the form of reduced filing requirements, as in Canada, the Netherlands and the United States, or allowing a small business to outsource their employment tax returns, as in Japan:

- Canada allows SMEs to benefit from reduced remittance and filing requirements for employer source deductions (including the Canada Pension Plan, the Employment Insurance and PIT) as well as corporate income tax and GST or HST. SMEs with average monthly withholdings of under CAD 3 000 may remit these deductions quarterly; between CAD 3 000 and 25 000, monthly, between CAD 25 000 and CAD 100 000, twice monthly, and over this limit, weekly.
- Self-employed individuals in the Netherlands can apply for exemptions to social security contributions by requesting a declaration from their local tax authority commissioner.

- In Japan, business operators with less than or equal to 50 employees (in the financial, insurance, real estate and retail sector) 100 employees (wholesale and service sector) or 300 employees, in all other sectors, can entrust payment of the labour insurance premiums and other matters concerning labour insurance to be conducted by the Labour Insurance Administration Association (associations of SMEs approved by the Minister of Health, Labour and Welfare). There is no distinction between corporations and natural persons operating SMEs.
- The United States requires employers to file quarterly returns of wages paid and withholding of income and payroll taxes. Small employers with an estimated employment tax of less than USD 1 000 may file on an annual basis.

Two countries report simplifications for small businesses for the payment of excise duties, allowing reduced filing requirements for SMEs. In Australia, small business can apply to defer settlement of excise duty and excise equivalent duties from a weekly to a monthly reporting cycle. In Canada, measures are in place to reduce the filing frequency of returns required of small remitters of federal excise levies. An entity may request in writing that the Canadian Revenue Agency (CRA) authorise a reporting period of a fiscal half-year rather than a fiscal month, if the total excise for the previous year is less than CAD 120 000. The person must also be licensed or registered with the CRA for over 12 months prior to authorisation and be in compliance with their excise obligations. This reduced filing requirement also applies to the Air Travellers Security charge.

## 4.3. Facilitating tax compliance for SMEs: where policy meets administration

Simplification measures can assist SME taxpayers to more easily meet their legal obligations under the tax system. Central to these measures will be the ability of the tax administration to facilitate compliance by delivering efficient procedures, good services, adequate guidance and taxpayer education. Tax policies and tax administration need to be aligned to be effective. Combining improvements in tax administration service delivery with streamlined regulatory arrangements and tax policy simplification measures is essential in addressing the compliance burden faced by SMEs.

Effective regulatory and administrative arrangements should recognise the specific circumstances of SMEs. In this sense, delivering a tax system that is tailored to some of the particular needs of SMEs is a challenge for many tax administrations. The heterogeneity of SMEs makes it difficult to administer the tax system in a way that effectively responds to the needs of SMEs. Many businesses, especially SMEs, find it difficult to grapple with the complexity and the relatively high compliance burden imposed on them when they enter the tax system. Equally, tax administrations face many challenges as they seek to provide services to reduce SME compliance costs and maximise tax compliance.

The OECD Forum on Tax Administration, over many years, has taken a more systematic approach towards SME tax compliance.[13] This section provides an overview of the various areas of a tax system that are important in fostering compliance by SME taxpayers and describes the main challenges that tax administrations face, in relation to SMEs, as they administer the tax system.

### *Tax compliance: a systemic approach*

The tax system should be seen as the whole of regulations, processes and actors that are involved in the process of taxation: policies and legislation, administrative regulations and procedures, administrative processes and compliance activities delivered by the tax administration, the compliance activities of taxpayers, and services from tax intermediaries as well as from other service providers (such as providers of accounting and filing software). Mechanisms to involve and engage the broader community are also part of the tax system. Supporting compliance by SMEs and preventing non-compliance will be the outcome of the interplay of all parties involved. In this context, the tax administration is responsible for its own service delivery, but also needs to act as a steward of the broader tax system.

### *Compliance Risk Management*

Tax compliance imposes demands in terms of the procedures and tax laws which must be followed, such as correct registration or payment rules. In broad terms, there are four categories of tax compliant behaviour (OECD, 2004):

- timely and correct registration;
- timely filing or lodgement of requisite taxation information;
- reporting of complete and accurate information (incorporating good record keeping); and
- payment of the right amount of tax on time.

For SME taxpayers observing tax rules involves significant costs relative to their turnover or income and requires specific knowledge and capabilities to fulfil all obligations correctly. The compliance burden that comes with entering the tax system may be an impediment to businesses moving from the informal to the formal economy or to fully comply with the tax rules once they have entered the system. The more a tax administration can provide services that make it easy to comply, the better the outcomes will be, both in terms of lowering the compliance burden and in observed compliance. It is however important to bear in mind that tax compliance is the outcome of the interplay of many factors and therefore attempts to improve levels of compliance need a comprehensive approach. Effective compliance strategies need to be multi-faceted and systemic.

Compliance refers to taxpayers' behaviour. This behaviour is the outcome of a wide array of variables, including the effect of deterrence (e.g. audits, perceived risk of detection and severity of sanctions); personal and social norms; opportunities for compliance or non-compliance (e.g. low compliance costs, easy rules or alternately, opportunities for evasion); fairness, related to outcomes and procedures, and trust, both in the government or the tax authority and in other taxpayers; and economic factors, including macroeconomic conditions, factors related to the business or industry and the amount of tax due (OECD, 2010).

To develop processes and interventions that effectively monitor and influence compliance, tax administrations need to follow a structured approach, which helps them to assess the strengths and weaknesses of the tax system and identify the relevant compliance risks for individual taxpayers or groups of taxpayers, such as SMEs. The OECD Forum on Tax Administration has a well-established framework, referred to as the Compliance Risk Management Model, which provides guidance in implementing such a structured approach (OECD, 2004).

Compliance risk management systematically assesses risks and opportunities in relation to specific tax laws, segments and industries, taxpayer behaviour and different tax processes. Strategies are designed to address those risks and include both upstream and downstream activities. "Upstream" refers to more preventive measures, such as taxpayer services, pre-filing audits, education and community outreach activities. "Downstream" are those measures targeted at detection and correction of flaws in tax returns after filing and will be more repressive. These strategies reinforce each other. Downstream activities such as audits have a direct effect in terms of revenue raised, but in the SME sector the indirect effects may be even more important: reinforcing social norms supportive of compliance and protecting fair competition by showing that the tax administration will deal with cases of deliberate non-compliant behaviour.

The compliance risk management model enables tax administrations to focus their attention on these domains and groups of taxpayers where non-compliant behaviour is more likely to occur. Interventions should take a systemic approach, looking at the causes for particular behaviours, if possible trying to adapt the processes and services, or the legislation, in such a way that they encourage desired future behaviour.

### *Right from the Start*

The OECD Information Note "Right from the Start: Influencing the Compliance Environment for Small or Medium Enterprises" (OECD, 2012) stresses the need to create an environment that is conducive to compliance. The focus of attention in that report shifts from risks for the tax administration towards supporting compliance from the perspective of the taxpayer. This also means shifting the attention from the stage after the filing of the tax return, to the pre-filing stage. The report addresses four perspectives:

1. Acting in real time and up-front, so that problems are prevented or addressed as they occur;
2. Focusing on end-to-end processes, rather than just focusing on the revenue body's processes;
3. Making it easy to comply (and difficult not to) by providing excellent services and streamlined processes to minimise error;
4. Actively involving and engaging taxpayers, their representatives and other stakeholders, in order to achieve a better understanding of the taxpayer's perspective and to co-operate with third parties.[14]

The "compliance environment" for SMEs includes stakeholders such as accountants and other tax intermediaries, industry organisations, providers of accounting software, banks and many others. Engagement of these stakeholders in the broader tax system will improve the outcomes and deliver better results for the SME taxpayer. Most tax administrations have only recently begun to develop strategies to more actively seek collaboration with these parties. A tax system which is "owned" by the broader society and in which stakeholders are involved and take responsibility, is likely to deliver better outcomes both for the taxpayer and for society as a whole. The co-operative compliance arrangements that the Netherlands Tax Administration has developed with businesses and tax intermediaries is an example of this.

## *Taking it one step further: emerging trends in SME tax compliance*

Recent developments in SME tax compliance include two major trends, both of which rely on technology:

- More focus is on building collaborative arrangements upfront, to ensure compliance right from the start and to reduce the costs of compliance to SMEs. The key to these approaches for SMEs is that compliance is "designed into" the business processes of the taxpayer and the value chain as a whole.

- Advanced business analytics enable tax administrations to make better use of the data they have available, or can obtain. This allows tax administrations to trace high risk taxpayers at an early stage and to detect high risk tax returns as they are lodged. It also enables the development of much better targeted services to ensure compliance and reduces the amount of information the SME is required to produce in order to comply.

### *Compliance by design*

Technology is changing the way SMEs operate. As the costs of software have fallen and the emergence of the "cloud" has enabled new ways of delivering technology, SMEs have gained access to new and sophisticated systems for managing their businesses. Most SMEs now use technology in some form to help them keep track of their business and to improve effectiveness. Information and payments are increasingly becoming digital. There is rapid growth of new payment systems using mobile devices and the use of electronic invoices is increasing. Electronic cash registers are used for handling cash transactions and a number of cheap and simple-to-use on-line accounting systems are available.

"Tax compliance by design" (OECD, 2014a) recognises these fundamental changes in the way SMEs operate and shows how tax compliance can become an integral part of the systems businesses use to carry out their daily transactions with one another and with their customers. Tax compliance can become easy and accurate if it is simply a by-product of the steps a business follows automatically to transact. "Tax compliance by design" assembles the different elements of technology associated with modern commerce into a system that delivers a seamless and secure flow of accurate tax information and tax payments.

There are two basic approaches to achieving tax compliance by design: the "secured chain approach" and the "centralised data approach" (OECD, 2014a). The secured chain approach creates a secured flow of information from the capture of business transactions to the final determination of the correct amount of tax being paid. The role of the tax administration is mainly to act as a facilitator of necessary environmental features in order to secure the flow of information from the taxpayer.

#### Box 4.4. **EasySME in Denmark**

An example of the secured chain approach is the concept of EasySME, which is being developed by the Danish Tax Administration (SKAT) in co-operation with accounting software developers in Denmark. The objective is to make it easier for small businesses to get an overview of the situation of their business and at the same time make it easier for them to comply with the tax legislation.

The concept requires that the taxpayer use one bank account for all business transactions. The system will use a standardised chart of accounts and is based on the use of certified accounting systems. This system will provide a help facility which provides guidance on tax issues. The content of this will be provided by SKAT. Tax returns are filed directly from the accounting system to SKAT.

The figure below depicts the main elements of the concept. To be certified as an EasySME accounting system, the system must show real-time updates of six key economic parameters, which gives the business a realistic and useful overview of the economic status and estimated taxes etc., for the entire fiscal year. After reporting of VAT and income, the Tax Administration recalculates the relevant key economic parameters and returns updated figures to the accounting system so that the business can make informed decisions. The EasySME concept is planned to be implemented step-by-step, starting in late 2016.

Box 4.4. **EasySME in Denmark** *(continued)*

**The concept of EasySME**

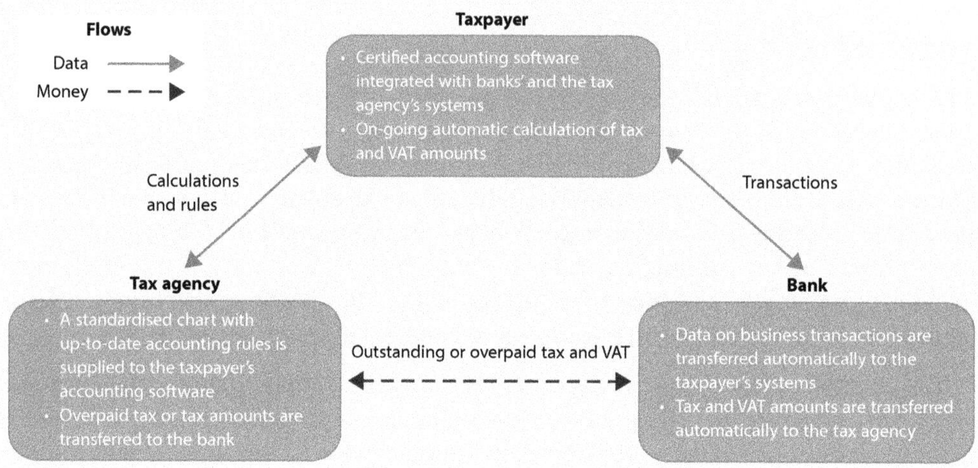


The benefits to SMEs do not just relate to tax compliance: the system will help them to use their bookkeeping system as a means to better run their business and at lower costs. At the same time it supports compliance by helping the taxpayer to file a correct tax return. Last but not least it will drive down costs for service and enforcement at the tax administration's end.

Under the centralised data approach, the tax administration captures relevant business transactions at their source in order to calculate the taxable income or VAT base, reducing the information sourced from the taxpayer and reducing the compliance burden. In this approach the tax administration plays a key role as "financial data centre". Although such an approach will most likely have difficulty capturing all data it can provide feasible compliance solutions, although this may depend on financial sector co-operation, the type of industry and the possibilities to capture cross-border transactions.

A key feature of both approaches is that tax processes are highly integrated with the underlying business processes. Tax compliance is to a large extent "embedded" in the daily business processes. This makes tax compliance processes more trustworthy and seamless, and makes it easier and less costly for the SME taxpayer to comply. As the tax administration will receive better and timelier information, it can follow-up more swiftly thus providing SME taxpayers with more certainty on their tax position.

### *Advanced analytics*

The availability of data and sophisticated analytical tools enable tax administrations to build more targeted and more effective approaches to securing and maintaining high levels of tax compliance. Tax administrations hold a vast array of data and over the last couple of years tax administrations have been able to bring these data from different legacy systems together by building an integrated data-layer, in a way that allows more in depth and continuous analysis of taxpayers' compliance behaviour. Data on past behaviour can help to predict possible future behaviour and assess whether a taxpayer would have a higher risk of non-compliance. The Australian Tax Office uses this kind of analysis in an online environment to decide whether a taxpayer is eligible for specific payment arrangements, or whether a further assessment is needed. This kind of analysis also helps to track down those taxpayers who may be involved in more severe tax fraud, such as carousel fraud and identity fraud. Advanced analytics is also helpful in identifying groups of taxpayers who would need a specific approach, based on their profile.

Tax processes for all companies, including SMEs, have traditionally been characterised by complex and formal regulations and came with relatively high compliance burdens. These regulations typically involved taxpayers filling out and filing tax returns, making formal appeals or following strict procedures for payment arrangements. Technology can make these procedures more real-time, more streamlined and less costly for the taxpayer and the tax administration. Technology can also help to tailor the work processes of the tax administration to the needs of the SME taxpayer, by facilitating compliance upfront and in more effectively addressing (or even preventing) non-compliance. These developments increase the amount of information held by the tax administration, which gives rise to questions regarding privacy, security and trust. Transparency, predictability and proportionality are key principles that can guide tax administrations in their approach to addressing these considerations in a balanced way.

### *Addressing tax evasion and fraud*

Addressing deliberate tax evasion and fraud is important for any tax administration to secure the tax base and help maintain trust and confidence in the integrity of the tax system. The strategies of tax administrations are not just targeted at helping the "willing" taxpayer by making compliance easier, but must also seek to drive out tax evasion by reducing the opportunities for deliberate non-compliant behaviour by making it difficult not to comply. In addition, strengthening the information available to the tax administration and deploying modern analytical techniques, open further opportunities to detect, address and stop tax fraud.

#### Box 4.5. Chile: Electronic VAT Invoicing System

The Electronic Invoicing System, launched in 2002, allows business taxpayers to issue and receive invoices, which are immediately available to the revenue body of Chile (SII). The system is available to all business taxpayers via commercial software products and in the "SII electronic invoicing system" offered for free in the SII's website. The "SII electronic invoicing system" seeks to provide taxpayers with a basic application to issue tax documents, which is especially useful for micro, small and medium enterprises.

The SII electronic invoicing system also provides both a simplified and complete accounting system for businesses, free of charge. The simplified accounting system is for businesses that choose to follow a special simplified taxation category and have sales under USD 2 000 000 per annum. The simplified system enables businesses to keep records of sales, purchases and other business expenses, such as salaries and wages, to calculate taxable income, to generate prefilled tax returns and to produce a standard financial report. The complete accounting system provides enhanced functionality for businesses including generation of complete financial statements on a monthly basis across the financial year and generation of prefilled monthly and annual tax returns, as well as other mandatory forms that are required to be submitted.

In order to process and cross check the information, the SII has implemented a system ("VAT PRO") which consolidates and compares the data on sales and purchases, provided to the SII through the e-tax documents, affidavits, other sources and the information obtained from the VAT declarations. Depending on the discrepancies detected, the SII defines the actions of control to implement.

### Box 4.5. Chile: Electronic VAT Invoicing System *(continued)*

In January 2014, the Government approved legislation that mandated the use of the Electronic Invoicing System by all businesses. A phased roll-out is underway, with all businesses scheduled to be using the system by early 2018.

**Chile's Electronic VAT Invoicing System**

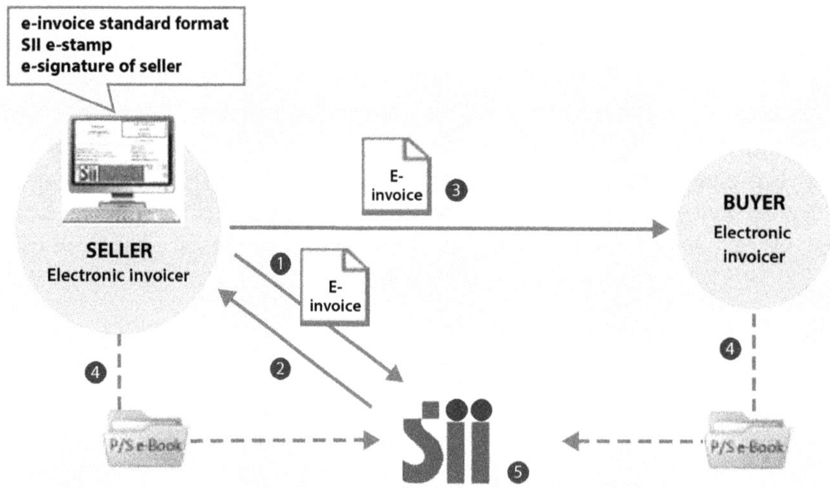


1. Seller, electronic invoicer, issues an electronic invoice.
2. Electronic invoice (xml format) is authorised online by the SII.
3. Buyer electronic invoicer receives the electronic invoice in xml format.
4. Both, seller and buyer, send the Purchase and Sales e-book to the SII on a monthly basis.
5. SII consolidates, cross checks and processes information provided by taxpayers and third parties.

*Source:* Electronic Documents: Solutions for Small and Medium Businesses, Chile Internal Revenue Service.

The SME sector includes elements of the "cash economy" or the "hidden economy". Technological developments as outlined earlier may also give rise to new threats to the tax system. Mobile payment services for example and the use of foreign bank accounts may help to hide income from the tax authorities. At the same time the growth of electronic payments provides better opportunities for tax administrations to obtain data on income and sales by SMEs. For example, some countries, such as Spain and Turkey, have introduced mandatory third party reporting on transactions via bankcards.

Tax administrations are deploying new strategies, which are based on a whole-of-government approach and by leveraging off the increased access of governments to information. Monitoring transactions real-time and analysing patterns of behaviour and network relations hold new opportunities to track down illicit activities, non-reported income or fraudulent schemes.

As tax administrations focus more on upfront strategies and improve their analytical capabilities, more costly downstream activities such as audits and investigations will be more targeted at high risk taxpayers. For some tax administrations a decrease has been observed in the number of audits that are carried out. Traditionally a desk or field audit would in many cases be a first response to any anomalies found in tax returns. Today tax administrations deploy a much broader set of strategies and treatments, focusing more on prevention and on effects on the behaviour of the broader group of taxpayers. A smaller number of audits may be more effective and deliver better outcomes, if part of a broader strategy.

## 4.4. Policy conclusions

### *Tax simplifications for SMEs*

There are a wide range of simplification measures for SMEs encompassing simplified single replacement tax regimes as well as simplification measures under specific taxes, including VAT, income taxes, employment taxes and excise taxes. These are summarised in Table 4.8.

The primary reason for simplification measures for SMEs is that tax compliance costs are disproportionately high for SMEs with regard to their turnover, making tax compliance costs regressive for many SMEs. These increased compliance costs may affect a number of the economic margins faced by SMEs, as summarised in Figure 4.1.

Figure 4.1. **Summary of impact of simplification measures on economic margins of SME owners**

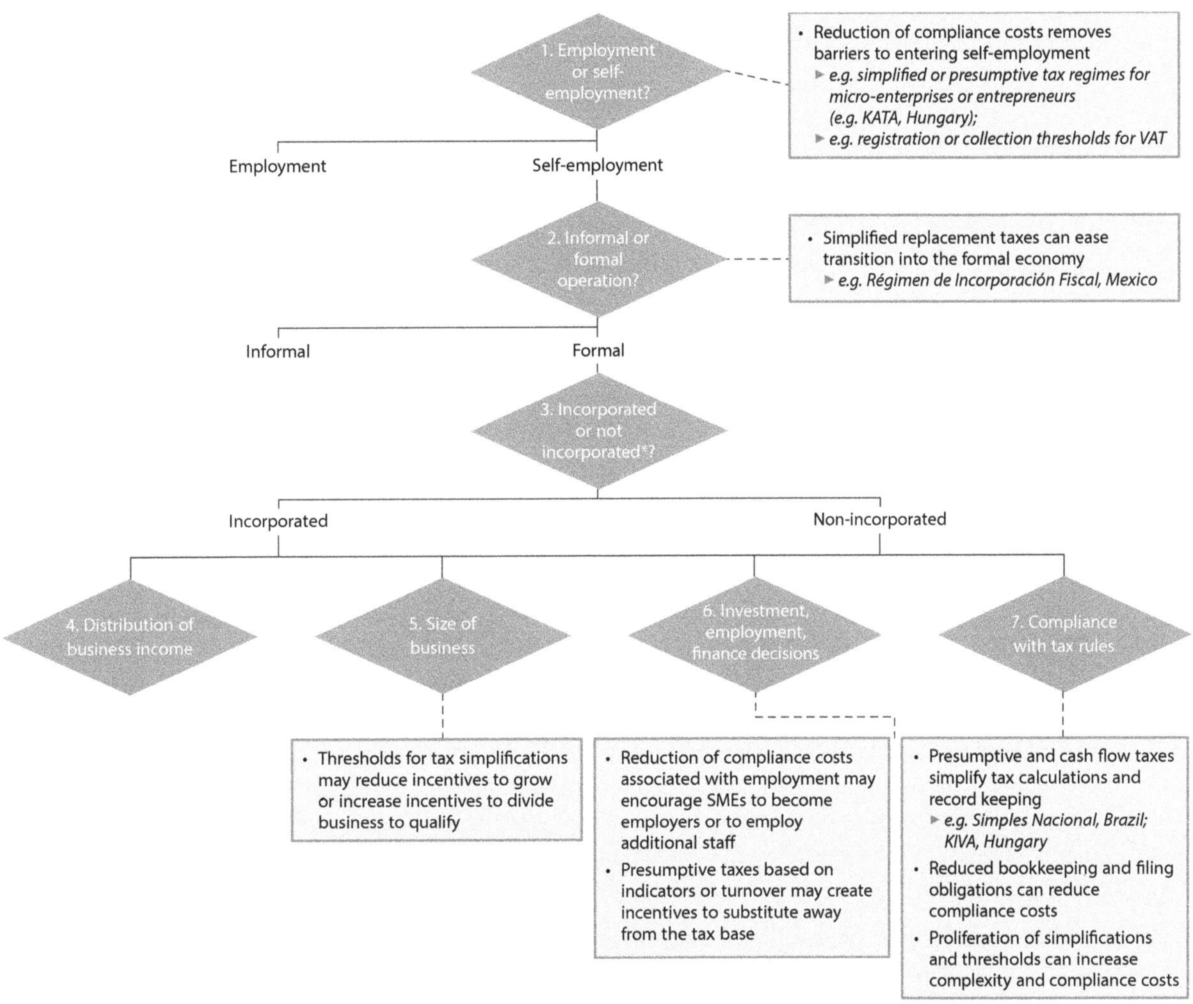

A disproportionately high compliance burden for SMEs may hinder business growth through the opportunity costs they impose. They can also distort business decisions, particularly those relating to employment. They can act as a deterrent to entry into self-employment. Finally, high tax compliance costs may be a deterrent to entering the formal sector, or to compliance with particular tax rules. Tax simplifications for SMEs may promote compliance to the extent that they reduce these costs, for example by providing relief from record-keeping and tax filing rules and assisting SMEs with their cash flow.

The simplification measures adopted by OECD and G20 countries in certain cases differ from the standard income or value-added tax regime only in matters of procedure, for example, permitting reduced frequency of filing and payment of VAT and income taxes, or simplified bookkeeping requirements. However in other cases, there is a pronounced departure from standard tax provisions. This is notably the case for presumptive tax schemes for the calculation of VAT or income tax liabilities, which result in a different tax base than standard calculations, or for VAT exemption thresholds.

Turnover is the most common criterion for determining eligibility for the different simplification measures observed in OECD and G20 countries. Its appeal relies on the fact that almost every SME will know the value of its total sales, therefore making it relatively easy to monitor and comply with. However, other indicators may be used to determine eligibility, for example, firms in particular sectors, or with a particular number of employees. Under presumptive taxes, eligibility criteria may encompass objective parameters such as electricity consumed, floor space or facilities, or total number of employees.

In principle, the different simplification approaches are often optional, allowing SMEs a varying degree of flexibility and in some cases avoiding some of the downsides of various simplification measures (e.g. cash flow accounting may reduce cash flow in circumstances where deductions must be deferred until the expense is paid). In these circumstances, SMEs may consider the impact of both the simplification and standard regime and decide accordingly, although this can in itself increase complexity. For instance, it is normal practice among the countries that replied to the questionnaire to allow firms below the exemption threshold to register voluntarily for VAT since exemptions that occur early in the transaction chain introduce a cascading effect as the non-deductible tax on inputs is embedded in the subsequent selling price and is not recoverable by taxpayers further down the supply chain. SMEs characterised by a high ratio of sales to private consumers are likely[15] to find it advantageous to be exempt from VAT. While SMEs selling to other registered firms would wish to register for VAT in order to benefit from the deduction of input VAT. Similarly, reduced VAT return filing schemes may not suit all businesses.[16] This is often the case for businesses that regularly claim refunds of input VAT because they will only be able to get a refund when they submit their return.

From a tax authority's perspective assessing the impact of a specific simplification measure may not be simply a matter of balancing between administrative cost savings and revenue loss. A number of other dimensions need to be carefully considered. Simplification measures may introduce distortions into the system by favouring eligible SMEs over businesses subject to the standard regime. In the case of exemption thresholds the distortion of competition could be addressed by setting a relatively low VAT threshold that would encourage participation by a greater number of firms. Similarly, presumptive taxes may also distort firm decisions as the amount of tax paid is not directly tied to income: for example, under a turnover based tax, a highly profitable firm will pay less tax, as a percentage of their income, than a less profitable firm.

The introduction of simplified measures may also provide disincentives for growth. For example, a SME close to the threshold for a presumptive tax or VAT exemption may prefer to keep the volume of its business below the threshold so as to continue benefiting from the simplified regime, both in terms of reduced compliance costs as well as tax payable. It therefore becomes critical to find ways to encourage borderline businesses to increase the volume of their economic activity and as a next step to smooth their transition to the standard regime once the conditions for a simplification scheme are no longer met. Flexible thresholds and gradual tax reductions are included among the means deployed by the countries that responded to the questionnaire.

Simplification schemes may also frustrate policy efforts to have all persons actively participate in the formal economy, in the sense that once outside the system it may be less likely for individuals to decide at some point to fully participate. This is notably the case for VAT exemption thresholds. This potential adverse effect could be partly addressed if SMEs below the exemption threshold (and not opting into the normal system) are required to pay another, simpler, form of tax (e.g. a simple lump sum patent, with minimal compliance costs) and thereby become part of the "formal" economy.

Caution should be taken to ensure that simplification measures do not reduce the integrity of the tax system by creating additional tax evasion risks. Putting in place the appropriate safeguards to avoid fraudulent use of optional simplification schemes should also be considered. For example to avoid VAT frauds by fly-by-night traders who may register for VAT and ask for a refund on an ad hoc basis several countries impose a minimum period of time during which taxpayers that have opted to register voluntarily must remain registered. Similarly, rules should be introduced to ensure that larger companies cannot benefit from simplification provisions or exemptions through the establishment of smaller companies.

Finally a key consideration is that the establishment of simplified schemes should not further increase the compliance burden of the tax system. The need to monitor compliance with eligibility criteria, to understand the different applicable rules and to calculate the benefit of simplified schemes against general rules, can introduce complexity rather than remove it. Further, simplified bookkeeping requirements may mean that SMEs maintain less comprehensive financial records, with detrimental consequences to the business.

Ideally, simplification measures should ensure that as far as possible taxes are not an impediment to SMEs' creation or growth, while minimising the distortionary effects that can be introduced by simplification measures themselves. This can be a rather complex exercise which requires careful consideration of many different parameters, including both the national context and SME characteristics.

## *Policy and administration: different sides of the same coin*

Both the OECD 2004 and 2012 reports emphasise that "…good compliance outcomes begin with good legislation." Regulations that are complex and burdensome can only be partially compensated by tailored services. Equally, simple legislation, or simplified tax requirements for SMEs, will have little effect if the tax administration does not administer the legislation in such a way that it supports the intended outcome, which is making tax procedures easier for SMEs.

Legislation that is clear and unambiguous provides a solid base for compliant behaviour, especially as this can be supported by online bookkeeping and filing systems that assure high quality tax returns. Such systems can capture business transactions by connecting to e-invoicing systems or scanning techniques. Legislation and other regulations can be expressed in "business rules", to be implemented in the system. As every transaction will follow the same predefined procedure and interpretation, reports and tax returns delivered by this system will have a high level of assurance. Such a strategy requires both legislation and tax administration policies to be designed and expressed clearly.

Table 4.8. **Summary of simplification measures for SMEs**

| | | Income tax simplifications | | | | VAT simplifications | | | | | | |
|---|---|---|---|---|---|---|---|---|---|---|---|---|
| | | | | | | | Calculation of VAT/GST liability | | Accounting, payment, filing | | | |
| | Single replacement tax regimes | Presumptive taxes | Simplified accounting | Reduced filing requirements | Other | Exemption thresholds | Presumptive tax schemes | Simplified input tax credit calculation schemes | Cash accounting | Reduced frequency of filing | Other | Other taxes |
| Argentina | | | | | | | Y | | | | Y | |
| Australia | | | Y | | Y | Y | | Y | Y | Y | Y | Y |
| Austria | | Y | Y | | | Y | | Y | Y | Y | Y | |
| Belgium | | | | | | Y | Y | | | Y | Y | |
| Brazil | Y | Y | | | | | Y | | Y | Y | Y | |
| Canada | | | Y | Y | Y | Y | Y | Y | | Y | Y | Y |
| Chile | | Y | Y | | | | Y | | | Y | | |
| China | | Y | | | | | Y | | | Y | | |
| Czech Republic | | Y | Y | | | Y | | | | Y | | |
| Denmark | | Y | | Y | Y | Y | | | | Y | | |
| Estonia | | | | | | Y | | | Y | | | |
| Finland | | | | | | Y | | | | Y | | |
| France | | Y | | | | Y | Y | | | Y | Y | |
| Germany | | | Y | | | Y | | Y | Y | | | |
| Greece | | | | | | Y | Y | | Y | | Y | |
| Hungary | Y | Y | | Y | | Y | | | Y | Y | Y | |
| Iceland | | | | | | Y | | | | | | |
| India | | Y | Y | Y | Y | | | | | | | |
| Ireland | | | | | | Y | | | Y | Y | | |
| Italy | Y | Y | Y | | | Y | | | Y | Y | Y | |
| Japan | | Y | | Y | | Y | | Y | | | | Y |
| Korea | | | | | | Y | Y | | | | Y | |
| Luxembourg | | | | | | Y | | | Y | Y | Y | |
| Mexico | Y | | Y | Y | | | Y | | Y | Y | Y | Y |
| Netherlands | | | | | | Y | | | | | Y | |
| New Zealand | | | Y | | | Y | | | Y | Y | | |
| Norway | | | | | | Y | | | | Y | | |
| Poland | | Y | Y | Y | | Y | | | Y | Y | Y | |
| Portugal | | Y | | | | Y | | | Y | Y | Y | |
| Slovak Republic | | Y | Y | | | Y | | | | | | |
| Slovenia | | Y | | | | Y | | | Y | | | |
| South Africa | Y | Y | | | | Y | | | Y | Y | Y | |
| Spain | | Y | Y | | | | Y | | | Y | Y | |
| Sweden | | | Y | | | | | | Y | Y | | |
| Switzerland | | | | | | Y | Y | | | Y | Y | |
| Turkey | Y | | Y | Y | | | | | | | Y | |
| United Kingdom | | | Y | Y | | Y | Y | | Y | Y | Y | |
| United States | | | Y | Y | | | | | | | | Y |

*Source:* Responses to an OECD questionnaire, *Survey on the Taxation of Small and Medium-Sized Enterprises*, 2015.

Reducing the compliance burden of SME taxpayers may necessitate reducing complexity of the different tax laws or introducing the types of simplification measures discussed above. It also relates to ensuring that more formal regulations, such as the procedures regarding filing, record keeping requirements, procedures for appeal or payment delays, are not unnecessarily complex. An effective tax system for SMEs is a system in which policy, legislation, compliance strategies and taxpayer services are carefully aligned. Such a system is the most likely to reduce compliance burdens for SMEs, promote SME compliance and lower costs for the tax administration.

## Notes

1. European Commission (2007), p 12.
2. See for example Hansford and Hasseldine (2012), Hasseldine et al. (2012) and PriceWaterhouseCoopers (2009).
3. OECD (2014b) and consultation with national officials.
4. For ease of reading, in this study, VAT (value added tax) refers to any national tax that embodies certain basic features, i.e. a broad-based tax on consumption which is collected through a staged process where each business in the supply chain takes part in controlling and collecting the tax, remitting the proportion of tax corresponding to its margin i.e. on the difference between the VAT imposed on its taxed inputs and the VAT imposed on its taxed outputs.
5. See for example European Commission (2012), where VAT was identified as the most burdensome area of EU regulation for both EU and non-EU SMEs.
6. A VAT compliance cost analysis in Sweden (Skatteverket, 2006) found that businesses with 1-4 employees had 35 times higher VAT compliance costs per employee than those with 50-499 employees.
7. See, for example, Harju et al. (2015), which found that the Finnish VAT threshold has notable effects in causing small firms to bunch just below the threshold, largely due to reductions in output.
8. The IMF proposes that the optimal turnover threshold for VAT collection should be increased, at the margin, if the benefits to the taxpayer in terms of reduced tax payments and compliance costs exceed the net cost to government of the same increase in terms of reduced tax receipts less administration costs, weighted by the value of public funds (Ebrill et al., 2001).
9. Special input tax deduction rules may apply depending on the country. This is the case for example in Chile and Spain. In the United Kingdom, a SME under the flat rate scheme may recover in the normal way the VAT incurred on the purchase of capital assets of a VAT inclusive value of GBP 2000 or more.
10. The base (reference year) for taxable sales (turnover) threshold is two years preceding the current year.
11. It has been argued (see European Commission, 2011) that this increases compliance costs – ironic when the scheme exists precisely to reduce them – as well as ensuring the maximum revenue loss for the government.

12. Temporary additional requirements shall be meet in 2015 (business income not exceeding UF 25 000 in the previous year) and 2016 (business income not exceeding UF 100 000 in the previous year)

13. Such strategies are further explored in a recent study by the Forum on Tax Administration, "Tax Compliance by Design", OECD (2014).

14. This is further explored in OECD (2013), *Together for Better Outcomes: Engaging and Involving SME Taxpayers and Stakeholders*, OECD Publishing

15. If it cannot pass the unrecovered input tax along to the buyer (perhaps because the demand for its product is highly elastic) then the real burden of the tax will have to be borne by the SME.

16. In South Africa, a facilitating provision for reduced frequency of filing for SMEs (every four months) with turnover less than ZAR 1.5 million was withdrawn due to limited use.

# *References*


Agha, A., and J. Haughton (1996), "Designing VAT Systems: Some Efficiency Considerations", *Review of Economics and Statistics*, 78(2), 303-308.

Australian Treasury (2015), *Stocktake of Regulation.* Australian Government, Canberra, www.treasury.gov.au/~/media/Treasury/Publications%20and%20Media/Publications/2015/Stocktake%20of%20Regulation%20Final%20Report/Downloads/PDF/Stocktake-of-Regulation.ashx.

Canadian Department of Industry (2013), *SME Regulatory Compliance Cost Report – September 2013*, Report of the Paperwork Burden Reduction Initative, Ottawa, www.reducingpaperburden.gc.ca/eic/site/pbri-iafp.nsf/eng/sx00146.html?Open&pv=1.

Corseuil, C., L. Henrique and R. Moura (2011), "O Impacto Do Simples Federal No Nível De Emprego Da Indústria Brasileira", *Instituto de Pesquisa Econômica Aplicada,* Texto Para Discussão, 1643, Agosto de 2011, www.ipea.gov.br/portal/images/stories/PDFs/TDs/td_1643.pdf.

Davis Tax Committee (2014), *Small & Medium Enterprises: Taxation Considerations, Interim Report,* www.treasury.gov.za/TaxReviewCommittee/DTC%20SME%20Report%20for%20Public%20Comment%2014%20July%202014.pdf.

Ebrill, L., M. Keen, J. Bodin, and V. Summers (eds) (2001), *The Modern VAT*, International Monetary Fund, Washington.

Erard, B. (1997), "The Income Tax Compliance Burden on Small and Medium-sized Canadian Businesses", *Carleton University Working Paper, 97-12*, www.collectionscanada.gc.ca/webarchives/20071205172155/www.fin.gc.ca/taxstudy/wp97-12e.pdf.

European Commission (2012), on "Top 10 most burdensome legislative acts for SMEs", http://ec.europa.eu/enterprise/policies/sme/files/smes/top10report-final_en.pdf.

European Commission (2011), *A retrospective evaluation of elements of the EU VAT system: Final Report,* http://ec.europa.eu/taxation_customs/resources/documents/common/publications/studies/report_evaluation_vat.pdf.

European Commission (2007), *Simplified Tax Compliance Procedures for SMEs – Final Report of the Expert Group,* EC Publishing, Brussels, http://ec.europa.eu/enterprise/policies/sme/files/support_measures/taxsimple/taxsimp_en.pdf.

Gale, W., and S. Brown. "Small Business, Innovation, and Tax Policy: A Review", *Tax Policy Center Urban Institute & Brookings Institution,* http://mpra.ub.uni-muenchen.de/57384/1/1001675-Small-Business-Innovation-and-Tax-Policy-A-Review.pdf.

Government of India (2006), *Definitions of Micro, Small & Medium Enterprises,* www.dcmsme.gov.in/ssiindia/defination_msme.htm.

Hansford, A., and J. Hasseldine (2012), "Tax compliance costs for small and medium size enterprises (SMEs): the case of the UK", *eJournal of Tax Research,* volume 10, number 2, https://ore.exeter.ac.uk/repository/bitstream/handle/10871/15816/hansford_tax%20compliance.pdf?sequence=2.

Harju, J., T. Matikka and T. Rauhanen (2015), "The Effect of VAT Threshold on the Behavior of Small Businesses: Evidence and Implications" Report prepared for the *CESifo Area Conference on Public Sector Economics,* https://www.cesifo-group.de/dms/ifodoc/docs/Akad_Conf/CFP_CONF/CFP_CONF_2015/pse15-van-der-Ploeg/Papers/Harju.pdf.

Hasseldine, J., C. Evans, A. Hansford, P. Lignier, S. Smulders and F. Vaillancourt (2012), *A comparative analysis of tax compliance costs and the role of special concessions and regimes for small businesses in Australia, Canada, South Africa and the United Kingdom,* www.charteredaccountants.com.au/~/media/Files/Industry%20topics/Tax/General%20Tax/A%20comparative%20analysis%20of%20tax%20compliance%20costs_RhodeIsland.ashx.

IBFD (2015), *IBFD Tax Research Platform,* accessed at http://online.ibfd.org/kbase.

IBFD (2013), *EU VAT Compass 2013/2014,* IBFD Publications, Amsterdam.

International Tax Dialogue (2013), *A Decade of Sharing Tax Experiences and Knowledge, Key Issues and Debates in VAT, SME Taxation and the Tax Treatment of the Financial Sector,* International Tax Dialogue, Paris.

Lignier, P., C. Evans and B. Tran-Nam (2014), "Tangled up in tape: The continuing tax compliance plight of the small and medium enterprise business sector", *Australian Tax Forum*, vol. 29, no.2, pp.217-247.

Lignier, P. and C. Evans (2012), "The rise and rise of tax compliance costs for the small business sector in Australia", *Australian Tax Forum* vol. 27, no.2, pp.615-672.

Monteiro, J. and J. Assunção (2009), "Outgoing the shadows: estimating the impact of bureaucracy simplification and tax cut on formality and investment", *Journal of Development Economics*, 99(1), 105-115,www.ie.ufrj.br/datacenterie/pdfs/seminarios/pesquisa/texto_05_09.pdf.

OECD (2015), *OECD Tax Database*, www.oecd.org/tax/tax-policy/tax-database.htm.

OECD (2014a), *Tax Compliance by Design: Achieving Improved SME Tax Compliance by Adopting a System Perspective*, OECD Publishing, Paris, http://dx.doi.org/10.1787/9789264223219-en.

OECD (2014b), *OECD Economic Surveys: Turkey 2014*, OECD Publishing, Paris, http://dx.doi.org/10.1787/eco_surveys-tur-2014-en.

OECD (2013), *Together for Better Outcomes: Engaging and Involving SME Taxpayers and Stakeholders*, OECD Publishing, Paris, http://dx.doi.org/10.1787/9789264200838-en.

OECD (2012), *Right from the Start: Influencing the Compliance Environment for SMEs*, Information Note, www.oecd.org/site/ctpfta/49428016.pdf.

OECD (2011), Supporting the Development of More Effective Tax Systems, *a report to the G-20 Development Working Group by the IMF, OECD, UN and World Bank.*

OECD (2010), *Understanding and Influencing Taxpayers' Compliance behaviour*, Information Note, www.oecd.org/ctp/administration/46274793.pdf.

OECD (2009), *Taxation of SMEs: Key Issues and Policy Considerations, OECD Tax Policy Studies*, No. 18, OECD Publishing, Paris, http://dx.doi.org/10.1787/9789264024748-en.

OECD (2004), *Compliance Risk Management: Managing and Improving Tax Compliance*, Guidance Note, www.oecd.org/ctp/administration/33818656.pdf.

President's Advisory Panel on Federal Tax Reform (2005), *Simple, Fair and Pro-Growth: Proposals to Fix America's Tax System.* Available at: www.treasury.gov/resource-center/tax-policy/Documents/Simple-Fair-and-Pro-Growth-Proposals-to-Fix-Americas-Tax-System-11-2005.pdf.

PriceWaterhouseCoopers (2009), *Small Medium Enterprises Total Tax Contribution Report* (Report Commissioned by the Australian Department of the Treasury, http://taxreview.treasury.gov.au/content/html/commissioned_work/downloads/pricewaterhousecoopers.pdf.

Skatteverket (Swedish National Tax Board) (2006), "Compliance Costs of Value-Added Tax in Sweden", Report 3B, Stockholm.

Terkper, Seth (2003), "Managing Small- and Medium-Size Taxpayers in Development Countries", *Tax Notes International*, 29, 13 January, 211-234.

The World Bank Group (2007), *Designing a Tax System for Micro and Small Businesses: Guide for Practitioners*, World Bank, Washington.

# *Annex A*

# Exchange rates

Table A1. **Exchange rates used in relation to the country responses to the SME tax questionnaire**

| Country (currency) [a] | Exchange Rate (currency/EUR) | Exchange Rate (EUR/Currency) |
|---|---|---|
| Australia (Australian dollar) | 1.4719 | 0.6794 |
| Brazil (Brazilian real) | 3.1230 | 0.3202 |
| Canada (Canadian dollar) | 1.4676 | 0.6814 |
| Chile (Chilean peso) [b] | 756.6335 | 0.0013 |
| China, People's Republic of (Chinese yuan) | 8.1510 | 0.1227 |
| Colombia (Colombian peso) | 2655.9387 | 0.0004 |
| Czech Republic (Czech koruna) | 27.5408 | 0.0363 |
| Denmark (Danish krone) | 7.4466 | 0.1343 |
| Hungary (Hungarian forint) | 308.6131 | 0.0032 |
| Iceland (Icelandic króna) | 154.9256 | 0.0065 |
| India (Indian rupee) | 80.9686 | 0.0124 |
| Indonesia (Indonesian rupiah) | 15742.6182 | 0.0001 |
| Israel (Israeli new shekel) | 4.7471 | 0.2107 |
| Japan (Japanese yen) | 140.5663 | 0.0071 |
| Korea (South Korean won) | 1397.1361 | 0.0007 |
| Mexico (Mexican peso) | 17.6363 | 0.0567 |
| New Zealand (New Zealand dollar) | 1.5993 | 0.6253 |
| Norway (Norweigan krone) | 8.3610 | 0.1196 |
| Poland (Polish złoty) | 4.1854 | 0.2389 |
| Russia (Russian rouble) | 50.9197 | 0.0196 |
| South Africa (South African rand) | 14.3992 | 0.0694 |
| Sweden (Swedish krona) | 9.1028 | 0.1099 |
| Switzerland (Swiss franc) | 1.2156 | 0.8226 |
| Turkey (Turkish lira) | 2.9037 | 0.3444 |
| United Kingdom (pound sterling) | 0.8063 | 1.2403 |
| United States (US dollar) | 1.3268 | 0.7537 |

*Source:* OECD database, available from: http://data.oecd.org/conversion/exchangerates.htm

*Notes:* a. Exchange rates reflect monthly averages across 2014

b. The rate of exchange used to convert the Chilean *Unidad de Fomento* (UF) to Chilean Peso was 1:25 626.15 (average of 6 months to 30 July). The rate of exchange of *Unidad Tributaria Mensual* (UTM) to *Unidad Tributaria Annual* (UTA) used was 1:12, the average for each month of 2014.

# *Annex B*

# Detailed SME characteristics from questionnaire responses

## B1. General caveats

General caveats that apply to all figures and tables from questionnaire data include:

1. Total employment, firm and taxable profit statistics for individual countries have been calculated through summation of incorporated and unincorporated data. Additional data provided by questionnaire respondents for country totals that differed from the data provided by categorised firm size (by employees or turnover) has not been included.
2. Exchange rates used to calculate Euro values are viewable in Annex A.
3. Totals may not add exactly due to rounding.
4. All data provided was from the latest available statistics unless specified otherwise in Table B1.

Table B1. **Country-specific notes to the figures and tables based on questionnaire responses**

| | |
|---|---|
| Australia | • Data is based on unit record (micro) tax return data for 2011-12 (employee counts are estimates based on payment summary data).<br>• Classification of firms by gross turnover is calculated in AUS Dollars [not EUR]. |
| Brazil | • Data for firms larger than 100 employees have been reclassified as 100-249 employees |
| Czech Republic | • Classification of firms by gross turnover is calculated in CZK [not EUR].<br>• Corporate income tax categories have been synthesised as follows:<br>*(i)* 0-1, 1-10, 10-100 = 0-100, *(ii)* 100-300 = 100-250, *(iii)* 300-500 = 250-500, *(iv)* above 1000 = 1000-2000<br>• Personal income tax categories have been synthesised as follows:<br>*(i)* 0-123 = 0-100, *(ii)* 123-191, 191-297 = 100-250, *(iii)* 297-421, 421-583 = 250-500 |
| Finland | • Data does not include information for businesses with no employed staff<br>• Gross turnover statistics were reclassified as follows *(i)* 0-39, 40-99 = 0-100, *(ii)* (100-399)*0.5 = 100-250, *(iii)* (100-399)*0.5 = 250-500, *(iv)* (400-2000)*0.33 = 500-1000, *(v)* (400-2000)*0.66 = 1000-2000, *(vi)* 10000-39999 = 10000-50000, *(vii)* 40000-199999 + 200000 |
| Germany | • Discrepancy between total firm numbers and Federal Statistical Office's figures as tax numbers are removed during aggregation process.<br>• The overviews and analyses include data only on those companies for which complete data were available. Data lacking clear identifiers were not taken into account (for data based on employment size class, this affected roughly two-thirds of companies covered under trade tax statistics; for data based on classification according to turnover, this affected nearly one-fourth).<br>• The breakdown into single-taxed and double-taxed entities does not take into account the special case of German *Personengesellschaften*. In this study, *Personengesellschaften* are categorised exclusively as single-taxed entities. However, in Germany corporations subject to double taxation participate in *Personengesellschaften*. Thus a clear classification of *Personengesellschaften* as either single-taxed or double-taxed entities is not possible |
| India | • Data excludes information on *(i)* employees whom are daily wagers or employees not subject to TDS (withholding tax) on salary, or where employers have not filed TDS statements, *(ii)* employees in entities not filing Income Tax returns for AY 2014-15, and *(iii)* data with incorrect Permanent Account Number |

| | |
|---|---|
| Ireland | • No data for firms with greater than 250 employees due to Irish Tax and Customs obligations to observe confidentiality of these firms |
| Japan | • Unincorporated businesses are defined as individual proprietorships<br>• Size of firm classifications adapted as follows *(i)* 100-249 = 100-299, *(ii)* 250+ = 300+ |
| Korea | • Size of gross revenue classifications adapted to *(i)* 100-250 = 100-300, *(ii)* 250-500 = 300-500 |
| Spain | • Employment statistics for unincorporated firms classified by number of employees were reclassified as follows: *(i)* 0, 1-2, 3-5, 6-9 = 0-9, *(ii)* 10-20, 21-49 = 10-49, *(iii)* more than 50 = 50-99 |
| Sweden | • Number of firms statistics classified by number of employees were reclassified as follows: *(i)* 0, 1-4, 5-9 = 0-9, *(ii)* 10-10, 20-49 = 10-49, *(iii)* 100-199 = 100-250, *(iv)* 200-499, 500+ = 250+ |
| United States | • Classification of firms by gross turnover is calculated in USD |

## B2. Detailed SME characteristics

Figure B1. **Relative number of firms at different entity sizes (by level of turnover) in each country**

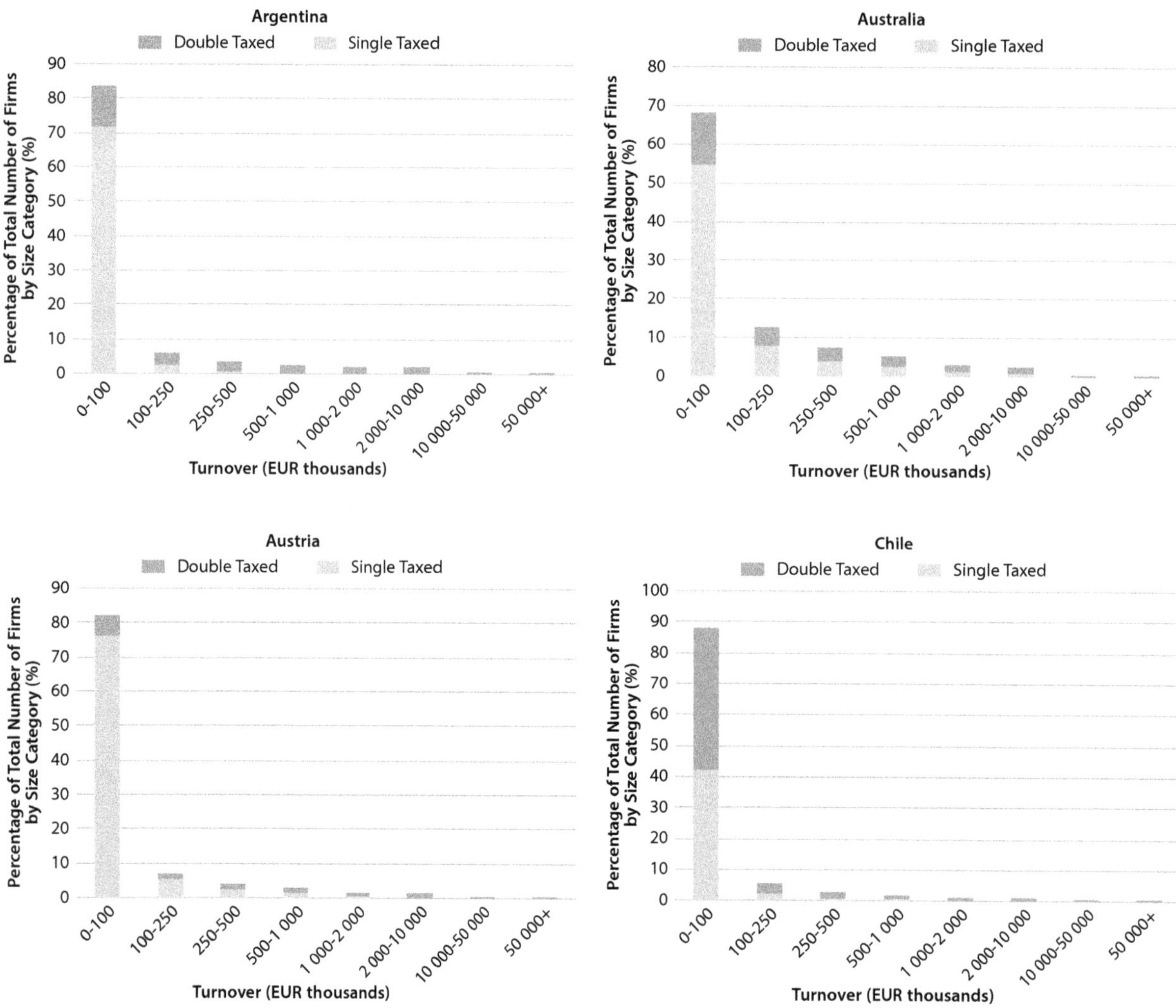

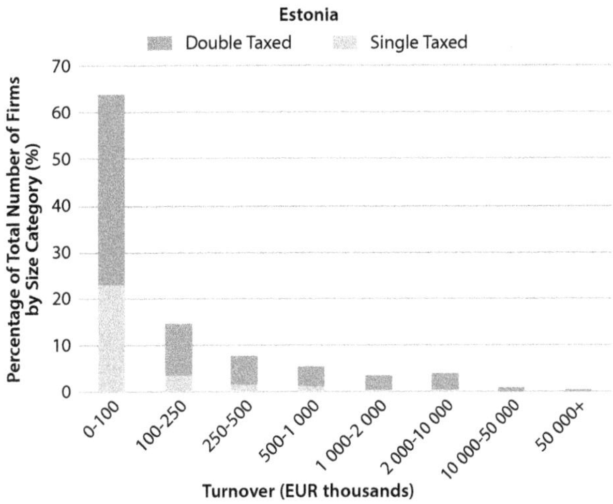
Estonia
Double Taxed
Single Taxed
Percentage of Total Number of Firms by Size Category (%)
0
10
20
30
40
50
60
70
0-100
100-250
250-500
500-1 000
1 000-2 000
2 000-10 000
10 000-50 000
50 000+
Turnover (EUR thousands)

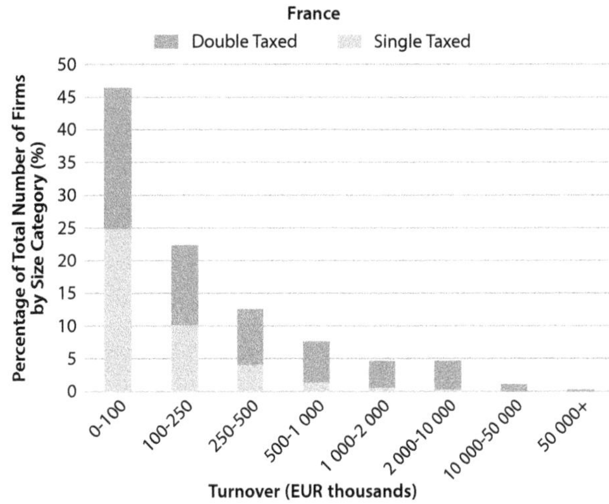
France
Double Taxed
Single Taxed
Percentage of Total Number of Firms by Size Category (%)
0
5
10
15
20
25
30
35
40
45
50
0-100
100-250
250-500
500-1 000
1 000-2 000
2 000-10 000
10 000-50 000
50 000+
Turnover (EUR thousands)

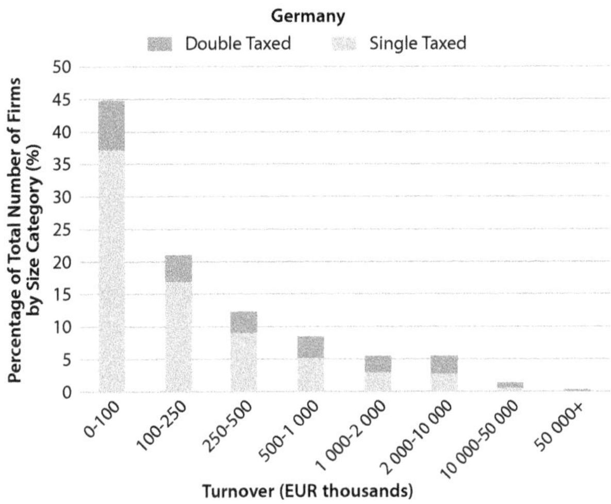
Germany
Double Taxed
Single Taxed
Percentage of Total Number of Firms by Size Category (%)
0
5
10
15
20
25
30
35
40
45
50
0-100
100-250
250-500
500-1 000
1 000-2 000
2 000-10 000
10 000-50 000
50 000+
Turnover (EUR thousands)

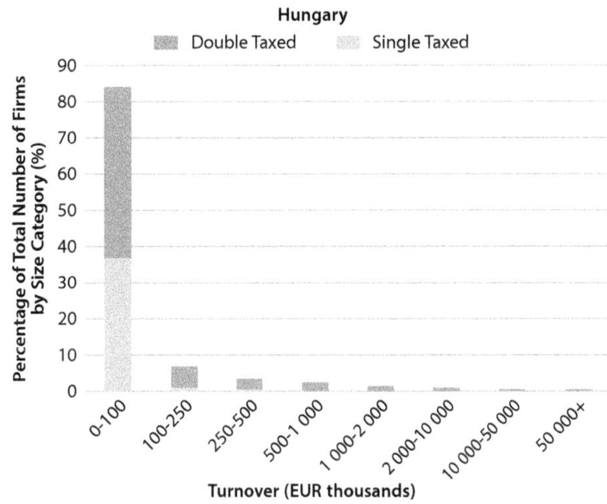
Hungary
Double Taxed
Single Taxed
Percentage of Total Number of Firms by Size Category (%)
0
10
20
30
40
50
60
70
80
90
0-100
100-250
250-500
500-1 000
1 000-2 000
2 000-10 000
10 000-50 000
50 000+
Turnover (EUR thousands)

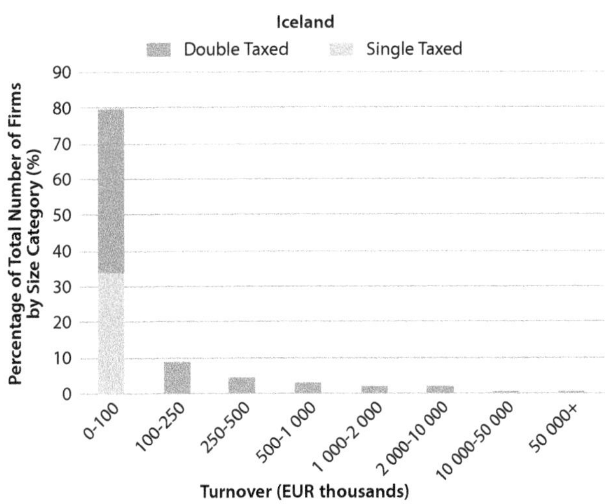
Iceland
Double Taxed
Single Taxed
Percentage of Total Number of Firms by Size Category (%)
0
10
20
30
40
50
60
70
80
90
0-100
100-250
250-500
500-1 000
1 000-2 000
2 000-10 000
10 000-50 000
50 000+
Turnover (EUR thousands)

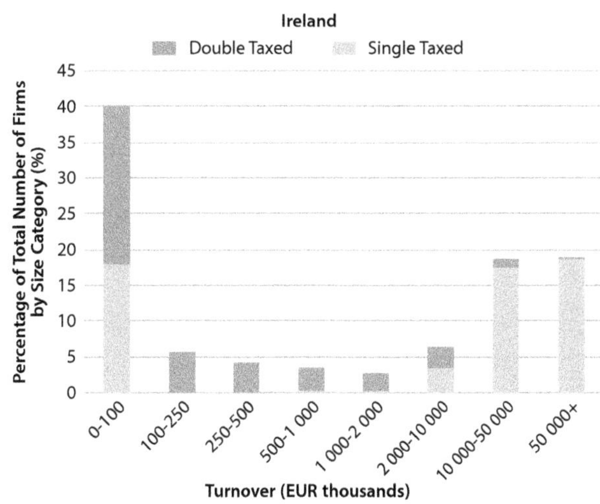
Ireland
Double Taxed
Single Taxed
Percentage of Total Number of Firms by Size Category (%)
0
5
10
15
20
25
30
35
40
45
0-100
100-250
250-500
500-1 000
1 000-2 000
2 000-10 000
10 000-50 000
50 000+
Turnover (EUR thousands)

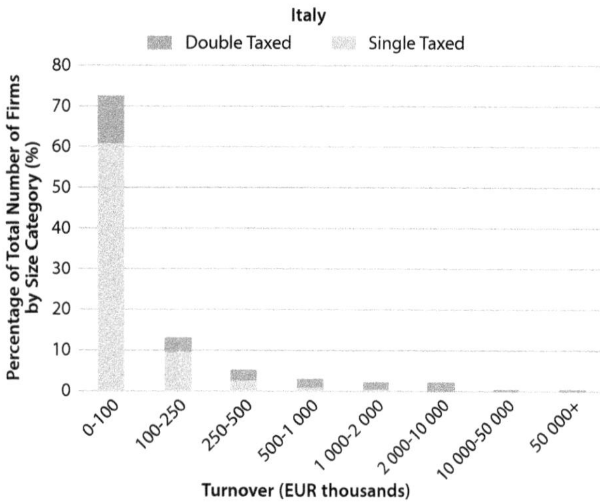
Italy
Double Taxed
Single Taxed
Percentage of Total Number of Firms by Size Category (%)
80
70
60
50
40
30
20
10
0
0-100
100-250
250-500
500-1 000
1 000-2 000
2 000-10 000
10 000-50 000
50 000+
Turnover (EUR thousands)

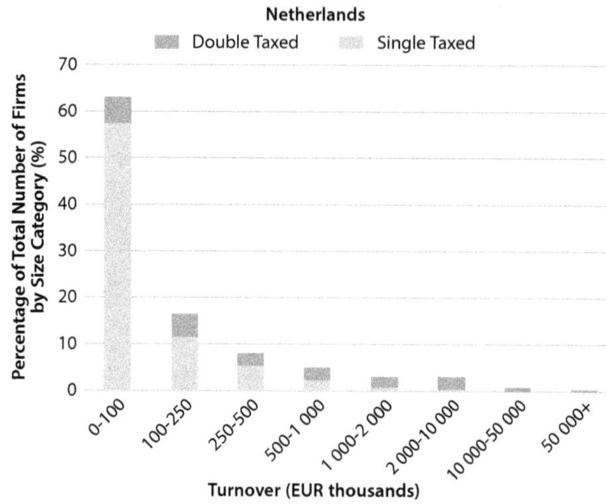
Netherlands
Double Taxed
Single Taxed
Percentage of Total Number of Firms by Size Category (%)
70
60
50
40
30
20
10
0
0-100
100-250
250-500
500-1 000
1 000-2 000
2 000-10 000
10 000-50 000
50 000+
Turnover (EUR thousands)

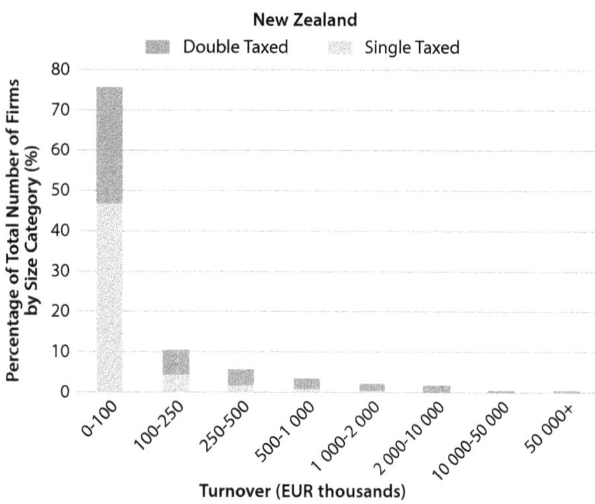
New Zealand
Double Taxed
Single Taxed
Percentage of Total Number of Firms by Size Category (%)
80
70
60
50
40
30
20
10
0
0-100
100-250
250-500
500-1 000
1 000-2 000
2 000-10 000
10 000-50 000
50 000+
Turnover (EUR thousands)

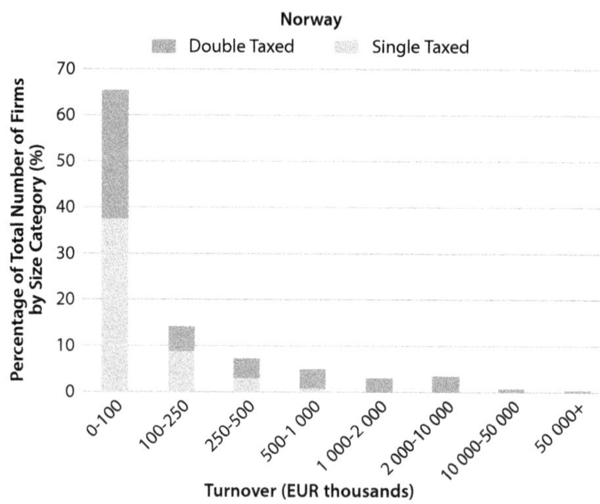
Norway
Double Taxed
Single Taxed
Percentage of Total Number of Firms by Size Category (%)
70
60
50
40
30
20
10
0
0-100
100-250
250-500
500-1 000
1 000-2 000
2 000-10 000
10 000-50 000
50 000+
Turnover (EUR thousands)

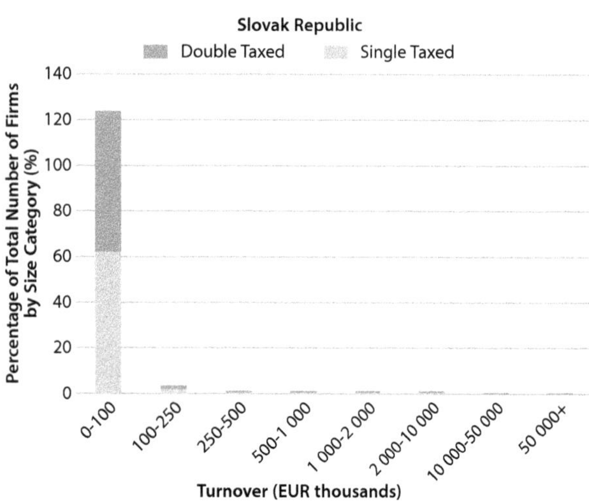
Slovak Republic
Double Taxed
Single Taxed
Percentage of Total Number of Firms by Size Category (%)
140
120
100
80
60
40
20
0
0-100
100-250
250-500
500-1 000
1 000-2 000
2 000-10 000
10 000-50 000
50 000+
Turnover (EUR thousands)

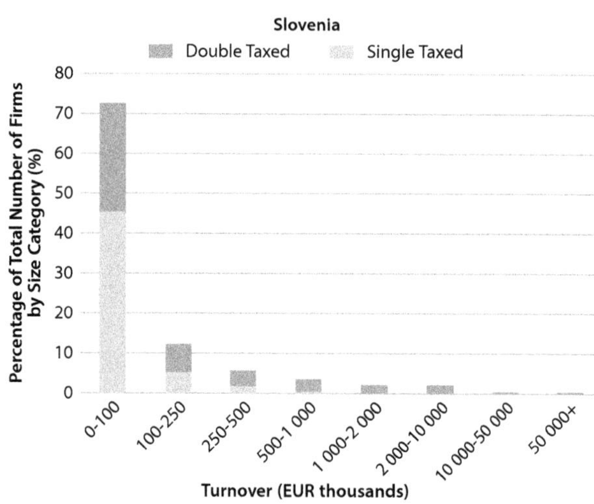
Slovenia
Double Taxed
Single Taxed
Percentage of Total Number of Firms by Size Category (%)
80
70
60
50
40
30
20
10
0
0-100
100-250
250-500
500-1 000
1 000-2 000
2 000-10 000
10 000-50 000
50 000+
Turnover (EUR thousands)

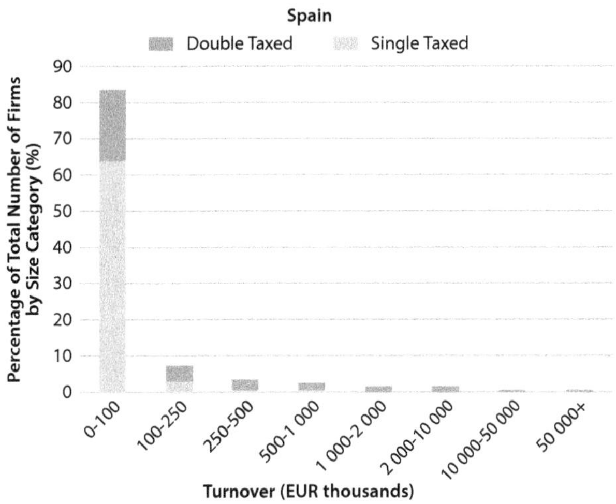


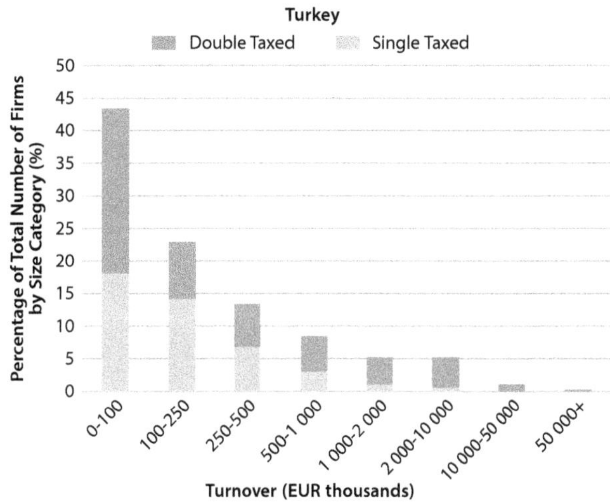


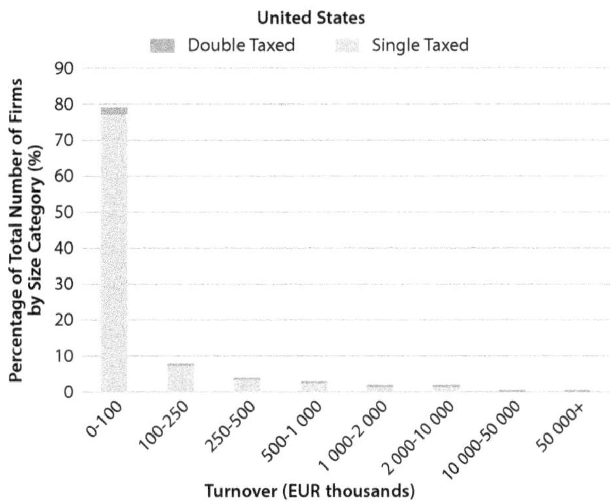


*Source:* Responses to an OECD questionnaire, *Survey on the Taxation of Small and Medium-Sized Enterprises*, 2015. See above for country details and caveats.

Figure B2. **Employment at different entity sizes (by number of employees) in each country**

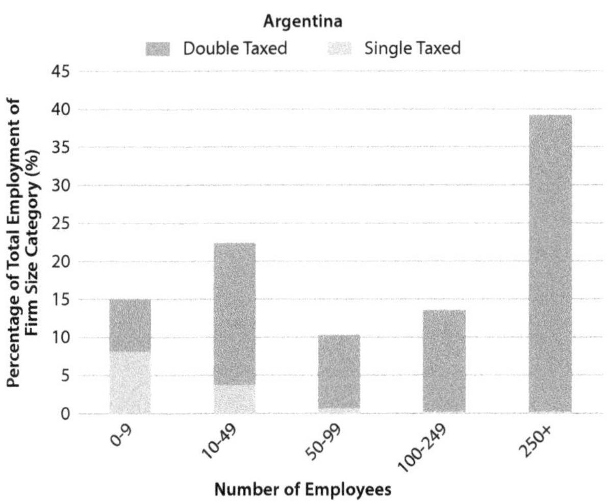


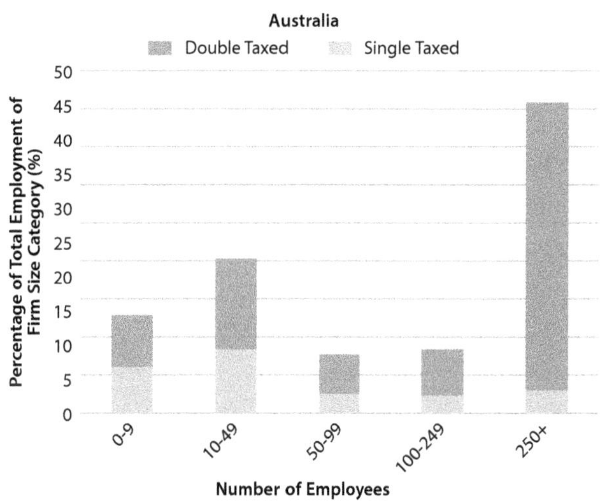

Austria
Double Taxed
Single Taxed
Percentage of Total Employment of Firm Size Category (%)
40
35
30
25
20
15
10
5
0
0-9
10-49
50-99
100-249
250+
Number of Employees

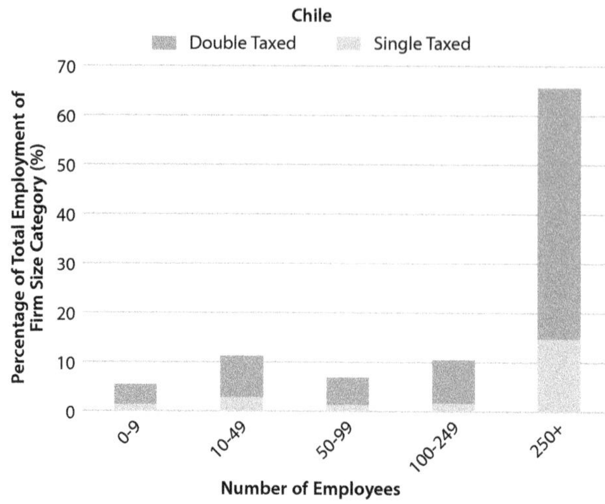
Chile
Double Taxed
Single Taxed
Percentage of Total Employment of Firm Size Category (%)
70
60
50
40
30
20
10
0
0-9
10-49
50-99
100-249
250+
Number of Employees

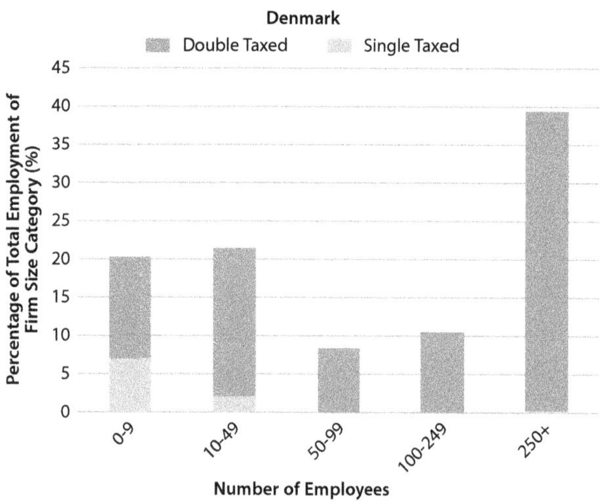
Denmark
Double Taxed
Single Taxed
Percentage of Total Employment of Firm Size Category (%)
45
40
35
30
25
20
15
10
5
0
0-9
10-49
50-99
100-249
250+
Number of Employees

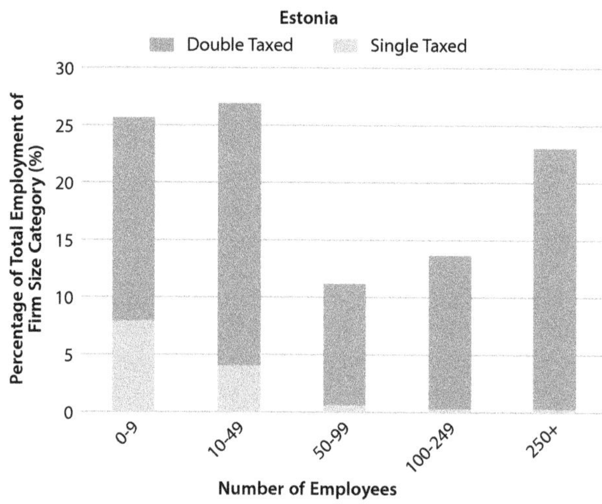
Estonia
Double Taxed
Single Taxed
Percentage of Total Employment of Firm Size Category (%)
30
25
20
15
10
5
0
0-9
10-49
50-99
100-249
250+
Number of Employees

France
Double Taxed
Single Taxed
Percentage of Total Employment of Firm Size Category (%)
45
40
35
30
25
20
15
10
5
0
0-9
10-49
50-99
100-249
250+
Number of Employees

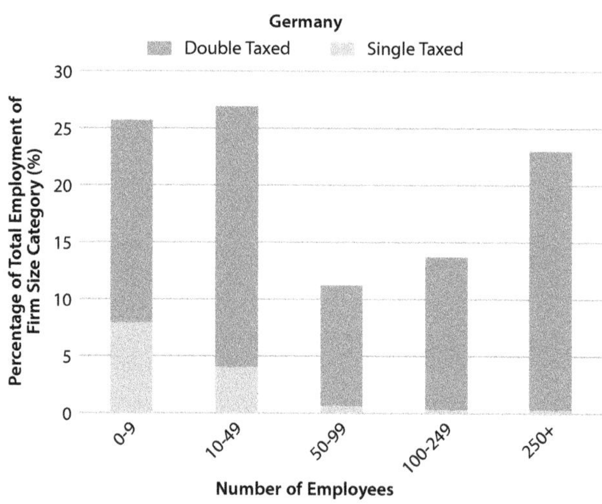
Germany
Double Taxed
Single Taxed
Percentage of Total Employment of Firm Size Category (%)
30
25
20
15
10
5
0
0-9
10-49
50-99
100-249
250+
Number of Employees

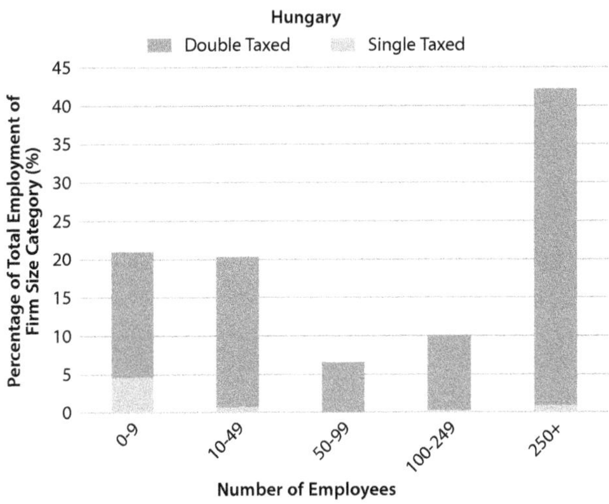
Hungary
Double Taxed
Single Taxed
Percentage of Total Employment of Firm Size Category (%)
45
40
35
30
25
20
15
10
5
0
0-9
10-49
50-99
100-249
250+
Number of Employees

Iceland
Double Taxed
Single Taxed
Percentage of Total Employment of Firm Size Category (%)
35
30
25
20
15
10
5
0
0-9
10-49
50-99
100-249
250+
Number of Employees

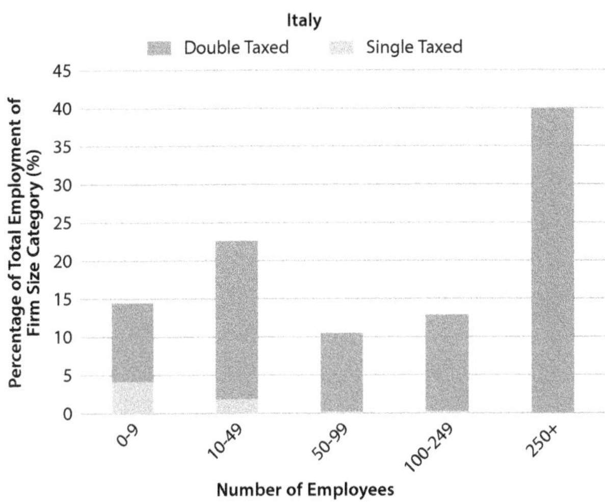
Italy
Double Taxed
Single Taxed
Percentage of Total Employment of Firm Size Category (%)
45
40
35
30
25
20
15
10
5
0
0-9
10-49
50-99
100-249
250+
Number of Employees

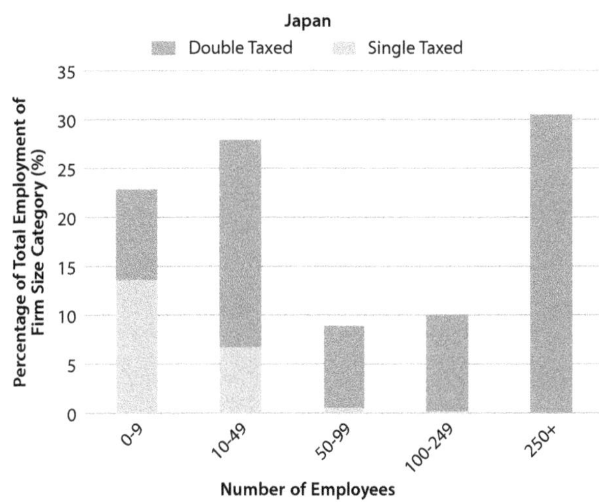
Japan
Double Taxed
Single Taxed
Percentage of Total Employment of Firm Size Category (%)
35
30
25
20
15
10
5
0
0-9
10-49
50-99
100-249
250+
Number of Employees

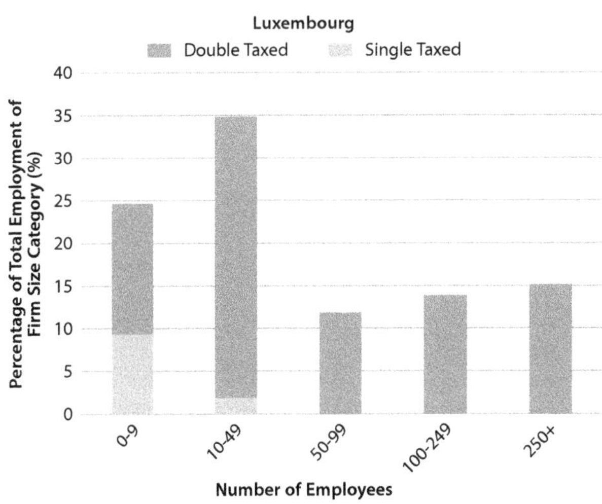
Luxembourg
Double Taxed
Single Taxed
Percentage of Total Employment of Firm Size Category (%)
40
35
30
25
20
15
10
5
0
0-9
10-49
50-99
100-249
250+
Number of Employees

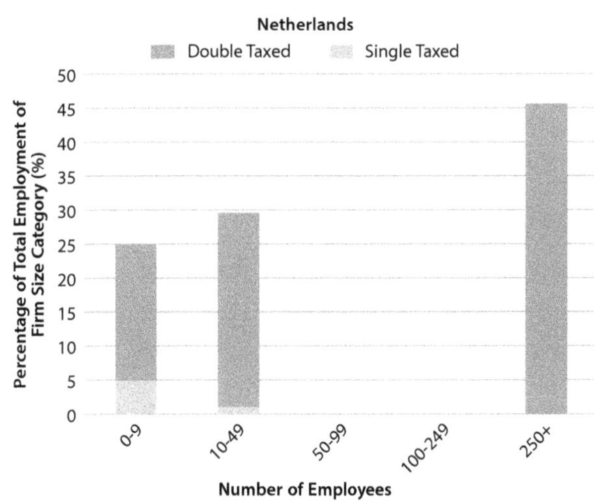
Netherlands
Double Taxed
Single Taxed
Percentage of Total Employment of Firm Size Category (%)
50
45
40
35
30
25
20
15
10
5
0
0-9
10-49
50-99
100-249
250+
Number of Employees

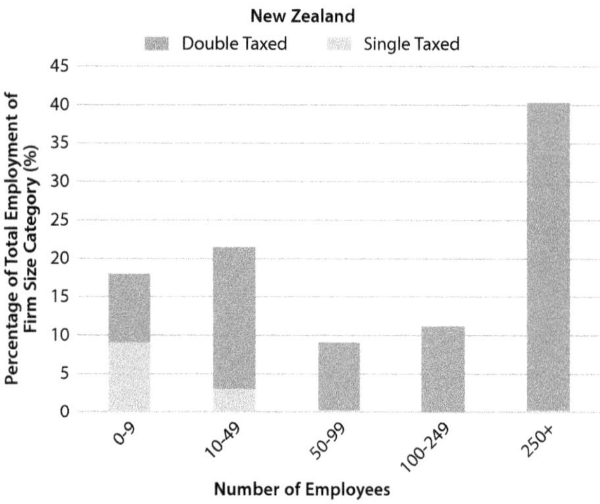


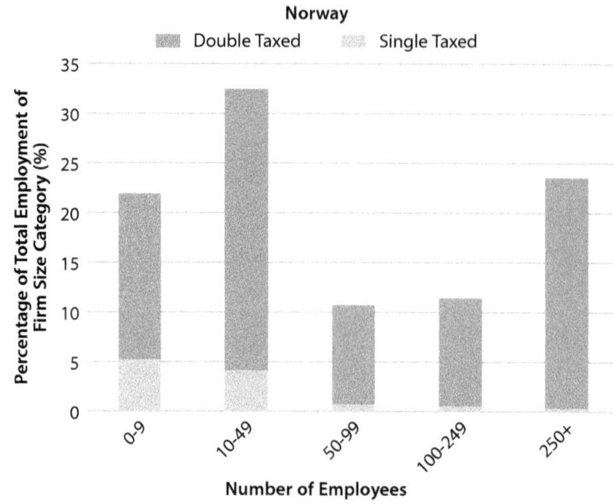


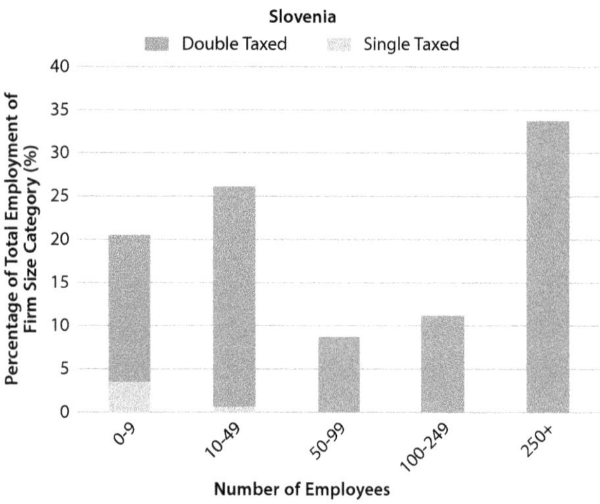


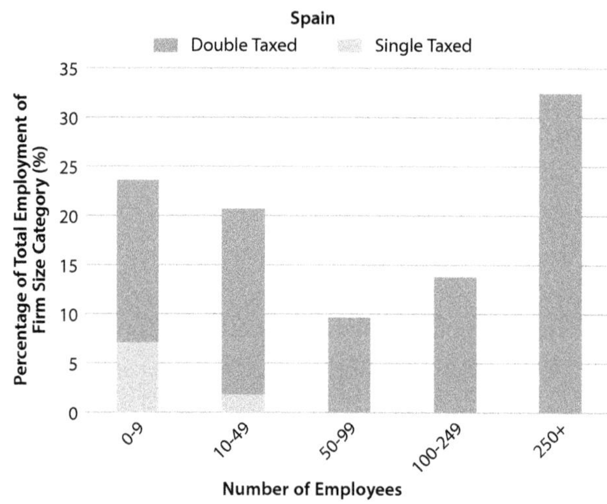


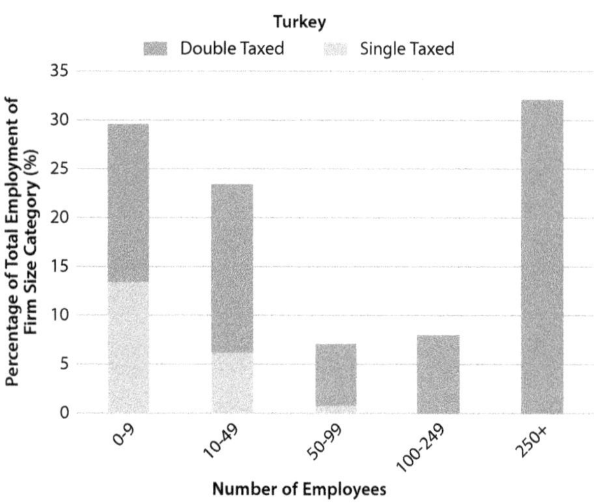


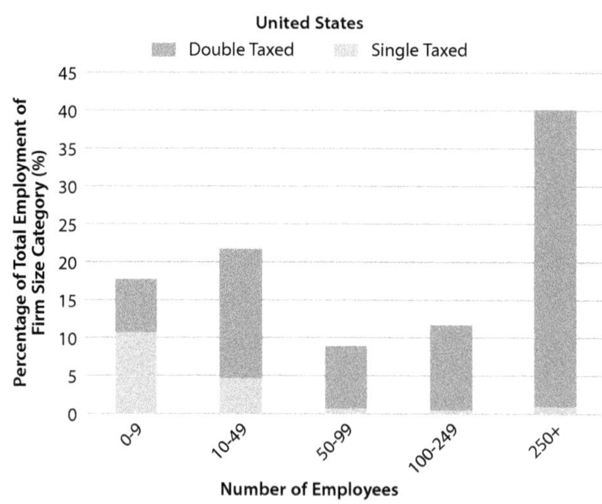


*Source:* Responses to an OECD questionnaire, *Survey on the Taxation of Small and Medium-Sized Enterprises*, 2015. See above for country details and caveats.

Table B2. **Average taxable income by firm size (by level of turnover, EUR thousands) in each country**

| | 0-500 | | 500-2 000 | | 0-2 000 | | 2 000 – 10 000 | | 10 000 – 50 000 | | 50 000 + | |
|---|---|---|---|---|---|---|---|---|---|---|---|---|
| **Country** | Double-taxed | Single-taxed | Double-taxed | Single-taxed | Double-taxed | Single-taxed | Double-taxed | Single-taxed | Double-taxed | Single-taxed | Double-taxed | Single-taxed |
| ARG | 104 000 | 21 000 | 1 005 000 | 828 000 | 275 000 | 24 000 | 4 199 000 | 3 209 000 | 20 558 000 | 19 908 000 | 233 298 000 | 55 974 000 |
| AUS | 13 000 | 13 000 | 93 000 | 103 000 | 26 000 | 18 000 | 328 000 | 288 000 | 1 359 000 | 1 095 000 | 29 116 000 | 9 058 000 |
| AUT | 51 000 | 28 000 | 71 000 | 91 000 | 55 000 | 30 000 | 212 000 | 137 000 | 946 000 | 1 356 000 | 7 008 000 | |
| CAN | 20 000 | | 107 000 | | 32 000 | | 291 000 | | 1 202 000 | | 18 243 000 | |
| EST | 22 000 | 10 000 | 90 000 | 60 000 | 30 000 | 13 000 | 281 000 | 132 000 | 942 000 | 812 000 | 2 218 000 | |
| FRA | | 17 000 | 27 000 | 110 000 | 4 000 | 21 000 | 116 000 | 374 000 | 491 000 | 1 882 000 | 7 875 000 | 11 991 000 |
| DEU | 4 000 | 25 000 | 43 000 | 83 000 | 15 000 | 31 000 | 168 000 | 235 000 | 616 000 | 1 026 000 | 1 694 000 | 6 706 000 |
| HUN | 5 000 | 1 000 | 59 000 | 38 000 | 8 000 | 1 000 | 229 000 | 107 000 | 814 000 | 563 000 | 7 900 000 | |
| ISL | 28 000 | 2 000 | 162 000 | | 38 000 | 2 000 | 408 000 | | 931 000 | | 11 088 000 | |
| IRL | 78 000 | 50 000 | 57 000 | 26 000 | 75 000 | 50 000 | 219 000 | 16 000 | 3 390 000 | 20 000 | 142 815 000 | 57 000 |
| ITA | | 17 000 | 25 000 | 55 000 | 4 000 | 18 000 | 98 000 | 84 000 | 601 000 | 309 000 | 12 864 000 | 1 867 000 |
| KOR | 0 | | 0 | | 0 | | 0 | | 1 000 | | 28 000 | |
| NZL | 20 000 | 24 000 | 65 000 | 130 000 | 25 000 | 27 000 | 340 000 | 438 000 | 1 960 000 | 1 536 000 | 18 455 000 | 22 920 000 |
| POR | 7 000 | | 42 000 | | 10 000 | | 191 000 | | 1 109 000 | | 11 000 000 | |
| SVN | 4 000 | 4 000 | 38 000 | 21 000 | 8 000 | 5 000 | 148 000 | 52 000 | 611 000 | 74 000 | 4 152 000 | |
| USA | 32 000 | 9 000 | 21 000 | 70 000 | 29 000 | 11 000 | 84 000 | 219 000 | 555 000 | 1 000 000 | 46 239 000 | 11 953 000 |
| Mean | 28 000 | 17 000 | 119 000 | 135 000 | 40 000 | 19 000 | 457 000 | 441 000 | 2 255 000 | 2 465 000 | 34 625 000 | 15 066 000 |

*Source:* Responses to an OECD questionnaire, *Survey on the Taxation of Small and Medium-Sized Enterprises*, 2015. See above for country details and caveats.

Table B3. **Average taxable income by firm size (by number of employees) in each country**

| | 0 – 9 | | 10 – 49 | | 50 – 99 | | 100 – 249 | | 250 + | |
|---|---|---|---|---|---|---|---|---|---|---|
| **Country** | Double-taxed | Single-taxed | Double-taxed | Single-taxed | Double-taxed | Single-taxed | Double-taxed | Single-taxed | Double-taxed | Single-taxed |
| ARG | 10 000 | 5 000 | 51 000 | 18 000 | 173 000 | 59 000 | 342 000 | 104 000 | 3 453 000 | 204 000 |
| AUS | 63 000 | 22 000 | 217 000 | 147 000 | 618 000 | 386 000 | 1 879 000 | 830 000 | 35 140 000 | 3 933 000 |
| AUT | 46 000 | 30 000 | 139 000 | 45 000 | 352 000 | 72 000 | 994 000 | 95 000 | 5 875 000 | 43 000 |
| DNK | 36 000 | 31 000 | 196 000 | 409 000 | 605 000 | 3 137 000 | 2 129 000 | 4 520 000 | 30 104 000 | 38 734 000 |
| EST | 29 000 | 13 000 | 128 000 | 40 000 | 424 000 | 62 000 | 711 000 | 84 000 | 2 913 000 | 42 000 |
| FRA | 20 000 | 27 000 | 97 000 | 159 000 | 263 000 | 816 000 | 891 000 | 1 093 000 | 7 841 000 | 7 598 000 |
| DEU | 8 000 | 48 000 | 79 000 | 165 000 | 421 000 | 715 000 | 1 093 000 | 1 538 000 | 3 858 000 | 7 824 000 |
| HUN | 8 000 | 1 000 | 101 000 | 24 000 | 300 000 | 0 | 612 000 | 1 000 | 4 459 000 | |
| IND | 25 000 | 18 000 | 288 000 | 158 000 | 1 141 000 | 235 000 | 1 943 000 | 305 000 | 19 579 000 | 1 313 000 |
| IRL | 130 000 | 40 000 | 323 000 | 103 000 | 959 000 | 139 000 | 1 973 000 | 111 000 | 26 147 000 | |
| ITA | 14 000 | 17 000 | 79 000 | 41 000 | 337 000 | 33 000 | 1 189 000 | 15 000 | 11 288 000 | 891 000 |
| NZL | 213 000 | 357 000 | 98 000 | 105 000 | 399 000 | 318 000 | 1 137 000 | 898 000 | 4 246 000 | 10 131 000 |
| SVN | 10 000 | 5 000 | 119 000 | 25 000 | 343 000 | 9 000 | 872 000 | 161 000 | 2 779 000 | |
| Mean | 47 000 | 47 000 | 147 000 | 111 000 | 487 000 | 460 000 | 1 213 000 | 750 000 | 12 129 000 | 7 071 000 |

*Source:* Responses to an OECD questionnaire, *Survey on the Taxation of Small and Medium-Sized Enterprises*, 2015. See above for country details and caveats.

# *Annex C*

# Employer, employee and self-employed social security contributions

| | Employer | | | | | | Employee | | | | | | Self-employed | | | | | |
|---|---|---|---|---|---|---|---|---|---|---|---|---|---|---|---|---|---|---|
| | | | Base | | Deductibility | | | | Base | | Deductibility | | | | Base | | Deductibility | |
| | Tax base | Marg. Rate/ lump sum | *Lower threshold* | *Upper threshold* | *Base* | *%* | Tax base | Marg. Rate/ lump sum | *Lower threshold* | *Upper threshold* | *Base* | *%* | Tax base | Marg. Rate/ lump sum | *Lower threshold* | *Upper threshold* | *Base* | *%* |
| Australia+ | - | - | - | - | - | - | - | - | - | - | - | - | - | - | - | - | - | - |
| Austria* | 14*MGE | 21.62857 | 5 534.34 | 63 420 | TY | 100 | 14*MGE | 0 | 0 | 5 534.34 | TY | 100 | AP | 26.15 | 0 | 63 420 | TY | 100 |
| | | | | | | | 14*MGE | 15.05714 | 5 534.34 | 17 444 | TY | 100 | | | | | | |
| | | | | | | | 14*MGE | 16.05714 | 17 444 | 19 026 | TY | 100 | | | | | | |
| | | | | | | | 14*MGE | 17.05714 | 19 026 | 21 420 | TY | 100 | | | | | | |
| | | | | | | | 14*MGE | 18.05714 | 21 420 | 63 420 | TY | 100 | | | | | | |
| Belgium | MGE | 34.79 | - | - | TY | 100 | MGE | 13.07 | - | - | TY | 100 | TY | 22 | 12 870.83 | 55 576.94 | 0 | 0 |
| | | | | | | | | | | | | | 0 | 14.16 | 55 576.94 | 81 902.81 | - | - |
| Canada* | AGE | 2.632 | 0 | 3 500 | 0 | 0 | AGE | 1.88 | 0 | 3 500 | 0 | 0 | AGE | 9.9 | 3 500 | 52 500 | TY/ TYs | 50 |
| | 0 | 7.582 | 3 500 | 48 600 | 0 | 0 | 0 | 6.83 | 3 500 | 48 600 | 0 | 0 | | | | | | |
| | 0 | 4.95 | 48 600 | 52 500 | TY | 100 | 0 | 4.95 | 48 600 | 52 500 | - | - | | | | | | |
| Chile+ | - | - | - | - | - | - | MGE | 7 | - | 1 735 932 | - | - | - | - | - | - | - | - |
| Czech Republic | MGE | 9 | - | - | TY | 100 | MGE | 4.5 | - | - | - | - | AGE | 6.75 | 155 652 | - | - | - |
| | MGE | 25 | 0 | 103 768 | 0 | 0 | MGE | 6.5 | - | 103 768 | - | - | AGE | 14.6 | 103 768 | 1 245 216 | - | - |
| Denmark+ | - | - | - | - | TY | 100 | AGE | 8 | - | - | TY | 100 | - | - | - | - | TY | 100 |
| | | | | | | | 0 | 0 | 0 | 0 | TY | 100 | | | | | | |
| Estonia* | MGE | 1 | 0 | 3 840 | TY | 100 | MGE | 2 | - | - | TY | 100 | MGE | 0 | - | 320 | TY | 100 |
| | 0 | 34 | 3 840 | - | TY | 100 | | | | | | | MGE | 33 | 320 | - | 0 | 0 |
| | | | | | | | | | | | | | MGE | 1 | - | - | TY | 100 |
| Finland | AGE | 23.6 | - | - | TY | 100 | TYs | 1.32 | - | - | - | - | AGE | 23.6 | - | - | TY | 100 |
| | | | | | | | AGE | 6.89 | - | - | TY | 100 | TY's | 1.32 | - | - | - | - |
| France* | AGE | 41.86 | 0 | 37 548 | TY | 100 | AGE | 14.05 | 0 | 37 548 | 0 | 100 | AGE | 46.34 | 0 | 37 032 | 0 | 0 |
| | 0 | 41.01 | 37 548 | 112 644 | TY | 100 | 0 | 12.35 | 37 548 | 112 644 | 0 | 100 | 0 | 28.6 | 37 032 | 148 128 | 0 | 0 |
| | 0 | 27.63 | 112 644 | 150 192 | TY | 100 | 0 | 3.4 | 112 644 | 150 192 | 0 | 100 | 0 | 20.6 | 148 128 | 185 160 | 0 | 0 |
| | 0 | 23.33 | 150 192 | - | TY | 100 | 0 | 1 | 150 192 | 0 | TY | 100 | 0 | 19.9 | 185 160 | - | - | - |
| | | | | | | | | | | | | | 0 | 45.8 | | 37 032 | 0 | 0 |
| | | | | | | | | | | | | | 0 | 28.8 | 37 032 | 148 128 | 0 | 0 |
| | | | | | | | | | | | | | 0 | 20.6 | 148 128 | 185 160 | 0 | 0 |
| | | | | | | | | | | | | | 0 | 19.9 | 185 160 | - | - | - |
| Germany* | AGE | 19.275 | 0 | 48 600 | 0 | 0 | AGE | 20.175 | 0 | 48 600 | 0 | 0 | - | - | - | - | - | - |
| | 0 | 10.95 | 48 600 | 71 400 | TY | 100 | 0 | 10.95 | 48 600 | 71 400 | TY | <100 | | | | | | |
| Greece* | MGE | 26.01 | - | 5 546.8 | TY | 100 | MGE | 16 | - | 5 546.8 | TY | 100 | 0 | 0 | 0 | 0 | 0 | 0 |
| Hungary | AGE+BEN | 28.5 | - | - | TY | 100 | AGE | 18.5 | - | - | - | - | TY | 27 | [1 370 250] | - | TY | 100 |
| | | | | | | | | | | | | | TY | 10 | [1 218 000] | - | - | - |
| | | | | | | | | | | | | | TY | 8.5 | [1 827 000] | - | - | - |
| Iceland+ | AGE | 7.59 | - | - | TY | 100 | TY | - | 1 624 601 | - | - | - | AGE | n.a. | - | - | - | n.a. |
| | | | | | | | AGE | 8 | - | - | TY | 100 | | | | | | |
| Ireland | AGE | 8.5 | 0 | 18 512 | TY | 100 | AGE | 4 | [18 304] | - | - | - | WGE | 4 | 5 000 | - | - | - |
| | 0 | 10.75 | 18 512 | 0 | TY | 100 | | | | | | | | | | | | |

| | Employer | | | | | | Employee | | | | | | Self-employed | | | | | |
|---|---|---|---|---|---|---|---|---|---|---|---|---|---|---|---|---|---|---|
| | | | Base | | Deductibility | | | | Base | | Deductibility | | | | Base | | Deductibility | |
| | Tax base | Marg. Rate/ lump sum | *Lower threshold* | *Upper threshold* | *Base* | *%* | Tax base | Marg. Rate/ lump sum | *Lower threshold* | *Upper threshold* | *Base* | *%* | Tax base | Marg. Rate/ lump sum | *Lower threshold* | *Upper threshold* | *Base* | *%* |
| Israel+ | MGE | 3.45 | 0 | 5 453 | TY | 100 | MGE | 3.5 | 0 | 5 453 | 0 | 0 | MGE | 9.82 | 0 | 5 453 | 0 | 0 |
| | 0 | 6.75 | 5 453 | 43 240 | TY | 100 | 0 | 12 | 5 453 | 43 240 | 0 | 0 | 0 | 16.23 | 5 453 | 43 240 | 0 | 0 |
| | | | | | | | | | | | | | 0 | 0 | 0 | 0 | 0 | 0 |
| Italy+ | AGE | 32.08 | 0 | 100 123 | TY | 100 | AGE | 9.49 | 0 | 46 031 | 0 | 0 | AGE | 22.2 | 15 516 | 46 031 | | |
| | | | | | | | 0 | 10.49 | 46 031 | 100 123 | TY | 100 | | 23.2 | 46 031 | 76 718 | TY | 100 |
| Japan* | MGE | 14.599 | 0 | 620 000 | TY | 100 | MGE | 14.119 | 0 | 620 000 | TY | 100 | - | - | - | - | TY/ TYs | 100 |
| | MGE | 5.98 | 620 000 | 1 210 000 | TY | 100 | MGE | 5.5 | 620 000 | 1 210 000 | TY | 100 | | | | | | |
| | MGE | 0.98 | 1 210 000 | 0 | TY | 100 | MGE | 0.5 | 1 210 000 | 0 | TY | 100 | | | | | | |
| Korea* | MGE | 10.291 | 0 | 2 203 200 | TY | 100 | MGE | 8.341 | 0 | 2 203 200 | TY | 100 | MGE | 9 | [240 000] | 3 890 000 | TY | 100 |
| | MGE | 5.791 | 2 203 200 | 0 | TY | 100 | MGE | 3.841 | 0 | 0 | - | - | | | | | | |
| Luxembourg*+ | AGE | 12.3 | 0 | 115 261.8 | TY | 100 | AGE | 11.05 | 0 | 115 261.8 | TY | 100 | AP | 23.2 | 0 | 5 763 | TY | 100 |
| | | | | | | | AGE | 1.4 | 5 763.09 | - | - | - | AP | 24.6 | 5 763.12 | 115 261.8 | TY | 100 |
| | | | | | | | | | | | | | AP | 1.4 | 115 261.8 | - | TY | 100 |
| Mexico* + | MGE | 0 | 0 | 0 | TY | 100 | MGE | 1.25 | 0 | 6 140.213 | - | - | - | 5 594 (A) | - | - | - | - |
| | MGE | 6.48 | 0 | 6 140.213 | TY | 100 | MGE | 1.65 | 6 140.213 | 51 168.44 | - | - | - | 7 200 (A) | - | - | - | - |
| | MGE | 7.58 | 6 140.213 | 51 168.44 | TY | 100 | | | | | | | | | | | | |
| Netherlands* + | AGE | 9.16 | 0 | 17 693 | 0.00 | 0 | TY | 31.15 | 0 | 33 363 | - | - | - | - | - | - | - | - |
| | 0 | 11.31 | 17 693 | 51 414 | TY | 100 | | | | | | | TY | 31.15 | 0 | 33 363 | - | - |
| | | | | | | | | | | | | | TY | 5.4 | 0 | 51 414 | - | - |
| New Zealand | - | - | - | - | - | - | - | - | - | - | - | - | - | - | - | - | - | - |
| Norway* + | AGE | 13 | 0 | 0 | TY | 100 | AGE | 8.2 | [39 600] | - | - | - | AGE | 11.4 | 39 600 | - | 0 | 0 |
| Poland+ | AGE | 16.78 | 0 | 112 380 | TY | 100 | AGE | 10.06 | 0 | 112 380 | TY | 100 | DMI | 29.02 | 2 248 | 112 380 | TY | 100 |
| | 0 | 4.17 | 112 380 | 0 | TY | 100 | 0 | 2.45 | 112 380 | 0 | TY | 100 | | | | | | |
| | | | | | | | AGE | 9 | - | - | TY | 100 | | | | | | |
| Portugal | MGE | 23.75 | - | - | TY | 100 | MGE | 11 | - | - | TY | 100 | MGEc | 29.6 | [628.83] | 5 030.64 | TY | 100 |
| Slovak | MGE | 30.4 | [352] | 4 025 | TY | 100 | MGE | 13.4 | /352/ | 4 025 | TY | 100 | MGE | 47.15 | 402.5 | 4 025 | TY | 100 |
| Republic* + | MGE | 0.8 | | | TY | 100 | | | | | | | | | | | | |
| Slovenia | MGE | 16.1 | - | - | TY | 100 | MGE | 22.1 | - | - | TY | 100 | MGE | 38.2 | 783.66 (913.91) | 5 331.13 | TY | 100 |
| Spain* | AGE | 29.9 | [9 036] | 43 164 | TY | 100 | AGE | 6.35 | /9 036/ | 43 164 | TY | 100 | AGE | 29.8 | [10 508.4] | 43 164 | TY | 100 |
| Sweden | AGE+BEN | 31.42 | - | - | TY | 100 | AGE | 7 | [18 781.2] | 459 183 | TC | 100 | AGE | 28.97 | - | - | TY/ TYs | 100 |
| Switzerland+ | AGE | 6.25 | 0 | 126 000 | TY | 100 | AGE | 6.25 | 0 | 126 000 | TY | 100 | AP | 9.7 | - | - | TYs | 100 |
| | 0 | 5.15 | 126 000 | 315 000 | TY | 100 | 0 | 5.15 | 126 000 | 0 | TY | 100 | | | | | | |
| Turkey (TRY)* | AGE | 20.5 | [[13 230]] | 85 995 | TY | 100 | AGE | 14 | /13 230/ | 85 995 | TY | 100 | AGE | 34.5 | [13 230]] | 85 995 | TY | 100 |
| United Kingdom* | WGE | 13.8 | 663 | - | TY | 100 | WGE | 12 | 153 | 805.0962 | 0 | 0 | AGE | 9 | 7 956 | 41 865 | - | - |
| | | | | | | | WGE | 2 | 805.0962 | - | - | - | AGE | 2 | 41 865 | - | - | - |
| | | | | | | | | | | | | | AGE | - | 5 885 | - | - | 50 |
| United States* | AGE | 13.65 | 0 | 7 000 | 0 | 0 | AGE | 7.65 | 0 | 117 000 | 0 | 0 | AGE | 15.3 | 0 | 117 000 | TY0 | 0 |
| | 0 | 7.65 | 7 000 | 117 000 | 0 | 0 | 0 | 1.45 | 117 000 | 2 000 000 | - | - | 0 | 2.9 | 117 000 | 200 000 | TY | 50 |
| | 0 | 1.45 | 117 000 | | 0 | 0 | | 2.35 | 200 000 | | | | | 3.8 | 200 000 | | | note |

*Source:* OECD Tax database (OECD, 2015). For the United States, the additional 0.9% SSC for the self-employed is not deductible, but 50% of the rest of the SSC is.

## Key to abbreviations

| | |
|---|---|
| n.a. | Data not provided |
| * | country specific footnotes |
| + | Non-tax compulsory payment (NTCP) |
| *Tax base* | |
| WGE | Weekly gross earnings |
| MGE | Monthly gross earnings |
| AGE | Annual gross earnings |
| BEN | Annual benefits |
| CPP | Canada Pension Plan |
| MGEc | Monthly gross earnings – Conventional |
| AP | Adjusted profits |
| DMI | Declared monthly income |
| *Deductibility Base* | |
| TY | Taxable income measured for central government tax purposes |
| TYs | Taxable income modified for sub-central government purposes |
| T | (Annual) central government income tax payable |
| Ts | (Annual) sub-central income tax |
| EMPR | Employer social security contribution |

## Explanatory notes

1. This table reports social security contribution rates and related provisions (using the representative case for those countries where social security provisions vary by locality). Threshold and maximum contribution amounts are shown in national currencies. For the purpose of this table, a dash (-) means "not applicable". Further explanatory notes may be found in the Explanatory Annex to *Taxing Wages* (OECD, 2015).

2. **Marginal rate:** The social security contribution marginal rates (flat or graduated) in many cases are aggregates over different rates for different social security contribution pools (e.g. for unemployment, health etc.) – see the note below on aggregation. In such cases, the disaggregated rates can be found by entering the applicable Excel cell.

– Where a flat rate system applies, the marginal rate applies to the tax base identified in column 1 (e.g. monthly gross earnings – see key to abbreviations) in excess of the lower threshold (base) amount, if any, up to the upper threshold (ceiling), if any.

– Similarly, where a graduated system applies, the marginal rates apply to the corresponding tax base band (lower threshold up to upper threshold) on the same line.

3. **Base: Lower and upper thresholds:** The base parameters (lower threshold and upper threshold) relate to the SSC calculation and the same time-frame (week, month or year) as indicated in the first (tax base) column.

– Where a lower threshold is shown without brackets, contributions are calculated as a percentage of gross earnings in excess of this threshold.

– Where a lower threshold amount is shown in square brackets [], the threshold is not a contribution-free amount deducted from the base but an amount which is used to determine whether the contribution is payable on the total amount of earnings.

– Where a lower threshold amount is shown in round brackets (), the threshold is decreasing with income. Where a lower threshold is shown in between //, the threshold is the deemed minimum SSC base for full-time workers. The impact of the minimum wage(s), if any, is not considered/ shown.

– Where an upper threshold value is shown on the same line as the top (or flat) marginal rate, the contributions are "capped" at this threshold (they are not imposed on the tax base in excess of this amount). The "lower" and "upper" thresholds (shown under "base") are relevant to the marginal rate, unless no marginal rate is shown, in which case the thresholds applies to the lump-sum charge.

4. **Maximum contribution:** In general, where a flat contribution rate applies, the maximum contribution (which excludes lump sum charge, if any) is calculated as the contribution rate multiplied by the upper threshold base amount.

– Where a progressive rate structure applies, the maximum contribution is determined in a similar fashion by applying the applicable marginal rates to the corresponding upper threshold.

– Lastly note that where an upper threshold does not exist, in general a maximum contribution would not exist.

– Where an upper threshold does not exist, but a maximum contribution is shown, explanatory notes may be provided in the Explanatory Annex to *Taxing Wages* (OECD, 2015).

| |
|---|
| 5. **Lump-sum charge:** The lump-sum charge (if any) relates to the time-frame (annual (A), monthly (M) or weekly (W)) as indicated in parentheses after the lump-sum amount.<br>– Where a taxpayer is exempt from the lump-sum charge if his/her earnings or income fall below a certain level, this amount is indicated in the "lower threshold" column, with the relevant measure noted in parentheses. |
| 6. **Deductibility – Base and %:** These columns consider the extent to which employer social security contributions are deductible against corporate taxable income.<br>– Where they are deductible against central government taxable income, the base is shown as TY and the deductible proportion of the contribution is given.<br>– If, in the representative case, sub-central government personal income tax is determined as a percentage of taxable income (TYs) which may differ from the definition used for central government purposes (TY) (see Table I.6), and if employer social security contributions are deductible from this base, then TYs and the deductible portion are shown.<br>– If contributions are deductible from both the central government tax base and (separately) the sub-central tax bases, then TY and TYs are shown on separate lines, along with the deductible portions. (Note that if sub-central income tax is determined as a percentage of central government tax or central government taxable income (with employer social security contributions indirectly deductible through this channel), this additional information would not be relevant). |

## Country-specific footnotes

| | |
|---|---|
| Austria | **Self-employed SSCs:** In 2014, the 26.15% rate consists of 18.5% for pension contributions and 7.65% for health contributions. The minimum base is 8 255.76 (=687.98*12) for pension contributions and 8 459.88 (=704,99*12) for health contributions. Additionally a monthly amount of 8.67 Euro for accident insurance. |
| Belgium | **Self-employed SSCs:** Since 2015, the social security contributions of self-employed persons are determined in two steps. Initially, advance payments are due on the inflation-adjusted taxable income of three years before (TY-3), e.g. provisional contributions of 2015 are based on the inflation-adjusted taxable income of 2012. In subsequent years, once the taxable income of the year (TY) is fixed by the tax administration, the final assessment of social security contributions uses the same rate schedule. Up till 2014 only the first step was applicable. |
| Canada | Information on the provincially-administered health care insurance plan and the contributions to the provincial worker's compensation plan which pays benefits to workers for work-related illness or injury is not included. |
| Chile | **Employee SSCs**: The contribution rates shown in the table relate to health care. In addition there are some other contributions paid by minority groups that are classified as taxes. See Explanatory Annex to *Taxing Wages* (OECD, 2015) for more details. |
| Estonia | **Employee and employer SSCs:** SSC are levied on total gross wage or salary including vacation payments, fringe benefits and remuneration of expenses related to work above a certain threshold. |
| Finland | **Employee SSCs:** There is an employees' pension insurance contribution which amounts to 5.55% of gross salary, an employees' unemployment insurance contribution equal to 0.5% of gross salary and a health insurance contribution for daily allowance equal to 0.84% of gross salary. For employees aged 53 and older, the pension insurance contribution amounts to 7.05% of gross salary. These contributions are deductible for income tax purposes.<br>**Self-employed SSCs**: The tax base is income as defined by the self-employed person for pension income insurance purposes. |
| France | **Employer SSCs:** social security contributions for work accidents are not included. These rates apply for non-managers.<br>**Employee SSCs:** These rates apply for non-managers. Social security contributions are fully deductible against personal taxable income.<br>**Self-employed SSCs:** the first set of rates (n.a.) apply for craftsmen, while the second set of rates (n.a.) apply for traders. |
| Germany | **Employer SSCs:** in addition, employers pay work injury contributions; no representative rate is available.<br>**Employee SSCs:** as of 1 January 2005, the lower ceiling rate increased by 0.25 percentage points for childless employees.<br>**Self-employed SSCs:** see the Explanatory Annex to *Taxing Wages* (OECD, 2015) for a description of the German system |

| | |
|---|---|
| Greece | **Employer SSCs:** the threshold shown applies to employees insured after 1 January 1993. A lower threshold of EUR 5,546.80 applies to employees insured before this date. See the Explanatory Annex to *Taxing Wages* (OECD, 2015) for more details.<br>**Employee and self-employed SSCs:** See the Explanatory Annex to *Taxing Wages* (OECD, 2015) for more details. |
| Hungary | **Self-employed SSCs:** the amount shown in column D is a minimum tax base for contributions and not a lower threshold. The child tax allowance may reduce the health and pension contribution payable (for details see the general description of the family tax allowance in the "*Taxing Wages*" country chapter). |
| Iceland | **Employee SSCs:** since January 2000, the compulsory payment to (privately-managed) pension funds, which amounts to 4% of wages, is deductible from taxable gross earnings. In addition, optional pension savings of up to 4% of wages may also be deducted. Although these contributions are not considered to be social security contributions (these payments are not made to a publicly-managed fund), they are included in the table in the case of Iceland. Please refer to the Non-Tax Compulsory Payment (NTCP) report on the OECD tax database webpage. (www.oecd.org/ctp/tax-policy/tax-database.htm#NTCP). |
| Ireland | **Employee SSCs:** Those earning less than EUR 18 304 are exempt.<br>**Self-employed SSCs:** additional 0.5% for income exceeding 100 100 euro per annum.<br>**Self-employed SSCs:** Lower rates are applied for workers younger than 21 years old. See the Explanatory Annex to *Taxing Wages* (OECD, 2015) for more details. |
| Japan | **Employer SSCs:** work injury social security contributions are not included (as no representative rate was available); the rate ranges between 0.3% and 10.3% of total remuneration. The employer's contribution rate depends on each industry's accident rate over the last three years and other factors.<br>**Self-employed SSCs:** because the national pension contribution is a fixed amount, it is described as a monthly "lump-sum" contribution. The National Health Insurance contribution depends on income, assets and the size of the household. Because the calculations are too complex to include, only the annual maximum contribution is shown |
| Korea | **Employer SSCs:** unemployment insurance premium is between 0.7% and 1.3% of gross income; work injury insurance premium is a specific rate for each industry (the representative rate applied in *Taxing Wages* is 1.95%, which is the rate shown here).<br>**Self-employed SSCs:** as the National Health Insurance contribution of self-employed depends on income, assets and the size of the household, it is not decided just as a rate of income; only the National Pension contribution is included. The data are applied for the second half of the year; the threshold were changed on July 1. |
| Luxembourg | **Employer SSCs:** for accident insurance, the employer's share ranges between 0.45% and 6%. The minimum contribution of 0.45% of gross earnings is included here (similar assumption is made in *Taxing Wages* (OECD, 2015)). |
| Mexico | **Employer SSCs:** the 1.10% rate applies to monthly earnings in excess of 3 times the monthly minimum legal wage.<br>**Employee SSCs:** For sickness and maternity insurance, 0.625% of the workers monthly wage, plus 0.40% of the amount in excess of three times the minimal legal wage (the amount that applies within the Federal District of Mexico City MWFD). For disability and life insurance, 0.625% of the monthly wage<br>**Self-employed SSCs:** self-employed taxpayers face two options in order to obtain social security. Under the first option, the self-employed pays a fixed rate based on an annual minimum wage. With the second option, the self-employed pays a fixed annual fee that depends on the number and age of the family members. The amount reported here corresponds to a couple (ages 30 to 39) with two children (ages 0 to 19). For 2014, the fees were updated by the Mexican Social Security Institute with a new breakdown of age groups. |
| Netherlands | Employer **SSCs:** in addition, employers pay 7.05% of gross earnings net of employees' pension premiums and unemployment social security contributions until a maximum of gross earnings of EUR 33 189. |
| Norway | **Employer SSCs:** The contribution is geographically differentiated according to the municipality where the work-place is. The standard rates are 14.1, 10.6, 7.9, 6.4, 5.1 or 0% of gross wages. The highest rate applies to central parts of southern Norway. Lower rates may apply under certain circumstances. The weighted average rate, which is included here, is approximately 13.1%.<br>**Employee SSCs:** Employees' contributions to the National Insurance Scheme generally amount to 8.2% of personal wage income. Employees do not make contributions if their wage income is less than NOK 39 600. Once wage income exceeds this floor, an alternative calculation is made where the contributions equal 25% of the wage income in excess of the floor. The actual contributions made would represent the minimum between the alternative calculation and 8.2% of the total wage income. |

| | |
|---|---|
| Poland | **Employee SSCs:** the additional 9% is levied on gross wages minus the social security contributions that already have been paid. |
| Slovak Republic | **All:** a minimum contribution is applicable: if the monthly income does not exceed the lower threshold value (minimum wage in the case of employment or 50% of average wage in the case of the self-employed), then the SSC rate applies to this value.<br>**Employer SSC:** does not take into account NTCP (4% rate) which further raise the final compulsory payment burden on labour income. See the detailed discussion of NTCP in the Explanatory Annex to the Tax Database (OECD, 2015).<br>**Self-employed:** SSC rates for the self-employed apply to adjusted assessment bases (thus effective SSC rates are lower compared to the statutory ones). The social and health insurance base is defined as the tax base (before allowances) in the previous year plus paid mandatory contributions (both social and health), divided by 1.6, taking into account the minimum assessment base (50% of average wage). |
| Slovenia | **Self-employed SSCs:** social security contributions for the self-employed are assessed on a monthly basis. There is no consolidation of payments on an annual basis. The table describes the figures for the illustrative months (May) in 2014. Only for the year 2014 there is one major difference in determining the minimum insurance base. If the self – employed person creates a loss or a profit (reduced by 30 % for the year 2014) that is less than the minimum wage (that is EUR 783.66) then it is the minimum insurance base equal to the minimum wage but only for pension, unemployment insurance and maternity leave (with contribution rate 24.75 %). If self-employed person creates a loss or a profit (reduced by 30 %) that is less than the 60 % of the AW, the base for the social security contributions for health insurance (with rate 13.45 %) is equal to the 60 % of the AW (in case of month May is the amount EUR 913.91). |
| Spain | A minimum contribution is applicable: if the annual income does not exceed the lower threshold value, then the SSC rate applies to this value. |
| Sweden | **Employee SSCs:** the contributions (including the maximum contribution) are rounded to the nearest SEK 100.<br>**Self-employed SSCs:** there is no lower threshold for SSC for self-employed, 28.97% is paid for all positive income although no income tax or employee general pension contribution is paid for earned income below basic allowance. Lower rates are applied to self-employed aged younger than 26 (14.89%) and over 65 (10,21%/0%). A general reduction of 7.5% on the SSC is applicable if the income exceeds SEK 40 000 per year. The maximal reduction is SEK 15 000 per year. |
| Switzerland | Self-employed **SSCs:** compulsory social security contribution for old age and disability insurance of 9.7% of gross annual earnings minus a percentage of invested equity capital. For yearly incomes of less than CHF 55,700 reduced rates apply. |
| Turkey (YTL) | **Employer and employees SSCs:** In addition, unemployment insurance fund contributions are also made (1% for the employee and 2% for the employer).Turkey changed the national currency unit as YTL as of 1 January 2005, where 1 YTL equals 1 million TL.<br>**Self-employed SSCs:** see the Explanatory Annex to *Taxing Wages* (OECD, 2015) for a description of the Turkish system |
| United Kingdom | **Employer SSCs:** the rates and thresholds shown are those in effect as of 5 April.<br>**Employee SSCs:** the rates and thresholds shown are those in effect as of 5 April.<br>**Self-employed SSCs:** the rates and thresholds shown are those in effect as of 5 April and only apply to Class 4 and Class 2 contributions (GBP 2.30/week). |
| United States | **Employer SSCs:** in addition, the employer pays a contribution to a state-sponsored unemployment plan which may generally be credited against the required federal percentage. For instance, the average unemployment insurance tax rate in Michigan was 4.9% of the first USD 9 000 of wages. |

**Non-tax compulsory payment (NTCP):** In these countries employers pay NTCPs. Detailed information on each country can be found on the *OECD Tax database* webpage (www.oecd.org/tax/tax-policy/tax-database.htm), under *B. Personal Taxes / 4. Non-tax compulsory payments.*

**Note on aggregation**: In some social security systems, both flat rate and progressive rate structures apply. Where these apply to the same base (e.g. gross earnings), the elements are aggregated for the purpose of reporting in this table.

– For example, assume a flat rate of 10.05% is applied to total gross earnings under one part of the social security contribution charge. Assume another element imposes a 1.5% rate on gross earnings between 0 and 97 200, and a 0.5% rate on gross earnings between 97 200 and 243 000. Given the same base (gross earnings), the various charges can be consolidated as follows: 11.55% rate applicable to earnings between 0 and 92 000; 10.55% rate applicable to earnings between 97 200 and 243 000; and 10.50% rate is applicable to earnings above 243 000.

# ORGANISATION FOR ECONOMIC CO-OPERATION AND DEVELOPMENT

The OECD is a unique forum where governments work together to address the economic, social and environmental challenges of globalisation. The OECD is also at the forefront of efforts to understand and to help governments respond to new developments and concerns, such as corporate governance, the information economy and the challenges of an ageing population. The Organisation provides a setting where governments can compare policy experiences, seek answers to common problems, identify good practice and work to co-ordinate domestic and international policies.

The OECD member countries are: Australia, Austria, Belgium, Canada, Chile, the Czech Republic, Denmark, Estonia, Finland, France, Germany, Greece, Hungary, Iceland, Ireland, Israel, Italy, Japan, Korea, Luxembourg, Mexico, the Netherlands, New Zealand, Norway, Poland, Portugal, the Slovak Republic, Slovenia, Spain, Sweden, Switzerland, Turkey, the United Kingdom and the United States. The European Union takes part in the work of the OECD.

OECD Publishing disseminates widely the results of the Organisation's statistics gathering and research on economic, social and environmental issues, as well as the conventions, guidelines and standards agreed by its members.

OECD PUBLISHING, 2, rue André-Pascal, 75775 PARIS CEDEX 16
(23 2015 42 1 P) ISBN 978-92-64-24346-0 – 2015

www.ingramcontent.com/pod-product-compliance
Ingram Content Group UK Ltd.
Pitfield, Milton Keynes, MK11 3LW, UK
UKHW051504290926
15471UKWH00008B/1404

9 789264 243460